FROM THE
DANCE HALL
TO
facebook.

FROM THE DANCE HALL TO

facebook.

⧽⧼

Teen Girls, Mass Media,

and Moral Panic

in the United States,

1905–2010

⧽⧼

SHAYLA THIEL-STERN

University of Massachusetts Press
Amherst and Boston

Copyright © 2014 by University of Massachusetts Press
All rights reserved
Printed in the United States of America

ISBN 978-1-62534-091-7 (paper); 090-0 (hardcover)

Designed by Sally Nichols
Set in Monotype Apollo
Printed and bound by Sheridan Books, Inc.

Library of Congress Cataloging-in-Publication Data

Thiel-Stern, Shayla, 1972–
From the dance hall to Facebook : teen girls, mass media, and moral panic in
the United States, 1905–2010 / Shayla Thiel-Stern.
pages cm
Includes bibliographical references and index.
ISBN 978-1-62534-091-7 (pbk. : alk. paper) — ISBN 978-1-62534-090-0
(hardcover : alk. paper) 1. Teenage girls—United States—Social conditions.
2. Mass media and teenage girls—United States. 3. Sex role in mass media.
4. Journalism—Objectivity—United States. I. Title.
HQ798.T45 2014
305.30973—dc23
2014008142

British Library Cataloguing-in-Publication Data
A catalogue record for this book is available from the British Library.

For Matt, Adelaide, and Miles Stern, with love

CONTENTS

Acknowledgments   ix

INTRODUCTION
Media, Panic, and Teen Girls in Recreational Space
1

CHAPTER 1.
The Dance Hall Evil, 1905–1928
24

CHAPTER 2.
The Rise and Fall of Girls' Track and Field, 1920–1940
56

CHAPTER 3.
The Elvis Problem, 1956–1959
91

CHAPTER 4.
Punk Rock and a Crisis of Femininity, 1976–1986
121

CHAPTER 5.
Policing Teen Girls Online, 2004–2010
145

AFTERWORD
173

Notes   179
Index   199

ACKNOWLEDGMENTS

During the four or so years from my starting to finishing *From the Dance Hall to Facebook,* I taught nearly two thousand students, co-advised two through their dissertations, participated in at least a hundred hours of meetings, authored and coauthored several shorter scholarly pieces, gave birth to two children, lost a beloved dog and cat, adopted two other cats, and now await a decision on tenure. Academic life, like other arenas, is notoriously difficult for full-time working moms, but I have been extraordinarily fortunate in the support of the people I acknowledge here, who have made managing work and life and writing a book far less difficult than it might have been. First and foremost, my loving, accommodating spouse, who (despite also working full-time) enjoys cooking dinner every night. Thank you, my dear Matt. Pia Foerster, our au pair, has provided critical support, as have various nearby family helping with child care. My parents and my brothers have unfailingly provided moral support.

I want to thank the scholars, writers, and mentors who have inspired and encouraged me as I moved forward with my research and writing: Carolyn Bronstein, Mary Vavrus, Rebecca Hains, Sharon Mazzarella, Catherine Squires, Kathy Hansen, Laurie Ouelette, Hazel Dicken-Garcia, Radhika Paramesewaran, Cynthia Lewis, Gigi Durham, Mary Trull, Jen Lancaster, and Mary Kearney. I am grateful as well to colleagues who gave me feedback when I presented my research, beginning in early days at the Association of Education in Journalism and Mass Communication conference in 2008 and continuing to the recent gathering of the Childhood and Youth Studies Across the Disciplines group at the University of Minnesota.

Members of my division, Critical and Cultural Studies, strongly encouraged me to consider expanding my research, and this was outstanding advice.

My sincere gratitude goes to the women who let me interview them for this book. Special thanks to Professor Jeffrey Smith for introducing me to his incredible mother (who was 103 at the time of our interview) and allowing me to talk to her about her memories.

I thank my colleagues in the School of Journalism and Mass Communication and my director, Al Tims, for their kind support. I owe a special debt of gratitude to the research librarians at Andersen Library at the University of Minnesota: Ryan Bean of the YMCA archives, and especially Linnea Anderson of the Social Welfare History Archives, who first piqued my interest in the topic of dance halls and continued to help me throughout this lengthy research process. Thanks also to Ruth DeFoster for her indexing skills.

A Mary Ann Yodelis-Smith Award from the AEJMC Commission on the Status of Women and a Grant-in-Aid from the University of Minnesota each covered portions of my research costs, and I am grateful to both institutions for this support.

My editor, Brian Halley, believed in my work and encouraged me to submit a proposal at a time when I was considering giving up on the project all together. This book would not have been published without him. Thank you to my copyeditor Susan Silver, Carol Betsch, Mary Bellino, Bruce Wilcox, and their colleagues at UMass Press for all their efforts on behalf of my book. Thanks also to the anonymous peer reviewers of the manuscript, whose critiques and suggestions were spot-on and whose expertise truly strengthened this work.

My belief in human equality and commitment to feminism propel my work here. I hope that by exposing how mass media historically have represented girls and young women in problematic ways, the book might lead media workers to question and change their own newsgathering and storytelling practices. Through this work, I would ultimately like to (albeit in a small way) make the world a better, more just place for my own children and students. Thank you for inspiring me.

FROM THE
DANCE HALL
TO
facebook.

✂

INTRODUCTION

છ<

MEDIA, PANIC, AND TEEN GIRLS
IN RECREATIONAL SPACE

IN 2006 A TV PRODUCER FROM ABC-7 CHICAGO called me at my campus office to see if I would agree to appear on a news segment to comment on how young people should be concerned about how what they post online might eventually cost them a job. This was my first-ever "media request" where, because of my research on adolescent girls and their use of the Internet and my position as a professor at a local university, I was considered an authoritative voice. I reluctantly agreed, worried about looking and sounding foolish on camera. Nonetheless, I was able to give my talking points—yes, young people should be very thoughtful about whatever they post online because it is in fact a public space accessible to all, even many years later, and even if what they posted was intended to be all in good fun, it could affect people's perception of them. Little did I realize at the time that I had been called on as an "expert" to help craft a particular narrative that fed into a larger, grand narrative about how the Internet was a wild, unrestricted space where young people needed to be policed because they could be stalked or mean to one another or exercise excessive sexual agency. More often than not, the small examples that fed into the grand narrative were gendered. Girls online appeared to be at the crux of this media-generated crisis, which started in the early part of the twenty-first century and continues through the present time (though for the purposes of this book, I ended the crisis in 2010, when there truly were still an abundance of mass media representations of teen girls using the Internet connected to crisis).

Although the common tropes of news-gathering and storytelling techniques have changed and adapted to changing media audiences and technologies within the United States over the past century or so, certain journalistic norms have stayed the same. Authorities and experts are needed to tell a fair, authoritative, and objective story, for example. The criteria for newsworthiness is almost entirely the same as it was a hundred years ago too: a story must be timely and impactful, concern prominent figures, hold geographic proximity to readers, contain an element of human interest, or demonstrate a conflict or something shocking or novel. These factors (among a few others mentioned less frequently in the journalism textbooks) determine "news value," and the way a story is told often determines whether an audience will truly buy it—in either a very literal way (for example, pay for a newspaper) or figurative way (for example, put faith in what the reporter states). Nonetheless, in the American mass media's reliance on criteria of newsworthiness and official sources to deliver the news, it also at times leaves certain voices out of the coverage entirely; these voices historically have been silenced based on their race, ethnicity, gender, or class.

This book examines one group of silenced voices within American mass media representations—those of teen girls. They are sometimes part of major news narratives, as this book demonstrates, but they are rarely interviewed as part of the story, and their quotes, if used, are often included to validate a narrative about the girl being foolish or naive. Reporters often incorporate the verbatim use of youth slang or an accent that denotes her race or class. While this practice is often simply part of journalistic reportage, it creates a grand narrative about teen girls that places them at the margins of society. Based on societal constructions of gender and youth as well as political and economic forces, their positionality within American culture certainly has changed in the span of 105 years, and yet teen girls are usually portrayed negatively (or not at all) within news and popular discourse and tend to appear insignificant in terms of making valued contributions as citizens.

Moreover, I see this marginalization as part of a historical pattern that has equated teen girls with crisis in even their most benign recreational pursuits over the past century and beyond in the United States. Nevertheless, leisure pursuits and recreational space are hardly a neutral topic. Raymond Williams famously located culture and leisure at the intersection of social structure and human agency. People endlessly reaffirm structure through their participation in a practice, he said, and the preexisting conventions of the practice shape and restrict their behavior. These conventions also provide the framework within which they understand and translate the practice in their own way.[1] In this context, it is significant that so many of the known media-fostered crises related to teenage girls over an extended period of history concern leisure and recreation. To better understand the problematic representation of teen girls and public recreational space, this book discusses femininity as a hegemonic cultural construct and explores why the performance of gender identity is central.

Performing Gender in Public

Judith Butler maintains that gender is not simply a biological condition that separates humans as males and females but rather an unstable cultural construct "performatively produced and compelled by the regulatory practices of gender coherence." In other words, women and girls learn to perform gender and maintain the performance based on dominant cultural understandings of what it means to be female. Because societal expectations that maintain the dominant norms of femininity and masculinity are somewhat fluid, this performance is constant and up for negotiation at all times. In many ways, the process is like a never-ending feedback loop in which the ways we understand "feminine" and "masculine" are represented, enacted, and embodied. Butler notes that the performance of gender has "clearly punitive consequences"—or that we "regularly punish those who fail to do their gender right."[2]

Antonio Gramsci's idea of hegemony provides a useful means to theorize how the media representation of teen girls' public recreational practices may re-create a worldview of heteronormative femininity and masculinity. Through hegemony, dominant cultural ideologies are formed and normalized to support ruling classes and their interests, and the larger population simply accepts the ideologies as natural or common sense.[3] Furthermore, the mainstream media uses imagery, text, and language to create entire systems of representation that contribute to hegemonic meaning.[4] These systems give power to often-harmful interpretations of gender and hierarchy. Dorothy Smith argues that hegemony works to anchor how the "ways in which we think about ourselves and one another and about our society— our images of how we should look, our homes, our lives, even our inner worlds" are represented to us through the media.[5]

In youth, the role of media in understanding gender roles is all the more pronounced. Much of media and technology usage is tangled up with young people's notions of what makes up the "real world." This age group is often brought into a patriarchal system of meaning making that is in large part an effect of the dominant mediated discourses surrounding them, and they use popular and mass media texts as sources for ways to behave, dress, talk, learn, and have fun. Teen girls in particular have a wide variety of sources from which to draw this information, including television shows and film, fashion magazines, and Internet media.[6] Despite the online media's many opportunities to resist these dominant discourses through interactivity and digital media creation, many teen girls still incorporate dominant hegemonic discourses about femininity and sexuality into their online media production.[7]

Over the course of the twentieth century, the general public has become more comfortable with female sexuality, but certain gendered expectations persist over time. Michel Foucault stated that sex gradually became an "object of great suspicion" within Western culture, provoking two cultural demands to emerge: "We demand that sex speak the truth (but, since it is the secret and is oblivious to its own nature, we reserve for ourselves the function of telling the truth of its truth, revealed and deciphered at last), and we demand that it tell us our truth, or rather, the deeply buried truth of that truth about ourselves which we think we possess in our immediate consciousness."[8] But when popular press has been tasked with demanding truth and telling stories about sexuality palatable to the American public, the suspicion that Foucault refers to is still evoked often. Sexuality is usually painted as deviant within American news stories, and often it connects (again) to whether gender is being performed in a way that is consistent within dominant patriarchal standards.

The media questions whether gender is being performed correctly as it relates to adolescent girls who are portrayed as too masculine and strong—or, conversely, too feminine and weak—and in this process the girls are often discursively punished for this performance—frequently by becoming victimized or sexualized. These themes become obvious within this book's analysis of how the U.S. press has presented narratives about teen girls and recreation over the past century. Another vital piece of the story, however, is the publicness of this gender performance within recreational practice.

Gendered Conceptions of Private and Public Space

The word "public" implies a "site" or "context" that society understands to be open to everyone.[9] But masculine and feminine worlds have historically been placed into separate spheres, casting the male into the public and female into the private domestic space. This relegation to private sphere can be traced in part to the feminine body being at odds—sexually, reproductively, and so on—with the masculine world. Smith says this means cultures historically have had to understand a "male world in its assumptions, its language, and its pattern of relating," where women have been historically excluded from participating in public life. Furthermore, the body itself is an important artifact in understanding this paternalist history, and "it is not necessary to deny the fact that the nature of the human body is also an effect of cultural, historical activity," writes Brian Turner. "The body is both natural and cultural." Susan Bordo argues that despite this, the feminine body has become docile, rife with a cultural imprint of standard beauty practices that cause women to feel that they must undergo constant improvement to fit the cultural ideals perpetuated through media discourse.[10] Women toil away to achieve a somewhat meaningless cultural ideal instead of pursuing more important, public achievements—political office, for example—and independence.

The cultural importance of motherhood, caregiving, and domesticity further sought to keep women in the private realm of the home (despite the fact that this work is not valued enough to be paid). The gendered nuclear family was established as a cultural ideal in the late eighteenth century, and it subsequently divided life into two distinct spheres—one public and one private.[11] Furthermore, relegating women to the home as the "natural" caregiver has turned families into "gendered institutions" in that their very traditional composition (wife as mother and homemaker, husband as father and breadwinner) reproduces gendered inequalities and differences in an everyday setting that is reaffirmed by the mass media, past and present.[12]

Contemporary readers are likely to find ideas of women's domesticity particularly antiquated and perhaps even quaint. Yet as we will see, concerns over women's roles in public persist in some form even today, although the tone of such concern has shifted from moralizing to worrying about young women's own health and safety. Both stances articulate an enduring protectionist approach toward young women, however. Because of this cultural acceptance of the feminine being equated with the private, girls and women who place themselves in public purview have been punished with harassment, depicted as members of a lower class, or viewed as sexually promiscuous. Even when females are only technologically "in public," they have been depicted negatively: Women telegraph operators in the late nineteenth century were represented as incompetent and sexually promiscuous in the telegraphic fiction written by their male counterparts, for example.[13] The gendered representation of the telephone—which blurs lines between public and private conversation—portrayed gabby, gossipy, unintelligent women and girls who lack the control to stay off of the phone and stay quietly out of the way.[14] American teenage girls in particular have been represented in popular culture and media as specifically beholden to the telephone, whether through the 1963 musical *Bye Bye Birdie* and its scene featuring silly teenage girls tying up their families' phone lines on "Telephone Hour," the T-Mobile cell phone commercial that debuted in 2007 depicting a shrill-voiced teenage cheerleader gabbing inanely on her phone for hours as scientists watch with bored expressions, to the depiction of the teenage Haley on the popular ABC sitcom, *Modern Family,* who was always talking her on cell phone obliviously and rolling her eyes at her family members. These representations of gender are in line with dominant norms of femininity and with certain dominant narratives about teen girls as insignificant, and it should be particularly concerning that this image persists within American popular media.

More specifically, girls are represented in two dichotomous (but often linked) ways within dominant cultural narratives and mass media stories about girls and public recreational space: victims and whores. On one hand, the story goes, girls will inevitably take advantage of their burgeoning adulthood and either intentionally or inadvertently "appear" sexual in public. (In most of the media narratives within this book, appearance is one of the most crucial aspects of performing femininity properly.) Some readers will undoubtedly point out that this narrative about the girl as whore might actually be celebrated in modern times—certainly as it is seen through advertising, where younger women flaunt their bodies and, as Rosalind Gill writes, are presented as "midriffs" represented as "empowered" by their playful sexuality. Gill warns this image is also a construct in which young women's "agentic capabilities are, it would seem, confined to be aestheticization of their physical appearances and tied to consumerism," noting that women today are "presented as active, desiring sexual subjects who choose to present themselves in a seemingly objectified manner because it suits their (implicitly 'liberated') interests to do so." Furthermore, M. Gigi Durham warns that this sexualized notion of girl power is now being applied to increasingly younger girls, particularly as it relates to the fashion and beauty products marketed to them.[15]

On the other hand, girls—unaware of their vulnerability, especially as it relates to their burgeoning public sexual development—can become victims. In the news narratives in this book, the citizens in each historical moment fear that girls could become prostitutes or juvenile delinquents, enter a life of promiscuity and violence, become lesbians, lose their ability to marry and reproduce, or be murdered or sold into slavery. These concerns are often tied to the feeling that the adolescent girls are not performing gender in a way that is consistent with the dominant understanding of girlhood in their own community, and this often fosters a cultural crisis that journalists might not necessarily start but do certainly foster and perpetuate.

Researching Adolescent Girls and Media

This line of inquiry fits into a relatively new field of research on girlhood, and specifically girls and media. In her groundbreaking 1978 essay, "Jackie: An Ideology of Adolescent Femininity," Angela McRobbie demonstrates how mass media discourses can foster certain subcodes associated with beauty and appearance, domesticity, and heteronormative romance that position the teen girl in a hegemonic state, where she literally buys into and enacts the particular values espoused in the magazine because they are culturally accepted as natural. This premise is seen in much of the analysis on adolescent girls that followed in the 1980s to the present. For example, Linda Christian-Smith's, Bronwyn Davies's, and Margaret Finders's research examines adolescent female book readers in and outside of school, each theorizing how gender is performed in the act of reading itself as well as in the pages of the books the girls choose and are assigned to read. In 1999 Dawn Currie conducted a critical analysis of readers of more contemporary U.S.-based teen magazines in *Girl Talk: Adolescent Magazines and Their Readers,* in which she grapples with whether these magazines prescribe the same kind of oppressive feminine ideology described by McRobbie or whether they are instead guilty pleasures that subvert and resist patriarchy. Sharon R. Mazzarella and Norma Odom Pecora's edited book, *Growing Up Girls: Popular Culture and the Construction of Identity,* features a variety of essays concerning girlhood from a feminist standpoint, bringing visibility to the way popular communication artifacts and media may shape identity among girls from a variety of backgrounds.[16]

These works within girls' studies influence and shape much of the later scholarship examining how adolescent girls use and make sense of the media surrounding them—from print to television to film to the Internet—and they provide a strong bedrock for the analysis conducted in this book. Many of the common threads among the historical case studies relate to how teen girls are associated with the proper cultural performance of femininity as it relates to domesticity, beauty, and romance and also to how American culture perceives and represents them as a troubled and often vexing demographic. Much of this scholarship has demonstrated—exhaustively and in many contexts—how teen girls' primary power is that of consumer and popular culture taste maker (although often they are seen as having little true "taste" in artistic terms)—an idea that is further explored in this book, especially in the chapters related to Elvis Presley, punk rock, and the Internet.

In *Girls Make Media* Mary Celeste Kearney demonstrates how girls who create music, film, websites and zines can speak back to the media that demean or marginalize them, often using these skills of production to gain entrée to the media industry as adults.[17] Indeed, it is easy to watch girls today produce media and cultural artifacts through the digital technologies that are a part of many of them—from creating Tumblr pages on their computers to short films shot with their smart phones. Even before the Internet was widely adopted, the irreverent zines produced by riot grrrls in the 1990s articulated a specifically feminist identity.[18]

I, too, want to advocate that young females be represented also as producers of media. Granted, this is a somewhat difficult point to argue within a book that attempts to demonstrate how the mass media has unfairly and systematically represented teen girls over the past century, because so much of this analysis hinges on girls being represented as consumers. Too often, they are seen in news coverage as mindless victims who embrace popular culture of their time—especially in the case of dance hall goers, Elvis lovers, and punk rockers—and consume that popular culture without a critical eye or producing any original cultural artifacts of their own.

But my research for this book demonstrates that adolescents historically produced their own cultural artifacts as well, in the form of scrapbooks, fan letters, and fan creations (one newspaper analyzed in this book showed photos of girls in the 1950s who had adorned their circle skirts with "I love Elvis," for example). Further, many adolescent girls used their own bodies to make a statement, most notably those who loved the punk and new wave aesthetic and expressed it through outlandish dress and hairstyles in the 1970s and 1980s.

Gender, Youth, and Technology

Technology plays a major role in the lives of adolescents today, both in how youth produce digital media and in how they manage their lives in general. Writer danah boyd notes that adolescents who grew up with the Internet do not differentiate between their "online" and "offline" worlds in the same way that members of Generation X and Baby Boomers might. Further, she and Alice Marwick say that teens today have created their own language and general understanding of what the Internet means in their lives; specifically, they curate their own social media postings and conceive of issues like privacy and "drama" in ways that are quite different than what most adults understand (and often in a way that is at odds with the panicked response of mass media to teens online).[19] Since the early part of the twenty-first century, scholars have studied adolescents' rather seamless capacity for integrating digital media use into their daily lives and routines. Sonia Livingstone, Cynthia Lewis and Bettina Fabos, and Rivka Ribak have studied adolescents engaged in interactive media use in their homes, noting that while they are articulating identity and negotiating gender on their computers, they are also maintaining a sense of personal privacy from others in their home. Susannah Stern has called for a more nuanced study of girls' Internet use to allow for a more thorough understanding of the different aspects of girlhood, from identity play to impression management to civic participation.[20]

Using a combination of traditional and online ethnography, Mary Gray accomplished this as she questioned how LGBT teens in the rural United States negotiated "queer visibility" within both their online and off-line interactions as a means of maintaining personal agency. In *Girl Wide Web: Girls, the Internet, and the Negotiation of Identity,* published in 2005, Sharon

R. Mazzarella presented a book of different research studies about how adolescent girls navigated the Internet and managed their lives in their various uses of digital technology, and she followed through in 2009 with *Girl Wide Web 2.0: Revisiting Girls, the Internet, and the Negotiation of Identity,* which demonstrated how much the Internet and girls' uses for it had changed in a relatively brief period. Again, girls had been positioned as beauty and fashion consumers through the growing commercialization of the Web, but girls also were increasingly able to seize the tools to produce cultural artifacts to represent themselves. Furthermore, the book acknowledged the important intersections of race, ethnicity, class, and religion figured into the analysis of girls online through pieces looking specifically at how Latina, Arabic, African American, Asian American, South African, and diasporic communities of girls articulated identity through technology.[21]

The research in my 2007 book, *Instant Identity: Adolescent Girls and the World of Instant Messaging,* used a combination of interviews and participant observation with American adolescent girls from a variety of backgrounds and analysis of their online conversations with peers to assess the role of instant messaging within their lives. I learned that the girls used interactive media technology (in this case, instant messaging, though it applied as well to other methods of online asynchronous chat) in an empowering way that often allowed them to transgress certain gender norms. But they also were somewhat unable to escape the hegemonic process of enacting what they felt was an acceptable performance of femininity—whether it related to beauty, sexuality, or other aspects of identity.[22] This performance was sometimes just a means of negotiating adolescent sexuality and gender identity, but it demonstrated that even though girls were productive in their online use, they often positioned themselves as objects of desire or commercialism.

Furthermore, girlhood online must increasingly be understood in the context of surveillance, because as girls continue to produce and share online, they increasingly become monitored and further wired in to corporations hoping to gain valuable market data from them. Leslie Regan Shade and Valerie Steeves each note how the iterative nature of girlhood in the age of social media should force us all to ask critical questions about privacy and youth. Moreover, we should also ask critical questions of what it means for girls to be empowered by media in the digital age and how girls might have internalized a more commodified ethic of "girl power" that, as

Rebecca Hains warns in her research, is not necessarily powerful in anyway. Furthermore, as Sarah Banet-Weiser adds, girls' "lives" online might actually be a product of the contemporary culture of "self-branding," where girls are simply reimagining themselves in a digital space and in effect offering their bodies as product and their work as labor within a neoliberal, postfeminist context; for example, as Banet-Weiser states, audiences can witness this branding being performed on YouTube when girls embrace hypersexuality while lip-synching to the commercialized pop of Katy Perry's "I Kissed a Girl."[23]

Looking Backward, Providing Historical Context

Despite the myriad fascinating research opportunities on girls as producers, consumers, and branding agents in the contemporary digital age, Mary Celeste Kearney encouraged girls' studies scholars to "look backward" and pay attention to a point in American history when adolescent girls were not studied or viewed as worthy of scholarly attention. Joan Jacobs Brumberg captured the voices of girls from past eras by studying diaries from which she learned that even teen girls in the early twentieth century were concerned about their changing bodies. Susan J. Douglas examined how U.S. media messages—from popular culture artifacts to advertising—intended for teen girls in the last half of the twentieth century targeted them in often-absurd, comical ways. Ilana Nash analyzed teen girl icons in twentieth-century America, including Gidget in the 1950s and Buffy the Vampire Slayer in the 1990s, and demonstrated how cultural constructions rely so heavily on media representations of fictional teen girls. Similarly, Kelly Schrum illuminated how young American teens after World War I were among the first to embody a teenage cultural identity and how high school girls became a powerful consumer demographic, especially for the beauty and entertainment industries.[24]

To further give voice to this generation of teen girls and their interactions with popular culture and media, Rebecca C. Hains, Sharon R. Mazzarella, and I conducted oral history interviews with thirty women from different backgrounds who grew up in postwar United States. Our work used the words of women remembering childhood interactions with media to identify specific narratives about memories of media from this period, including such a strong identification with historical and generational forces (such as the Great Depression, World War II, the development of radio and television, and their love of adventure stories) that shaped every facet of their relationship with the media itself.[25] One goal of this book is to indeed look backward on the girls who lived in generations past and bring needed illumination to their untold history, but I also aim to demonstrate how the representations of them by various media tend to misrepresent them in many ways and why this misrepresentation occurs so systematically throughout the history investigated. Often, this process is related to news-gathering practices that capitalize on difference—in this case, gender, youth, and often socioeconomic status—perhaps in an effort to sell papers or gain viewers.

Media, Deviance, Moral Entrepreneurship, and Panic

I argue in this book that certain narratives about teen girls have cycled through the past century, effectively maintaining this population at a constant point of crisis that sometimes is elevated to the point of moral panic. This is usually a gendered, exaggerated crisis that depends on certain journalistic devices and, in many cases, on the advocacy of experts and authorities whose personal agenda (whether rooted in religion, ethics, politics, economics, personal duty, or occupation) relies on either the preservation of this crisis or its elevation to panic.

This book looks at several distinct historical cases of crisis and panic over teen girls and public recreational space that take place over just more than a century in the United States. They are not intended to become exhaustive case studies but rather cultural snapshots in time that illuminate significant points in the past century or so when the news media significantly increased coverage of teen girls—and arguably fostered increased social concern that limited girls' opportunities in cultural space. The historical snapshots include

1. the popularity of dance halls with working-class teen girls in the early 1900s and social reformers' efforts to reform and outlaw dance halls;
2. the perceived problems associated with teen girls participating in "sports of strife," or strenuous athletics—specifically, track and field (including a fear of hurting girls' ability to reproduce in the future and the issue of participants appearing too "masculine" while running);

3. teen girls' public demonstration of emotion and sexuality in their adulation of Elvis Presley in the mid-1950s and the perceived link between juvenile delinquency (specifically, promiscuity) and enjoying his music;

4. the concern in the late 1970s and early 1980s that teen girls who embraced punk rock music and fashion were not feminine enough and that their physical rebellion (which in the media was tied almost entirely to their appearance in public) could be linked to their own moral decay, cultural deviance, or inability to one day conform to dominant cultural notions of femininity; and

5. teen girls' widespread use of social networking sites such as Facebook and MySpace since 2004, with special attention paid to issues of sexual predation, sexting, and cyberbullying and to the general fear that girls either show excessive sexual agency or are victimized online.

The news media focused a disproportionate amount of attention on all these narratives, as Mary Douglas Vavrus reveals is often the case within media narratives regarding femininity, where media workers do "not make much of the very small and homogenous group of women used to tell" the stories and do not bother to look for alternative interpretations of the statistics used to bolster their claims.[26] This book analyzes how these historical snapshots are linked by authorities and moral entrepreneurs who crusaded on behalf of or against teen girls concerning their participation in these activities. The snapshots are also connected to one another through the mass media's policing of gender performance and calling out teen girls when they are not enacting proper femininity in their public leisure pursuits.

Some would describe these various crisis points as related to "moral panic," very basically (and perhaps, uncritically) defined as an irrational cultural overreaction about a phenomenon deemed deviant.[27] The more classic understanding of moral panic comes from the theory's original author, Stanley Cohen, who says it occurs when a "condition, episode, person or group of persons emerges to become defined as a threat to societal values and interests; its nature is presented in a stylized and stereotypical fashion by the mass media; the moral barricades are manned by editors, bishops, politicians and other right-thinking people; socially accredited experts pronounce their diagnoses and solutions." Cohen explains the nuances available within the definition of moral panic too, noting the subject is sometimes "quite novel" and other times commonplace. He says it might pass quickly and be forgotten or might have severe social consequences in terms of legal and social policy change or "even in the way society conceives itself."[28]

Often, a moral panic is distinctly connected to mass media reporting, perpetuating, and reproducing its discourses. Cohen specifically noted that when journalists exaggerate in reporting an issue by overblowing or distorting data, repeat fallacies that seem believable but are incorrect, and use misleading photos and headlines that are flashy or moralistic, they foster moral panic. Stuart Hall, Chas Critcher, Tony Jefferson, John Clarke, and Brian Roberts in *Policing the Crisis: Mugging, the State, and Law and Order* remind us that "novelty" is in fact a traditional and conventional news value that journalist use to determine whether a story is newsworthy, and stories of the "novel" frequently may be classified as leading to moral panic.[29] The authors attest that moral panic must be intrinsically connected to Marxist ideology to understand moral panic as part of a larger phenomenon within a range of media institutions and the texts they produce. Furthermore, the authors connect their analysis of moral panic to Gramsci's theory of hegemony, or the idea that certain discourses can become normalized through a process of consent and naturalization. This idea is more complicated than the simplistic notion that journalists—who often work for large, corporate media organizations—simply reproduce and spread the dominant ideology of their elite organizations in their news coverage. Instead, it suggests that audiences, even active audiences who make sense of media based on their own cultural background and beliefs, become so accustomed to certain representations that they accept them as fact.

Additionally, Hall and his coauthors write that media practitioners are frequently not the "primary definers" of news events, but their professional relationship to sources allows them to play a crucial role in reproducing the definitions of those who have access to the media to serve as "accredited sources."[30] Journalists are steered toward specific topics by regular institutional sources: politicians, government officials, law enforcement officers, scholars, cultural experts, and others. Through this reporting process, conservative—and arguably patriarchal—social agendas can be disseminated through the media. Again, a hegemonic process is enacted: the social condition of consent is necessary for this broad cultural construction of negative meanings, or threats, that stimulate crisis and in some cases, panic. The research and analysis in this book links sources—often the moral authorities and entrepreneurs within their distinct historical moments—to the news media reports that perpetuate the moral panic and in turn stereotype and marginalize girls.

Despite their ability to perpetuate and spread moral panic, media workers should not be blamed as the sole arbiters. Instead, the dialectical process directly and indirectly involves audiences. Hall also explains reporters "freely" formulate questions "on behalf of the public," and through this practice they establish "a logic which is compatible with the dominant interests in society." He concludes, "ideology is a function of the discourse and of the logic of social processes, rather than an intention of the agent," and in fact "ideological formulations remain largely unconscious to both the speaker and the receiver," which leaves the ideology of moral panic critically unexamined and therefore are all the more potent.[31] This is not a new way of doing journalism nor is it entirely the fault of journalists who tell the stories. Rather, this is part of a hegemonic system rooted in dominant cultural discourses, which in the United States are often tied to mass media, but they are also inextricably linked to other important forces—specifically, history, politics, economics, established social hierarchies, and local and national culture.

Furthermore, media is not a one-way flow but rather a complicated process of meaning making between message and receiver, and the message sometimes isn't interpreted in an expected way. In fact, people often find personal agency and empowerment within their own resistant readings of mass media messages. Nonetheless, mass media representation is inarguably part of how people make judgments about the world around them, and it also provides something of a template in the case of many, especially adolescent girls who turn to texts that they find authoritative, if not just helpful, to negotiate and articulate identity as they move from childhood to adulthood. This relates to the process of hegemony, which makes it difficult to question normalized meanings of what it means to be feminine or a teenager living at a particular point in history in a certain part of the world.

Many cultural studies scholars, most notably Angela McRobbie and Stuart Hall, have linked moral panic to the marginalization of women and minorities, and Cohen, Charles Acland, and Dick Hebdige delve into panic over youth culture, but not specifically female youth (in fact, almost exclusively *male* youth). Media-fueled crises and moral panics arguably have been created to maintain the power of the status quo and in turn affect the social construction of reality for all media audience members. Given the historical discrimination against females as well as the remarkable amount of news devoted to the coverage of the activities of teen girls, it is vital to examine how media discourses portray gender and youth. Often, gender seems to relate directly to widespread public social anxieties within the larger U.S. population, and published and broadcast news often feed these anxieties.

Although deviance is often an underlying concern in historical and contemporary U.S. media coverage of teen girls in public recreational space, the media coverage of and public discourse about deviance never reached the levels that most moral panic scholars would define as truly a panic. They might argue that Cohen's definition of moral panic suggests it happens in a defined, tightly bound period, and although the cases in this book were limited to periods of two to twenty years, they are not as brief and defined as he prescribes. While scholars including Erich Goode and Nachman Ben-Yehuda describe moral panic as more historically cyclical, Cohen and even Hall and his colleagues see it as more episodic and culturally distinct. Moreover, Kenneth Thompson's claim that moral panics are becoming more frequent and pervasive is in direct contrast with McRobbie and Sarah Thornton's assertion that they are becoming less frequent and harder to constitute because folk devils now are savvy enough to fight back.[32]

Most moral panics related specifically to gender and femininity would not even be covered by its strict definition. After all, gendered moral panics are recycled, redistributed, and reconstituted in a nearly constant historical cycle. Moreover, panics related to teen girls might be seen as so insignificant as to hardly count as arousing societal anxiety. Nonetheless, the same concerns about the appropriate performance of femininity and girlhood and the same cultural worries about teen girls' behaviors (and the potential consequences of those behaviors) continue to be the same, even over more than a century. Embedded patriarchy makes it nearly impossible to theoretically employ moral panic to these repeated crises about teen girls in public recreational space as a result. Still, many of the components of media-generated moral panic are at work in the analysis of American teen girls in public recreational space over the past century.

At the least, an underlying media discourse of crisis pervades the coverage and works as an effective classification for how the mass media—first, only through print and, later, through broadcast and interactive media—has represented teen girls in much of its coverage of them. Although crisis is related to moral panic, it is conceptually distinct. As Charles Acland notes, "Panics, as the concentration of popular concern, trigger the structured responses of social institutions and do not occur in an isolated manner on an irregular basis. Certainly, crises differ from one another in the scope and intensity to which they shake up the social apparatus and are experienced at a popular level. Yet crisis, or at least the threat thereof, is equally a normal and everyday aspect in many arenas; otherwise, there would not be enough need for such regulatory bodies as the police, the military, the judiciary, and religious orders." Acland criticizes cultural studies scholars for "fetishizing youth" in so much of their research but reiterates that the "the significatory power of youth-as-problem is always at the fore" and has been within American culture since the beginning of the twentieth century.[33] I argue in this book that female youth are even more powerful signs of youth-as-problem because when they do not publicly perform femininity in a way that adheres to the dominant cultural norms of their historical time, media narratives latch on to the performance as an indication of crisis.

In his work, however, Acland is talking about a genuine crisis of sorts because he is talking about young people committing crimes (and the perception that it could be a crime wave, etc.). In the historical snapshots discussed in this book, although the mass media has represented teen girls in something of a constantly cycling historical crisis of whore verses victim in its coverage, they are not committing crimes but rather enjoying their leisure and experiencing recreation by dancing, running, listening to music, attending live events, and using the Internet to communicate with the world. The fact that these somewhat benign (but public) pursuits were covered so problematically by the mass media solidifies the point that the teen girl is a troubling cultural figure. She is criticized for looking too pretty or sexy or young (all characterizations foisted on her, even though they are also cultural expectations associated with the performance of gender) or seeming too masculine, unladylike—and in both cases she invites trouble. Society is conditioned to see her as a victim who must be policed and saved, and this is the dominant narrative told by a variety of American media from the early twentieth century to contemporary society.

Within the construction of crisis and panic, the mass media's narratives must be bolstered by authorities and experts who can attest to the problem at hand, and these people are what Howard S. Becker called "moral entre-preneurs." Moral entrepreneurs tend to possess social power and position-ing that enables them to enforce rules, he says, noting that "distinctions of age, sex, ethnicity, and class are all related to differences in power, which accounts for differences in the degree to which groups so distinguished can make rules for others." Some moral entrepreneurs create rules and others enforce rules, with the former usually being what Becker calls a "crusading reformer." He writes of the rule creator: "The existing rules do not satisfy him because there is some evil which profoundly disturbs him. He feels that nothing can be right in the world until the rules are made to correct it. He operates with an absolute ethic; what he sees is truly and totally evil with no qualification. Any means is justified to do away with it. The crusader is fervent and righteous, often self-righteous."[34] This is the moral entrepreneur seen in many of the cases in this book, though journalists do not rely only on moral entrepreneurs to police the various crises related to teen girls in America. Other experts—academics (like myself), persons with political motivations, leaders in nonprofit organizations related to the issue at hand—serve as authorities on stories about teen girls' public recre-ation. Notably, however, teen girls themselves rarely serve as authoritative sources within these stories.

This book demonstrates how panic and crisis are often perpetuated by journalists, often in an attempt simply to gain a wider viewing audience or sell newspapers, and often this moral panic is at the expense of marginal-ized communities—the poor, women, young people, people of color, and immigrants.

Teen Girlhoods in America

There is no single, universal girlhood but rather, as Mazzarella, Hains, and I write, "there are girlhoods—cultural constructs that vary by race, class, nationality, generation, regionality, sexual identity, and so on."[35] But the mass media in the United States often does represent primarily either the white middle- to upper-class girlhood or the girlhood of those who need to be "saved," which during the Progressive era were immigrant and work-ing-class girls. This makes that type of teen girl seem "normalized," further marginalizing girls of color and lower socioeconomic means and placing them in the position of "Others."

In choosing the term "teen girl" rather than "adolescent girl" or "young woman," I make a deliberate choice. It means something very different to be a fifteen-year-old in 1906, and even in 1956, than it does to be a teen girl in the 2000s. In the early 1900s most fifteen-year-old girls were not expected to attend school beyond their elementary years, and in fact they were often preparing to work (often, as a physical laborer at a factory), support their parents and siblings, and find a suitable husband. In the 1950s the teen girl was viewed as an ingenue, expected to complete high school but not necessarily college and perhaps work for a time in an "acceptable" career (secretary, teacher, nurse) until she married and had children. Moreover, the term "teenager" itself was not regularly used until the 1940s.[36] In the contemporary United States, many people (including the journalists whose stories are included in this book) classify college women as "girls," perhaps as a nod to the extended adolescence that sociologist and digital media scholar Sherry Turkle feel has marked middle-class American life in the age of the Internet.[37]

Nonetheless, "teen girl"—which limits the age group I am studying to the teen years of thirteen to nineteen—is a social construct that conjures a specific image for most audiences. I see this analysis an opportunity to play with our understanding of the teen girl and to historically contextualize how she became what she is today. Most important, even though a fifteen-year-old girl is quite different today from the presuffrage period of the United States, the mass media has consistently treated her the same way. She has always been represented as a "crisis." Her leisure choices outside of her home have always been represented as somewhat problematic. She has always been a site of contestation—whether because of her choice to dance all night in a public dance hall in the middle of urban Chicago or because of her choice to post a digital photo of herself wearing a tiny bikini to her Facebook page. Some media scholars, including Hains, note that girls choosing to engage in recreation during their free time are often portrayed by the media as "empowered," or demonstrating their "girl power"; however, this "girl power" is often a commodified, commercialized idea that entails purchasing the right kind of beauty products and clothing and appropriating the right kind of public appearance to be truly acceptable.[38] Catherine Driscoll notes that the analysis of adolescent girl culture is often an exercise in the "opposition between pleasure in consumption figured as conformity," where "resistance is often just another form of conformity and conformity may be compatible with other resistances."[39] This opposition is evident in the historical snapshots in this book. I attempt within each chapter, however, to provide historical and cultural context to what it meant to be a teen girl at the point of analysis—from the sociological meanings behind girlhood and femininity within specific U.S. cultures to the mass media landscape and journalistic practices in the years examined.

The Goals of This Book

Although important scholarship on the media representation of adolescent girls has emerged during the past two decades, much of this work concentrates on examples from the 1990s to the present day with little or no historical context about how girls have been represented in media. Furthermore, most of this work looks at popular texts—teen magazines, popular television shows, film, and websites—rather than news discourses from the dominant media of their times. This book attempts to fill this gap.

Over the past fifteen or so years many studies have been conducted on the role of the Internet in young people's lives. Some has focused on the gender, race, and class differences within Internet usage. Fewer studies have focused on how the mass media represents young people, and girls in particular, in their use of the Internet. Very little has been said about how these studies of youth and the Internet fit into American culture and history. My own research started in the present, looking both at how teen girls interacted in a virtual environment and how the mass media interpreted their interactions. Looking backward allows for reflection about how the past influences our understanding of gender, youth, and technology. Even though so much is new within new media studies, many of our cultural attitudes about it are rooted in the past.

McRobbie argues that one of the weaknesses of most media critiques lies in their analysis of just one type of media as if it exists in a vacuum. She writes, "we do not exist in social unreality while we watch television or read the newspaper, nor are we transported back to reality when we turn the TV off to wash the dishes or discard the paper to go to bed."[40] In this book's research, I was careful to include newspapers, magazines, radio and television broadcasts, and the Internet and to describe their relationship to audiences as they existed within each historical period. Stuart Hall suggests that the reader has to work to detect, interpret, and potentially resist the ideological aspects of a text, and this can be accomplished only through critical, careful reading and negotiation of meaning.[41] Although the intention of my analysis is to take a critical, qualitative look at the media within different historical periods, the news media analysis is quite extensive, especially in terms of the print media, as I made an effort to find and read every article printed on each of the topics as they related to teen girls. Moreover, popular media texts (such as discussions of popular TV shows or radio broadcasts) are sometimes included to add further cultural context to the analysis when appropriate.

Although this project is limited in scope to English-language American media (meaning that ethnic and immigrant presses are excluded, unfortunately), it does attempt to look at how the African American press, particularly the *Chicago Defender* but also other prominent black newspapers, responded to the historical case studies and represented teen girls in its coverage. The analysis in this book demonstrates that the narratives were somewhat different from their mainstream counterparts that serve primarily white, middle- and upper-class audiences—especially, and unsurprisingly, in the first half of the twentieth century. The chapters in *From the Dance Hall to Facebook* each explore various aspects of recreation within their historical context, comparing and contrasting the stories told by the mainstream news media with the stories told by authorities, experts, and activists (who are often quoted in the stories) and teen girls themselves (who are very rarely quoted in the stories).

Feminist scholars including McRobbie and Carol Gilligan remind us that in disciplines ranging from psychology to cultural studies, early youth scholars studied only boys yet applied their findings to boys and girls alike. The fact that female voices have rarely been a part of official history and scholarship presents a challenge to scholars who seek to understand girlhood and girls' lives in the past. Girls have not been granted official agency to speak for themselves, and the dominant mass media of the various times usually spoke about them or for them. As a result, as Ilana Nash points out, teen girls in American history tend to be described as "types" and, all too often, stereotypes, or "an iconic abstraction representing dominant culture's desires or nightmares."[42]

Although this work is not ethnographic, it was important to me to incorporate actual voices of the girls and women who lived during these periods of gendered crisis. In some cases I was able to conduct oral history–style interviews with women who were teen girls at the time of the crisis. Paul

Thompson writes, "since the nature of most existing records is to reflect the standpoint of authority, it is not surprising that the judgment of history has more often than not vindicated the wisdom of the powers that be. Oral history by contrast makes a much fairer trail possible: witnesses can now also be called from the under-classes, the unprivileged, and the defeated."[43] These women relied on their memory to recount their girlhood stories—some of which were in the distant past, as in the case of an interview I conducted with a 104-year-old woman remembering the outdoor dance halls of her youth, and others in the recent past, as in the case of the young women discussing their experiences with social media as young teens. This allows for teen girls to retroactively speak back to the history and media and provide context and clarification that is often absent from the dominant narratives about teen girls in the United States. To capture direct quotations I culled library archives for diaries, journals, and oral histories, as well as previously published interviews and documentaries. I attempted to weave all these quotations into the overall narrative of the book without detracting from the story I wanted to tell.

Still, finding legitimate, unmediated voices from diverse sources, especially in the earliest historical periods, was often a challenge. In many cases the diaries and letters that are available for study were bequeathed to library archives. The women who did this were usually Caucasian. They were typically wealthy (for example, Yvonne Blue and Emma Young Dickson, whose journals and diaries were used in my research) or famous (such as Babe Didrikson and Florence MacDonald, well-known athletes who participated in oral histories preserved in museum archives). These accounts are helpful, but the teen girls described in news reports, especially in the first two chapters of this book, were working class or poor, and their viewpoints were generally not included within official history nor found in library archival materials. Although some of their voices were included in scholarly research of the time, even this research was conducted by researchers who clearly looked down on their subjects. Most often, these girls were spoken about or spoken on behalf of by moral entrepreneurs, scholars, and reporters. In this way, they are mediated voices, and it can be difficult to say whether true agency and self-representation is taking place in the quotations used to represent their points of view. Nonetheless, I made every attempt to incorporate the actual voices of teen girls throughout history whenever possible within each of these chapters' historical moments.

As Susan Douglas has pointed out, research on girlhood is important as ever, even as it relates to their leisure pursuits and pop cultural preferences. In her discussion of teen girls and the 1990s all-female pop group, the Spice Girls, she writes, "When adolescent girls flock to a group, they are telling us plenty about how they experience the transition to womanhood in a society in which boys are still very much on top. Girls today are being urged, simultaneously, to be independent, assertive, and achievement oriented, yet also demure, attractive, soft-spoken, fifteen pounds underweight, and deferential to men."[44]

Indeed, the conflicting messages the mass media tells about girls must be critically examined if we wish to expose the sexist undertones in so much of it. I believe this book's research has the potential to make a strong theoretical contribution to the literature on gender performance and mass media representation as well as to feminist media scholarship and the growing field of girlhood studies. Ultimately, however, I hope the book reaches audiences outside academia as well. Parents, educators, media practitioners, policymakers, and girls themselves should be concerned that the way girls are represented within media often does not align with reality, and this misalignment limits both their political and cultural power. Perhaps this exposure could lead to reform.

I also hope this book demonstrates that this is a historical pattern of sexism in which crisis becomes a both a cultural distraction and the means by which American teen girls are robbed of power and agency. Even more, though, I hope that it allows a space for those girls' voices to be heard within the margins of these dominant narratives and gives them much-deserved visibility as the intelligent, creative, culturally productive citizens that they are.

CHAPTER 1

༖

THE DANCE HALL EVIL,
1905–1928

༖

Decent girls are attracted there by the dance, the freedom of coming alone, and in nearly every instance making dangerous acquaintances both among the men and women, and very soon lose the attractiveness which they possessed when they first went there.

—Mrs. Charles H. (Belle) Israels, chair of the Committee of
Amusements and Vacation Resources of Working Girls

We danced until 5 o'clock this morning and had the finest time.

—Seventeen-year-old "Sophie" from Minneapolis, quoted in the
Minneapolis Tribune, March 22, 1908

IN THE EARLY PART OF THE TWENTIETH century, teenage girls from many walks of life found themselves drawn to the sound of ragtime. Ragtime music, popularized for many by Scott Joplin's "Maple Leaf Rag" in 1899, used a ragged rhythm that was a syncopated modification of the classic concert march, which was often instrumental. A precursor to other kinds of jazz music that developed after 1915, "rags" are seen as some of the earliest pop-jazz tunes. Middle- and upper-class teens listened on the family phonographs to their favorite rags. Dance styles developed around the music, and just as in later years with the jitterbug, the Lindy Hop, and the hustle, girls taught one another the steps. In 1918 wealthy eighteen-year-old Emma Young told of the fun of dancing to popular music on the bow of a ship to a Victrola, and Dorothy Smith recalled getting dressed up as a middle-class teen to dance under the stars at regular street dances in the 1920s in her hometown of Rockford, Illinois.[1]

But it was primarily the urban working-class teen girls—already largely on their own earning wages and no longer attending school—who were able to go out and dance to the live versions of rags in their cities' dance halls.[2] The majority of these dance halls opened in urban residential areas in the early 1900s. Admission was cheap or often, for ladies only, free. The ragtime music in dance halls was usually performed by musicians and was a lively backdrop for couples who would one-step while holding each other close. For many of the girls who went to dance halls, the ability to get out on the dance floor represented a rare opportunity for autonomy—a moment to let loose to music and feel free from the responsibilities of supporting their families. And unlike dancing at home or at a community center dance, parents and chaperones would not monitor their dancing (or anything else that they might choose to do, from speaking to men to smoking cigarettes and drinking alcohol).[3] "Dance madness" reached a peak with working-class girls between the years of 1880 and 1920, according to the historian Kathy Peiss.[4] This chapter covers the period of 1905 to 1928, because those years represent the American press's heaviest coverage of dance halls.

Peiss describes dance halls as thriving in the "back rooms of dingy saloons, in large neighborhood halls, and in the brightly lit pavilions of amusement parks," with the character of each type of hall varying wildly from organization to social composition.[5] The majority of historical scholarship on dance halls focuses on their cultural function within major cities, specifically New York and Chicago. Smaller regional dance halls, dances in barns, and "open air ballrooms" set up on streets and lake beaches throughout the country also existed but have been less documented than their urban counterparts.

Media coverage of dance halls in the early twentieth century primarily conjured one word: evil. Whether in a story about government regulation or crime, the dance halls in major metropolitan areas provided reporters with salacious fodder that seemed intended to strike fear in their audiences. These stories, which ran frequently in papers across the country, almost always focused on girls and how they would be corrupted or hurt by dance halls.

"This Is No Place for Ladies?"

The newspaper coverage of American dance halls between 1905 and 1928 demonstrates how a discomfort—specifically the perceived poor influence of dance halls on girls who were mostly in their teens—became a pervasive social issue that both supported and reproduced dominant cultural discourses related to gender. How this came to be was largely a product of historical circumstance. Despite lacking the political power of the vote, women were increasingly in the public eye, due to the suffrage movement and to the growing acceptance of women's participation in the workplace, civic clubs, and leisure pursuits. This early appearance of women outside the domestic sphere caused a certain amount of consternation in U.S. society. Publicity or publicness was still connected to promiscuity as it related to women and girls.[6] Many people connected women being in public with women who walked on the streets as prostitutes. Further, many people were concerned that girls and women who went into public urban spaces would be victimized.

This connection is visible in a 1905 story in the *Minneapolis Tribune* about how a Christian preacher and his wife entered a dance hall with the hope of evangelizing the people inside. The article reinforces the cultural belief that women—even religious women with husbands—were ill equipped to handle situations that required them to be in public. The preacher's wife, identified as Mrs. Asher, attempted to quiet a man in the dance hall in her "quiet, womanly way":

> She approached the unruly member and attempted to subdue him in her quiet, womanly way, but without success. "My dear man," she said. "I am sure that you will behave like a gentleman when you realize that there are ladies present. You wouldn't willingly offend a woman would you?"
>
> "Not me," said the fellow. "But this is no place for ladies. Why don't you go home where you belong? I have the greatest respect for ladies. I have a wife and two daughters of my own, but I do not allow them to frequent saloons."[7]

News stories were far more unrelenting in their coverage of the working-class girls who went to dance halls, suggesting that by merely showing up in them, they would be susceptible to corruption. Although anxiety over teen delinquency in the United States most likely did not reach its nadir until after World War I, newspaper articles in the early 1900s suggest audiences were growingly concerned about it. For example, a parade of adolescent girls from juvenile detention custody were brought to the

Chicago mayor's office in June 1905 by a prominent social reformer to put a human face on the dance hall problem for him in a story headlined (in attention-demanding caps), "GIRLS TESTIFY TO DUNNE. VICTIMS OF DANCE HALL BROUGHT BEFORE THE MAYOR."[8]

Another example is found in the story "Girls Worse Than Boys," in a January 3, 1906, *Chicago Daily Tribune* article. Official sources (directors of juvenile detention centers) were called on to discuss how dance halls were to blame for the increase in "bad girls":

> The bad boy is disappearing; the bold, bad girl is taking his place. She is the girl who wears her hat on one side, swings along the street smiling at every man she passes, whisks into the dance hall, whirls through the throng, tipples wine, snaps her fingers disdainfully in her mother's face, ignores her warnings. She is society's problem; compared with her the street gamin with the tangled shock is like a cherub with its face turned toward the sky. That is what William O. LaMonte, for five years clerk of the Juvenile Court, told the members of the Social Economics club yesterday.
>
> "Do you mean to say that delinquency is increasing among girls?" demanded an aggrieved member, amazed.
>
> "I do," asserted Mr. LaMonte. "I mean that and I mean that delinquency among girls is increasing much more rapidly than among boys; it is increasing at an alarming extent."

Noting the sharp increase in cases of delinquent girls brought to Juvenile Court over the past year, he charged the women activists in attendance to "work day and night" to abolish dance halls in order to save girls in the future from such a fate.

Another *Daily Tribune* story featured a quote from Mrs. John B. Sherwood explaining the dance hall's function: "Young people need some sort of safety valve. They must have amusement or they will get in trouble," she said. "The commercialized dance hall caters to this desire for amusement, this longing for pleasure. They encourage it; they feed upon it, and by lax supervision, often fan it into a dangerous flame."[9] These viewpoints further reinforce the notion that dance halls and teen girls were a dangerous combination because of the opportunity they presented for gender negotiation and sexuality articulation in the public sphere.

One of the earliest waves of coverage surrounding regulation and prohibition of dance halls started with a strange incident in Chicago: in 1905
a young woman named Mabel Wright reportedly went to a dance hall,
danced for a few hours, and then committed suicide by taking poison (she
left a suicide note in her pocket and told a man who attempted to help her
she had taken chloroform and wanted to die). The first news story the *Chicago Daily Tribune* published about her death suggested that even though
the twenty-two-year-old was a wholesome young woman living with her
mother, she had secretly visited dance halls, where she met a man who she
eventually secretly married. The reporter noted that the dance hall (rather
than the man, who is later revealed to have broken her heart) was her
downfall: "Mrs. Wright apparently was surrounded with all the care and
refinement it was possible for a loving parent and brother to bestow. And
yet, unknown to her family, she visited dance halls."[10] The third deck of the
headline about the article notes, "Young Girls Frequent Hall," as if to provide a final connection between death and the notion that simply attending
a dance hall could place a girl at risk to become brokenhearted and suicidal.

An excerpt from "Want Law to Govern City Dance Halls: Committee
for Working Girls Says Many of These Places Are Now a Menace (with a
second capitalized deck, "LIQUOR SOLD IN SOME," and a third deck reading, "Young Girls Also Make Undesirable Acquaintances There") exemplifies how descriptive language could be used to concern readers. "The girls
found in these halls ranged from 16 to 24, and over 80 percent of them were
unescorted," the reporter wrote. "On an average Saturday night fully 2,000
unescorted young girls enter the dance halls of the city, in many cases
without the knowledge of their parents."[11] Dance halls were portrayed as
"vice dives" and bait, luring girls into a life of drinking, drugs, and prostitution.[12]

The girls who went to them usually were portrayed as neither sophisticated nor intelligent enough to navigate their way in the world outside their
homes. In a 1905 *Chicago Daily Tribune* article, Mrs. E. Cornelia Clafin, a
delegate from the Promotion of Health Club, said, "when a woman is alone
in a great city, with no home to welcome her, and the open doors of a dance
hall shed a warm light across her path, she cannot be blamed if she goes
inside."[13]

Moreover, the increasing public furor over dance halls was evident
in articles that had little or nothing to do with dance halls. For example,

in an article about upcoming aldermen elections in Chicago, a member of the Women's Civic League, was quoted asking candidates, "What method would you suggest for the protection of girls from the dance hall and saloon evils?" The reporter noted in the article that the dance hall evil ranked second behind the issue of enfranchisement of women in Illinois and just ahead of the "garbage problem."[14]

Although the press coverage often suggested that all girls were potential victims of the dance hall evil, class often seemed to mark girls as more vulnerable (both because working-class girls were more likely to go to them but also because they were often represented as ignorant and childlike). Given this, it might seem remarkable that both the penny press papers and tabloids, which were read by a largely working-class audience, and the prestige papers, such as the *New York Times,* which targeted upper-class readers, took the same journalistic approach in covering dance halls. The frenzied crisis fostered by the media's dance hall coverage likely also worked to scare the upper-class readers into believing that their daughters might also be susceptible to the "dance hall evil." After all, the *New York Times* also wished to sell newspapers and gain advertising too.

Newspapers in the Early Twentieth Century

Moral panic could not exist without mass media's stereotypical or stylized presentation of the topic causing the panic.[15] As such, the dance hall panic could hardly have existed before the establishment of the penny press in the middle to late 1800s. The penny press is a term that refers to the amount charged for most major city papers but also refers to the ability of newspapers to reach a mass audience. Thanks to the invention of steam presses, urban and regional newspapers became popular among the middle and working classes because of their low cost and sordid subject matter often revolving around crime, adventure, tragedy, and gossip.[16] Although these newspapers were not necessarily viewed as competition to more elite newspapers—such as the *New York Times,* which was six cents—historians often credit them with increasing rates of literacy among working classes and fostering a hunger for news and increased journalistic competition among all newspapers of the day.[17] Although the period of the penny press is generally thought to have ended in the 1860s, some of its hallmarks—specifically its splashy style and concentration of sordid crime stories—remained as a regular part of daily papers in cities nationwide for decades to come, including during the period of the dance hall panic.[18]

Competition continued to increase, especially for New York newspapers, as they entered the era of yellow journalism. Both a practice and an era in which the type of journalism was practiced, yellow journalism used fear-mongering headlines, sensational and questionably ethical stories, and a sympathizing tone for the underdog and commoner. It was made especially famous by *New York World* publisher Joseph Pulitzer and *New York Journal* publisher William Randolph Hearst, who competed fiercely with each other through increasingly sensational stories and cheaper newspapers.[19] The height of yellow journalism is often thought to be around 1890–1900, when the competing New York dailies increased coverage of Cuba in such a way that stirred up the public and political sentiment that most likely led to the Spanish-American War.[20] Although the yellow journalism era was thought to be winding down by the time reporters latched on to the dance hall crisis (and the *World* and *Journal* were no longer the dominant newspapers in New York City), its sensational tone and lack of objectivity arguably influenced both the headlines and impassioned tone of the dance hall news coverage described in this chapter.

The period of yellow journalism made way for investigative, undercover reporting called "muckraking," which emerged and peaked around the time that dance halls became fashionable among working-class teen girls, specifically in the late nineteenth century into the first decade of the twentieth century. The practice, which often borrowed from the sensationalism of yellow journalism reporting, is described as investigative journalism involving social issues (often exposing corruption of elected officials or corporate leaders and crime). One of the most famous stories of the genre was "The History of the Standard Oil Company: The Oil War of 1872," by Ida Tarbell, a famous muckraking journalist who published the piece in *McClure's Magazine* in 1908, the same time as most of the negative dance hall news coverage took place.[21]

Muckrakers' journalistic accounts were usually featured in magazines, where a longer format allowed for sprawling, thorough storytelling, but the style of muckraking journalism—specifically, the concern that the press and others uncovered stories of a sordid nature for the concern of the average, middle-class individual—is noticeable in newspaper coverage of social issues such as dance hall reform. Not only are the social issues covered in newspapers at this time indicative of the concerns of prominent social reformers and government officials, but reporters often used undercover accounts within the stories. For example, an article about women social reformers in New York describes how a young female social reformer visited dozens of dance halls to talk to young women and men who attended them as part of an "investigative report."[22] In a *Chicago Daily Tribune* story the reporter takes on a first-person "investigation" of the city's fruit stands (which he called "kindergarten wine rooms" and contended they were a kind of social training ground for the more evil dance halls).[23]

In the early 1900s newspapers provided citizens with an official record of news events that were most pertinent based on geographic location and interests, along with an opportunity to glimpse how others lived and what they believed. Transportation still consisted primarily of horse and train travel, and there were few opportunities outside of actually visiting a place and witnessing cultural norms associated with that location to learn about others' morals, values, and interests. The newspaper—especially regional newspapers with a fairly large readership—could provide documentation for those who could not visit and witness themselves. Newspaper accounts reinforced cultural beliefs tied to an individual's understanding of morality, politics, and the important issues of the age. Newspapers took part in a social construction of reality that reinforced cultural norms as well as gender norms.[24] With this in mind, understanding how newspapers approached coverage of dance halls demonstrates how they ultimately played a large part in creating what became known through early twentieth century news headlines and cultural discourse as the "dance hall evil."

Constructed by the mass media, the mythology of the dance halls generally evolved from the crime reports and commentary by prominent social progressives published in the papers, in which a vivid picture of debauchery was revealed: dancing, drinking, carousing, fighting, and in some cases prostituting. Mythology might not be a fair description. Indeed, the big-city dance hall did often seem to provide police with plenty of work, according to newspaper accounts. But to readers who never would have considered entering an actual dance hall, the newspaper stories, opinion pieces, and crime reports painted a morally repugnant picture. Their reality was constructed using the most sordid elements of dance halls, from their selling of liquor to the overtly sexual dancing that many believed took place in them. Furthermore, even though some social reformers sang the praises of wholesome leisure and dancing, newspapers did not run any stories about the potential positive outcomes of visiting a dance hall. Arguably, the news frame associated with working-class girls going to dance halls to have fun dancing was not considered to be newsworthy. The news frame that positioned dance halls as dangerous public space probably was far better at selling papers.

In some ways news stories in the early twentieth century resemble journalistic storytelling conventions in contemporary times—for example, the way that facts appear in order of importance and are illustrated with quotations. But certain differences exist that make stories from the period unique. For example, the reporter would sometimes tell the story in first person or the imagined words of a source rather than quote the source. Moreover, loaded and fairly subjective terms—"evil," for example—are peppered throughout the coverage without contextualization or attribution, giving the impression that journalists were not particularly critical of their sources or their political motivations.

In the following excerpt from the *New York Tribune,* under the headline, "East Side Dance Halls That Play Havoc with Morals," it is difficult to tell where the reporter is getting information about girls who go to dance halls. The following excerpt, like much of the article, reads like an authoritative first-person account that leaves no question about whether the reporter believes dance halls are dangerous spaces for girls:

> The drinking may not be heavy, but a girl heated and excited by dancing when induced to take even only a sip of beer, is bound to be in not the best condition to take care of herself. Most of the men drink freely, and language becomes unbridled and conduct is not of the chastest. The men who run these dance halls do not do it for the moral improvement of the community. Anyone who pays is admitted, and no questions asked. Thus a lot of vicious riffraff of both sexes will find their way into even the most respectable dance halls, and will mix with Innocent girls and young men.[25]

Like this *New York Tribune* story, most of the stories did not contain bylines. In an era before professionalism was an established value for journalists, bylines were simply unnecessary. The ethical implications of this particular reporting practice are somewhat obvious: because audiences could not hold reporters individually accountable for their work, reporters arguably had more leeway to stray from the objectivity and fairness that is associated with journalism in the middle and later parts of the century.

Conversely, one could argue that this practice shielded reporters from vindictive city officials, allowing them to perform duties without being beholden to certain sources and their agendas. But the analysis of the news articles in this chapter suggests the reporters returned to the same official sources repeatedly in their coverage of the dance hall problem and reform movement; they rarely presented the viewpoint of dance hall supporters and never presented the viewpoint of the young people actually going to dance halls. Moreover, news organizations' policy of publishing without bylines allowed them to put forth an "anonymous, authoritative voice" that was difficult to question.[26] This made for incredibly effective publicity on issues that reflected social progressives' notions of morality and evil, particularly their crusade against dance halls. These social progressives, often women with a higher socioeconomic status, were positioned by reporters as experts who could comment on the degenerate influence of dance halls on girls.

The Dancing School Type

The socioeconomic status of the girls who went to dance halls in the early twentieth century is a consideration in every news account written. In this *New York Tribune* article, the "dancing school girl" from the East Side is vulgar and rough: "The vulgarizing effects of the generally vicious dance hall cannot be overrated. The dancing school girl is a type on the East Side, and can easily be recognized by the boldness of her star, roughness of her speech and vulgarity of her manners. But, above all, the dance hall cheapens the worth of her own body. She does not resent even the most vulgar touch. It is not therefore surprising that cases of ruin are frequent and illicit connections widely prevalent." In other words, this East Side girl was not educated or taught manners in the first place, and this lack of fine breeding and wealth is partially responsible for her having gone to the dance hall. Then, the dance hall itself "vulgarized" her further—simply by virtue of her having been there. The reporter then makes a larger connection: "Many of the fallen women of the city are graduates of the East Side dance halls." In other words, girls of a lower class were prone to go to these dance halls, and when they did, they became disreputable, which further led to them becoming prostitutes. A police officer was quoted saying a large part of his job between the hours of midnight and one in the morning was to use a skeleton key to let in girls into their families' locked apartments after leaving the dance halls.[27]

In another *New York Tribune* article discussing working-class girls' preference for dance halls (this time West Side girls), a sixteen-year-old New Yorker named Josie, who went to public dances "three out of every seven nights of the week," said, "When I'm eighteen or nineteen I won't care about it anymore. I'll have a 'friend' then and won't want to go any-wheres."[28] Although this quote is really quite delightful, it was taken from a research report, *The Neglected Girl,* written by Ruth Smiley True about the grim plight of poor and working-class girls, including many who were served by the Hartley Settlement House. True described dance halls as a welcome escape: "Many of the older girls—I mean girls over sixteen—have found their way to the dance hall. Two of them go together as a rule. They must have a little money—carfare and a quarter for entrance, but that is all that is needed; no chaperone and no escort. Bonds are off; freedom is absolute; the range of possibilities is almost limitless."[29]

In this article the girls' working-class status is important to the narrative, but True's research is far more nuanced and detailed than what appears in the news article. Her report speaks mostly about how the girls live in abject poverty and go to work to support their families at a young age. Further-more, a different meaning emerges from that delightful quote—one that questions whether a sixteen-year-old girl should be thinking about getting married at such a young age: "A party of this kind is not the single carnival of the year. Once a week, if not twice or thrice, the girl who goes to the dance hall goes through its round of excesses. The most startling fact in this connection is that it is the little girls who are doing the dancing in the public places of amusement in New York. The young girl usually settles down to keeping steady company some time before her early marriage, and goes less to the dance halls."[30] Again, this more depressing piece of True's report likely did not fit into the preferred narrative by the *New York Tribune* reporter who wrote the story. Instead, the girls described sound ignorant and silly.

Similarly, in a 1908 column in the *Minneapolis Tribune* "Tribune Girl" quotes the seventeen-year-old girl, "Sophie," who cleans her house: "A bunch of us girls go down town to the hall and it don't cost nothing and

"The Whole Story: The Dance, the Drink, the Man, the Girl": "Dance hall evil" illustrated in *The Survey*, vol. 22, no. 3, July 1909. Photo by Hine. (Social Welfare History Archives, University of Minnesota-Twin Cities)

we go in and the fellows ask us to dance and we just have lots of fun . . . If you don't let [fellows] kiss you [after they take you out to eat after the dance] they sometimes get mad and then you have to go home alone. I ain't scared and I have enough fun at the dance to make up for it."[31] With its lack of grammar and use of slang, the girl's quotation would expose her class even if readers did not know she was a housekeeper (and, moreover, the author refers to her home in the tony Lowry Hill neighborhood of Minneapolis and Sophie battling the traffic in northeast Minneapolis, a more industrial section of the city at that time). The column was written as a response to a strict ordinance against dance halls intended to show how dance halls could be a source of cheap recreation for girls with few other opportunities for fun and relaxation. It is unclear whether the columnist actually did interview her housekeeper or, as the headline "The Dance-Hall Evil as Tribune Girl Sees It through Others' Eyes" suggests, just made up the quote as if it were spoken by a typical dance hall goer. Furthermore, it would have been unusual to have interviewed an actual working-class girl for a news story.

Additionally, ethnicity also was an important consideration in the media's coverage of the dance hall issue because many of the girls discussed were immigrants or children of immigrants. In response to a question of whether her mother knew she frequented dance halls until the wee hours of the morning, the seventeen-year-old in *Minneapolis Tribune* story replied, "O, sure, Ma knows but she is too busy with the young kids to bother about me, and anyhow, she don't care for she used to go to dances in the old country herself and she knows a girl has to have some fun." The inclusion of a quote about the "old country" lets the audience know her mother is an immigrant and that she is the first-generation immigrant daughter. To further this point, the writer later laments her naive parents not realizing that the big-city public dances are not the "same innocent pastime that it was in the foreign hamlet where they spent their youth."[32]

In a muckraking-style piece from *McClure*'s titled "The Daughters of the Poor," George Kibbe Turner explored the suffering and victimization of young working-class and poor women. In a section focusing on the overtly sexual dancing ("tough" dancing) that takes place in dance halls, Turner described a "new Jewish immigrant girl": "She arrives, pays her nickel piece, and sits—a big, dazed, awkward child—upon one of the wooden benches along the wall," he wrote. Despite most social reformers' concern that liquor seduces girls into dancing and leaving with strange men, Turner instead blamed the fact that the girls are "lonely and poverty-stricken" and "ignorant and dazed by the strange conditions of a new country."[33] The words "ignorant and dazed" as applied to a new immigrant create a media narrative that constructs immigrants as stupid and amusingly unassimilated. Although the main point of Turner's story was to implicate the infamous Tammany Hall political machine in sanctioning citywide illegal establishments, his description of the girl at the dance hall illustrates the normalization of statements that are clearly sexist, classist, and racist. This sort of language was not even questioned by the editors of the time.

Turner's article also discussed the role of dance halls in the practice of "white slavery," which today would be known as human sex trafficking.[34] "White slavery" is itself a documented moral panic, wherein the late nineteenth- and early twentieth-century press published mostly (if not entirely) fabricated reports about Caucasian girls and young women taken by degenerate gangs of Chinese immigrants who would introduce them to opium and prostitution. The "white slavery" panic was very much a product of the racism of the time, wherein low-paid Chinese immigrant labor was viewed as a threat to Caucasian workers who demanded more pay for their work.[35] The white slavery panic also effectively racialized and marginalized all people of color who might be viewed as threatening simply because of the fear that African Americans, Asians, and Latinos would harm Caucasians if given the opportunity. Although largely a myth perpetuated by city tabloids, white slavery functioned as an ongoing crisis that had the social effect of public acceptance for increased law enforcement.[36] The white slave panic is associated with "dance hall evil," but it is only a component of the problematic narrative of teen girls' corruption and victimization through their attendance of dance halls.

Clearly, working girls' sexuality on public display was more of an issue within the prevalent media coverage of dance halls. An article published in the *Chicago Daily Tribune,* "Women to Fight Dance Hall Evil," more explicitly connected "saving" girls from the evils of the dance halls as they flaunted their sexuality. The article included many long quotes from Mrs. John B. Sherwood, who was displeased with the failure of the police to "suppress the vicious dance hall by law." The Women's Club planned to start its own girls-only dance hall that would be patrolled by chaperones and held only during daylight hours. The article's author deemed dance halls a "new brand of competition for the proprietors of the 'girl traps'—a competition actuated, not by a debased commercial instinct, but by a conviction that girls have a right to the pleasure of the dance without the subsequent sorrow which often comes to them under the soft lights of the commercialized dance hall." Mrs. Sherwood, in speaking for the club, noted that it was not dancing that they opposed: "Few persons—even those who are opposed to it—think there is anything wrong in dancing itself. It is the attendant consequences which they dread." In other words, dancing in private (and dancing among other women) was not necessarily the problem; rather, the sexuality associated with dancing with a male partner was their concern. This femininity, especially as it was articulated by lower-class girls, needed to be policed.[37]

This belief is also clear in a *New York Times* article quoting Mrs. Charles H. (Belle) Israels, the chair of the Committee of Amusements and Vacation Resources of Working Girls. Israels, who is one of the frequent sources referred to in this chapter, said, "Home conditions of most of the young working girls in New York are such that they cannot undertake to carry on the social life which they crave within the limits that are prescribed for the young women of other environments. The dance hall is naturally her club. Here she meets boys and men who are attractive to her and to whom she in turn can be attractive."[38] Israels—a former settlement worker—was a common source for *Times* stories because of her visibility within the Progressive movement and involvement with numerous organizations dedicated to the "amusement problem" facing working-class girls. Her comments suggest that the dance hall, in all its vulgarity, was one of the only venues where working-class girls could meet men of an appropriate social class. (Note that she did not suggest that affluent country clubs offer affordable fees and entrance requirements that would allow a girl to meet non–working-class men because these were not "within the limits that are prescribed for the young women" of these environments.) She also explained that working-class girls may lose their "attractiveness," or virtuousness, after going to a dance hall alone: "The iniquity of such places is that decent girls are attracted there by the dance, the freedom of coming alone, and in nearly every instance making dangerous acquaintances both among the men and women, and very soon lose the attractiveness which they possessed when they first went there."[39]

Dance halls that serve liquor were far worse than the ones that don't because it allows girls to become all the more corrupted, she suggested. "The young man who wishes to spread himself dissuades the girl from drinking 3-cent drinks, such as beer or soft drinks, because he wants to show his ability to buy more expensive ones—whisky at 15 cents," she said in the *Times* story. "The girl begins by being unwilling to drink it, but she soon follows the example of the less scrupulous or more hardened girls she sees about her." In Israels's estimation, girls were so witless that they were impressed at the seeming wealth of a man willing to buy her drinks and influenced to move on to harder liquor by merely seeing "hardened girls" around her drinking it.[40]

Settlement Workers, Progressives, and Moral Entrepreneurship

In a 1907 *Chicago Daily Tribune* article, "War against City's Vice Centers on Dance Hall: Women Members of the Law and Order League's Special Committee Will Concentrate Attack on Resorts," women are the "crusaders" in a war where they say they will recruit other "mothers and other women desirous of ridding Chicago of vice breeding places" to take part in a mass meeting to shutter the city's dance halls.[41] The suggestion that mothers should be the type of people who care about vice ties in to the age-old ethic of care associated with women—because women are mothers they should specifically care about these issues, and men who are fathers should not be concerned with such trivialities or emotional pursuits. Reporting from a press conference in the office of Lucy Page Gaston, a prominent anti-to-bacco activist who convinced the Illinois legislature to impose a statewide ban on cigarettes in 1907, a journalist writes that although "they cannot crusade against every vice at once," the women "intend to secure a fund of $25,000 to defray the expenses of stamping out the evil" of the dance halls.[42]

Indeed, much of the narrative about dance hall and evil rooted from the social reformers of the time, most of them political Progressives, who were quite savvy at being quoted in the press to further their cause. Most of these dance hall crusaders, including Israels, Sherwood, and Gaston, were women who perfectly fit Howard S. Becker's description of "moral entre-preneur," particularly in the way that their social position enabled them to enforce rules. Even though their gender precluded them from having real political power, they did have special power in their moral crusade against girls and dance halls because they were white, wealthy, and socially connected, and the girls were working class or poor and often immigrants or first-generation Americans.[43] These social reformers were constantly included in media coverage on dance halls, usually in connection with a social reform organization. In fact, only such organizations in Chicago (Promotion of Health Club, Catholic Women's League, Nike Club, Teachers Federation, Visiting Nurse Association, Law and Order League, and Evan-ston Women's Club) and New York (Women's Conference of the Society for Ethical Culture, New York Women's University Club, National Council of Jewish Women, New York Section, plus a handful of others) appeared to generate most of the events and discussion around the corrupting influence of dance halls in the one hundred or so newspaper articles published on the topic.

Although many of the women members and leaders in these clubs were married to men who were wealthy or politically connected, a number of them were educated single women from middle-class families. They were unusual in that they had careers—during a period when most middle-class women did not work—that involved progressive initiatives to help the poor and immigrants. Most of these unmarried women had previous experience working in late nineteenth- and early twentieth-century settlement houses, and their experience made them perfect advocates for immigrants, the poor, and especially for the women and girls who lived in the communities they served.

The settlement house movement encouraged wealthy and lower-income Americans to live interdependently and more closely together in urban areas, with one of the goals encouraging mixed-income living and abandoning slum areas. Settlement houses provided poor residents with food, shelter, and basic education, all funded by a city's wealthy donors, and middle-class settlement workers lived with them there, sharing their own wisdom and knowledge of culture and serving them directly as teachers or social service providers; during the period studied for this chapter, 413 settlements were active in thirty-two states. Early settlement workers are often credited in contemporary times with pioneering the profession of social work.[44] The majority of settlement workers were women, and many of these women were passionate social reformers—many of whom appear in the news coverage of the anti–dance hall crusade and many of whom attempted to influence social policy and antipoverty initiatives associated with less "moral" causes than dance halls. Their connection to the work of the settlement movement gave them moral authority but also positioned them as qualified to discuss the poor, working class, and immigrants in the media coverage of dance halls.

Although the majority of sources for news stories in the American press historically have been male, reporters did not seem to question the fact that women made up the majority of the quoted sources in their coverage of dance halls.[45] Given the sociohistorical issues revolving around gender at this point in history, the Progressives' political work with regard to young women naturally had to be undertaken by women activists because such work was deemed inappropriate and too trivial for Progressive men activists.

In New York the most visible female reformers were Jewish, and in fact dance hall reform largely emerged from the National Council of Jewish Women, New York Section, which spent much of its energy in the early 1900s on rescuing "wayward" Jewish girls. Many, including Israels and Julia Schoenfeld, were former settlement workers who first attempted to save teen girls from corruption by teaching Sunday school in state reforma-

Dance hall alternative: Working-class girls dancing and socializing inside the Hartley Settlement House in Manhattan, ca. 1915. (Social Welfare History Archives, University of Minnesota-Twin Cities)

tories.[46] After realizing that preaching had not made their intended impact, the councilwomen opened a recreation room in a downtown district with the hope of attracting girls to a wholesome environment.[47] This endeavor was covered in one story by the *New York Times,* but most of the newspapers' coverage focused on the crime and illegalities associated with dance halls rather than social organizations' proposals for solutions.

Seeing a need to present more compelling data regarding the corruption of working-class girls, the National Council of Jewish Women, New York Section, under Israels's leadership conducted survey research and in their efforts became more convinced that the dance hall was often the source and site of corruption for this seemingly vulnerable population. More than two hundred girls they surveyed cited dancing as their favorite pastime above all other pastimes and said they would prefer to go to a city dance hall to do so.[48] In 1905 the group's early survey research blossomed into a project for a full city committee, the Committee of Fourteen, which composed a lengthy document titled "The Social Evil in New York City." The committee, a mix of male and female social reformers and government officials, was not concerned primarily with the welfare of working-class girls but rather with the larger task of convincing the public that the government should repeal the Raines Law.[49]

The Raines Law was passed by the New York State legislature on March 23, 1896, and exempted saloons with attached hotels from a statewide drinking ban on Sundays. Since most men worked six days a week, this provision was popular. Many saloon owners were able to take part in this loophole by purchasing adjoining apartments (which were often used as brothels) and applying for a hotel license. These were known as Raines Law hotels and were the scourge of many social reformers concerned about the uptick in prostitution and other immoral behavior.[50] Much of the coverage of dance halls referred to these Raines Law hotels because they were often associated with dance halls—sometimes fairly and sometimes simply because dance halls were perceived as "gin palaces," as social reformer Jane Addams referred to them.[51] Although dance halls were popular during the last five to ten years of the nineteenth century, the apex of dance hall coverage did not occur until nearly a decade later, when the issue of reforming them was pushed as both as a way to repeal Raines and to stop the "corruption" of working-class girls who attended them. Furthermore, it served as an early rumbling of the latest iteration of the pre–Prohibition Temperance Movement in the United States, which many years later involved numerous social Progressives who had been involved in the settlement movement and various social reform issues.

In 1905 a committee of concerned citizens and government officials was formed in New York with the task of repealing the Raines Law exemption. Israels, a committee member, published a summary of the report in *The Survey* titled "The Way of the Girl."[52] In the report she and fellow committee member Schoenfeld note they had visited dance halls all over the city to better understand the topic. A word-for-word accounting of Schoenfeld's findings was available to readers of the *New York Tribune* in its story on the meeting. The following is an excerpt from Schoenfeld's presentation:

> In the vilest parts of Paris I saw no more vulgar or low dancing than I have seen at the "rackets" in New York . . .

> Girls come alone and in groups of twos or threes. They return with anyone they can pick up at a dance. They are young, seldom far in their twenties, most of them eighteen and nineteen, though I have seen many girls not much over fourteen in one hall. I conversed with a group of girls under fourteen and found out that they go weekly to a dance and stay till midnight. In this instance the parents knew where their girls were.[53]

In addition to establishing the extent of the dance hall problem among younger girls, she also seemed to rebuke their parents for allowing them to stay out so late. The *Tribune* continued to quote Schoenfeld as she made a very clear distinction between good girls and bad girls, noting they came from "all walks of life" but meaning they came only from a lower socioeconomic status:

> Girls come from every walk of life, the shops and factories, the burlesque and chorus, domestics and waitresses. Even the girl in the home who is not employed is on the streets searching for fun. In the Casino many good girls are seen, but in the lowly saloon dance halls they are seldom found. Manners and customs are as loose as morals. Between the dances the girls flock to the dressing rooms, some to smoke, some to powder and paint. The men flock to the bar. The girls drink, but not to the extent that is naturally expected. The men are usually drunk before the evening is over.[54]

Only the more general points of Schoenfeld and the Committee of Fourteen's report were covered by the *New York Times* in its story, "Want Law to Govern City Dance Halls: Committee for Working Girls Says Many of These Places Are Now a Menace." But the headlines and word choice made clear the danger and evil girls encounter at dance halls: The second-deck headline read, "LIQUOR SOLD IN SOME," and the third deck reported, "Young Girls Also Make Undesirable Acquaintances There—Has a Benefit When Well Run." In choosing to use words such as "menace," to emphasize that some sell alcohol, and to note that "undesirable acquaintances" abound for young girls, the reporter essentially buried the women's point that a dance hall did not always have to be a dangerous or corrupting place for girls (a point suggested in the lowest subheading of the story). The *Times*'s reporter also added a line that Schoenfeld soon would be attending graduate school, perhaps to reassure readers that a single young woman who had entered dance halls was in fact a trustable authority. This also provides another indication that socioeconomic status matters enormously in the media narrative about dance halls, particularly as it was covered by an elite news source like the *Times*. Journalists' reliance on socially prominent and official sources reinforces Stuart Hall's point that the news media are partly responsible in perpetuating certain ideologies that reinforce upper-class values.[55]

Not all the women social reformers specifically blamed the naive, ignorant working-class girls for their susceptibility to dance hall evil. In a *Chicago Daily Tribune* article, settlement worker Corinne Browne noted that it was the "man evil" rather than the dance hall evil leading to the corruption of young ladies: "It is not the dance hall, nor the dancing, that leads the girl to her destruction, but the men that frequent these places. There is a law which prohibits the sale of liquor to minors. It should be enforced. I would arrest every man who buys a drop of liquor in a dance hall. See that the present laws are enforced—see that no liquor is sold in the dance halls, and see that they are closed at midnight. With these two things carried out the evil will be eliminated. Surround the dance halls with good environment." But even her testimony was trumped by a higher authority, the better-known authority Lucy Gaston, who responded, "If the women's clubs haven't brains and heart to think of some substitute for the dance hall, I do not know who will be found that has," a quote that placed the onus of vanquishing the dance hall evil specifically on other women.[56] Although the articles always mentioned gender as it related to the patrons of dance halls, this was the only occasion where a source within the article gendered the problem *and* the responsibility for solving it.

Setting the Agenda of the Dance Hall Evil

Social reformers against dance halls were able to use the press to their advantage to spread Progressive messages to a variety of audiences, but journalists also were able to appropriate these messages to craft their own narrative about dance halls as they related to young girls. They were able to find many opportunities to pull meaty quotations from the reformers' fiery rhetoric, including the speeches they gave at conferences. For example, the

National Conference on Social Welfare presented the early twentieth-century newspapers with an opportunity to both cover a large news event and present a narrative about dance halls that would appeal to (and scare) their readers.

In the speeches throughout the 1912 conference, themes of moral corruption abound. Israels's conference speech described in specific and colorful terms how girls are corrupted even just from hearing about a dance hall. The *New York Times* reported on her speech in an article titled, "Polite Dances are Shown to Society," making special references to the "Turkey Trot" and the "Bunny Hug" as particularly offensive.[57] Excerpted here, the original speech is specific in how boys who attend dance halls corrupt girls, even when they do not go to dance halls themselves: "The boy who is seated at the burlesque show . . . and is hearing in the latest slang the nearest approach to ribald language, is tomorrow presenting these things as the latest smartness to the girl with whom he is dancing—perhaps at the church sociable. He forms his standard of taste, and he forms the girl's standard of taste, in other places besides the dance hall. And what he likes, she likes. What he wants her to do and what she believes will make him anxious to have her for a companion and a friend, is what she will do."[58]

Also speaking at the national convention was Beulah Kennard, the educational director of the Department Store Education Association and another frequent source for the *New York Times* articles on topics related to appropriate recreation and leisure choices for young and teen girls.[59] In her remarks, titled "Emotional Life of Girls," she explained that as girls were granted more freedom from parental control and other authorities, it became more necessary to ensure "self control and inner restraint necessary to their safety." She said that despite the fact that girls and young women were "sophisticated to some extent," they were still "too young to regulate their emotions.[60] Much like the news story about the preacher's wife in the dance hall suggests, girls and women cannot be trusted because they are too emotional and vulnerable.

Furthermore, Kennard repeats the theme that girls who venture into public for leisure should be saved: "They meet on the street, in dance halls and skating rinks or by appointment at theatres and restaurants. Much of their intercourse is innocent enough but there is a growing laxness and an astounding indifference on the part of parents. We often wonder if girls no longer have any mothers . . . There is no alternative but to guard them from premature and hasty judgment so far as we may and to train them to some sense of their high calling."[61] Kennard's focus on safety and protection of girls and the notion of self-restraint reverberate throughout the news coverage and opinion pieces on girls' competitive sports, Elvis Presley, the punk rock movement, and Facebook that are explored in the next several chapters. These chapters further demonstrate a connection between the journalistic discourse that enables moral panic and gendered paternalism that spans over a century.

One prominent conference speaker was Joseph Lee, a wealthy philanthropist who later became the president of the Playground Association of America (PAA). Lee was one of the few men associated in the press with anti–dance hall sentiment and was quoted as the primary source for three *New York Times* articles linking recreation to immorality.[62] At the conference, he discussed the potential evil found in "rhythm," which he describes as "pervasive" and a "female instinct."[63] In his discussion of how dancing had become a "national obsession, amounting almost to a mania" that "had invaded the very ballroom and captured professional 'society' itself,"[64] he notes that girls' participation in dancing makes it an act of "sex expression."[65] The role of rhythm was paramount, Lee said: "the effect of rhythm has important bearing on the dance hall problem . . . The great evil of the dance hall is not in what it leads to but what it leaves out in the lost chance for a finer romance, a deeper poetry. The worst side is not their surreptitious nature but their lack of beauty."[66]

In his remarks Lee said that girls should find a new outlet to replace the dance hall, suggesting they create art (though not too sexually provocative art), read novels, and participate in girls-only sports (though people must guard against them becoming unladylike "tomboys"). He finally concluded that, above all, "girls should be taught dressmaking, the art in which most interest is taken and most money spent at the present day, the true intention of which, from Praxiteles and Botticelli down to Worth, is, and has been, not to banish beauty but to interpret it. Such teaching will both release a power of expression and emancipate from foreign fashion-makers and the monstrosities they now impose upon us."[67] In other words, a young woman's true recreation should be working in the private space of the home, participating in rituals of domesticity.

The Survey, the same publication that published Israel and Schoenfeld's dance hall report, was also a common bond among the social reformers who attended the National Conference on Social Welfare and crusaded against dance halls. The journal often functioned as a platform for dance hall reform. Widely regarded by social reformers, progressive activists, and settlement workers as required professional reading, *The Survey* fulfilled the need for a space to discuss issues affecting working-class women and girls in reformers' own words. The articles often provided more depth and nuance on the issue of the dance hall than the shorter, event-focused news stories in the major newspapers, and they were written by insiders, often practicing social workers, reform leaders, and members of prominent social organizations devoted to cultural improvement. Although this chapter does not focus extensively on the articles of *The Survey* or its predecessor *Charities* (known for a time as *Charities and the Commons*), the journal was widely read and influential among the social reformers interested in regulating or outlawing dance halls. It focused broadly on issues of working-class leisure, recreation, and betterment, especially among the young, and is further explored in chapter 2 in the discussion of teen girls' leisure and sports in the 1920s and 1930s.

One of the most famous social reformers to become involved in the issue of girls and dance halls was Jane Addams, who was also credited with using her own inheritance to found one of the best-known settlement houses, the Hull House in Chicago (and later was the first woman awarded a Nobel Peace Prize). Also known for her work as a suffragist and pacifist, Addams's visibility lent gravity to any issue. In 1908 she voiced concern over dance halls and their roles in the lives of working-class teen girls in an editorial in *Charities and the Commons:*

> In every city arise so-called "places"—"gin palaces" they are called in fiction—in Chicago, we euphemistically say merely "places" in which alcohol is dispensed not to allay thirst, but, pretending to stimulate gaiety, it is sold solely in order to empty pockets. Huge dance halls are opened to which hundreds of young people are attracted, standing wistfully outside a roped circle, for within it five cents will procure for five minutes the sense of allurement and intoxication which is sold in lieu of innocent pleasure . . . As these overworked girls stream along the street, it is easy to see only the self-conscious walk, the giggling speech, the preposterous clothing. And yet through the huge hat, with its wilderness of feathers, the girl announces to the world that she is

here. She demands attention to the fact of her existence, she states that she is ready to live, to take her immemorial place in the world.[68]

Addams's prominence and visibility lent validation to Progressives' and other social reformers' concerns about the corrupting power of dance halls on working-class teen girls. Her public condemnation of dance halls' influence on girls might have given the story added traction among the newspapers that provided such heavy coverage of the subject. Addams's statement on the importance of finding activities that are less "soul-destroying" for working-class teen girls was an important statement within the movement.

When comparing the news articles with the speeches, particularly in the case of Addams, it is important to note that reporters tended to draw quotations about soul-destroying gin palaces and ignore arguments about social justice for the poor, better labor conditions for workers, and gender equity. Perhaps these points did not fit into the news frame of either the penny press style tabloids or the prestige papers like the *New York Times* and therefore were not included.

The Black Press's Coverage of Dance Halls

African American audiences might have been offered a different viewpoint from the black press of the time. Contemporary readers might be surprised to learn about the power and reach of the black press within early twentieth-century America, particularly the reach of the *Chicago Defender,* which was founded in 1905 and viewed as a very influential newspaper in its dealing with the changing race relations in the United States during the period of the dance hall coverage.[69] With a circulation of 230,000 (which did not account for informal circulation, where the publication was passed around among families, church members, and neighbors who could not afford the subscription), the paper was the largest black newspaper in the country in the early 1900s. By billing the paper on the front page of each issue as "The World's Greatest Weekly," editor Robert S. Abbott sought to "speak boldly on behalf of Black America."[70] Although the chapters in this book use a variety of African American publications in the analysis of media coverage of teen girls and public recreation, the *Defender* is cited most often, especially in the case studies in the early part of the twentieth century, when newspapers in general were a primary source of news for readers.

The coverage of dance halls by the black press was indeed different from other newspapers' coverage. Specifically, journalists questioned the strong narrative of panic. Instead, stories suggested that dance halls were in need of oversight and regulation rather than shuttering. The *Chicago Defender*'s dance hall coverage from 1905 to 1920 was decidedly less concerned with sexuality on display and more concerned with preserving the safety and enjoyment of dancers. A settlement house worker identified as Alice P. Vanston also noted that despite their serving as places where girls can have "good general exercise, which she can enjoy with music and among her equals," the dance halls should have some municipal direction. Vanston reacted negatively to raising the dance hall age limits to twenty-one because "this would cut out from the enjoyment of a very innocent recreation a very large number of young people."[71] She defended her viewpoint in the interest of healthful recreation and "not paternalism," and among the settlement workers and Progressive activists of the time, she seemed remarkably plainspoken and undramatic. Similarly, an article from the same period discussed how a community betterment group made up of reformed boys had kept the dance halls "in check."[72] Both the sources and their quotations in these news articles provide a contrast to those included in the articles discussed earlier in the chapter, where the quotations used colorful rhetoric to describe dance halls and unapologetically advocated for paternalism in every way.

Furthermore, the *New York Amsterdam News* broached the topic of racism in an editorial that questioned whether political Progressives' condemnation of dance halls was related to their allowance of "mixing of races." The opinion piece, harshly worded and critical of the dominant rhetoric associated with dance halls, also criticized the moral panic associated with "white slavery" and dance halls:

> One would think . . . that white women were imbeciles who are absolutely unable to choose their own associates and that if the superiority of the race is to be maintained they must not be permitted to mingle with men of other races. We believe that the average, rational individual of any race, civilized and uncivilized, superior and inferior, is able to pick out his own associates, even in a dance hall, and we are opposed to barring of Orientals from dance halls simply because they are Orientals. They are not accused of forcing white girls to dance

with them, and those who do dance with them do so of their own free will. IS THIS A CRIME?[73]

Several years later, however, the *New York Amsterdam News* reporter covering the Committee of Fourteen's second report in 1928 did take up the rhetoric of the women crusading against dance halls, describing dance halls as a "serious and growing menace" where the "hostess of the night club and speakeasy is the American counterpart of the Geisha girl . . . employed for the main purpose of increasing the sales of liquor, food and other drinks, and incidentally she is to provide . . . entertainment for the men customers." The article focused on illegal dance halls that also functioned as brothels, but the reporter did not make a clear distinction between legal and illegal dance halls and instead wrote an article that might have run in any of the white-dominated media coverage.[74] Perhaps this has less to do with racial differences and more to do with the general professionalization of journalism that was beginning to take hold at the end of the 1920s—a historical shift that is explained in the next chapter.

Searching for Girls' Voices

The news stories reported during the period of the dance hall crisis primarily consist of sources speaking on behalf of working-class girls. Most reporters would not have thought to interview a working-class girl in the early twentieth century for her view on the dance halls. It is unclear whether the columnist writing the *Minneapolis Tribune* story at the beginning of the chapter was presenting a fictionalized account of what a dance hall girl might have said (the language in the column suggests this might be the case) or whether she actually asked her housekeeper about dance halls. Quotes in the *New York Tribune* article were actually pulled directly from Ruth Smiley True's *Neglected Girl* report and not from journalists' interviews with girls who went to dance halls. Although a diary entry of one very wealthy seventeen-year-old from the era was quoted talking about her love for dancing, there are no journals or diaries from poor or working-class girls in archives that talk about their visits to dance halls.

Some working-class girls' words were recorded in academic literature from the period, however. For example, a large body of interviews with working-class girls who went out to dance halls can be found in Paul

Cressey's ethnographic study, *The Taxi-Dance Hall,* research that focused on an especially notorious type of dance hall that proliferated in urban areas. Cressey started his research as a doctoral student at the University of Chicago in the mid-1920s, perhaps after learning about them through the extensive media coverage on dance halls in the preceding decade or so. His work included dozens of long interviews with girls and women who frequented taxi dance halls and his own observations of dance halls, but it is riddled with judgments about race and ethnicity, class, and gender that by contemporary standards are problematic. An excerpt from his field notes on the dance hall girl "type" follows:

> The dance-hall girl, on closer inspection, seems to represent more a type in more than appearance. She may be either blond or brunette, but apparently she is required to be slender, lithe, youthful, and vivacious. She perhaps need not be thought virtuous, in the conventional sense; she must at least be considered "peppy." Occasionally a girl more brazen than the rest, with cynically curled lips and too generously applied rouge, dances by, exhibiting in her actions a revolt against the conventional. But for the most part the dancers appear to be giddy young girls in the first flush of enthusiasm over the thrills, satisfactions, and money which this transient world of the dance hall provides. Their stock in trade seems to be an ability to dance with some skill a great variety of dance steps, and more important, sufficient attractiveness to draw many patrons to the hall. They apparently seek to enhance their attractiveness by every female device—rouge, lipstick, and fetching coiffures.[75]

Nonetheless, Cressey's work is one of the places where girls could speak at length about their lives. In his interviews with the girls and women who found "their way to these questionable places," Cressey asked about their family background and their thoughts on whether going to dance halls would be consequential for them. In the text the girls and women were referred to as "cases" who mostly had never attended or dropped out of high school. Many of them referred to themselves as "dance instructors at a dance school"[76] (dance halls were frequently classified as dancing schools, and many functioned as such during the day and held regular public dances, charging admission, at night).[77]

Several of the girls said they simply felt more welcome and at home at the dance hall than in their own homes. One girl related,

> You can't imagine how happy I felt to get back to the "school" again after two weeks at home in Wisconsin. Of course I was glad to see my mother, but then you know we don't have so much to talk about any-more . . . But up at "school," I just feel at home . . . I know how things go, I have my friends who are always glad to see me come back, and who are really interested enough to spend their money on me. There are a lot of fellows up there who don't amount to much, but—just the same—I have more real friends there than in all the rest of the world put together.[78]

Cressey described sixteen-year-old Sophie Zelinski as the daughter of ambitious Polish parents who expected her to graduate from high school and attend college, but her love of dancing and adventure had given her "different ideas." She was "sick of this school bunk" and wanted to see a different kind of life but did not believe the dance hall was a wholesome environment in any way:

> My mother tells me that if I gotta go out to dances, I oughta go to the big dance places. But I tell her that I'm not just going to dances—I'm now a dancing teacher, giving private lessons in a dancing school. I tell her: "You always wanted me to be a teacher, didn't you?" Well, I'm already a teacher, making good money. Then she don't say nothing more. She thinks it's all right because I'm a "dancing instructress." Why, she even brags to her friends about me. What'd she do if she knew what kind of a joint this really was?[79]

Zelinski's answer demonstrated an awareness of her actions and environment that belied the message of social reformers and other anti–dance hall crusaders who described the girls going to them as naive and unaware of the evil associated with dance halls. On the contrary, Cressey did not find many girls or women who regretted their experience at the taxi dance hall or other dance halls, and most of them seemed aware of the potential dangers posed within them.

Like Cressey, other early dance hall researchers from the University of

Chicago positioned themselves as objective cultural observers conducting sociological research grounded in anthropological methods. Often, their field notes read like scientists on safari writing notes about the wildlife they studied. In *Dance Hall Days,* McBee quotes from a female sociologist student's report on dance halls about how men "stood around between dances with their arms around the girls in a much more open fashion than they do at the dances to which I am accustomed, and the girls accepted it in a calm, matter of fact way that showed they were quite used to it."[80] This observation that girls were not alarmed by physical attention they received from men, and in fact might have truly enjoyed their time with men in dance halls, belies the social norms of the historical period that dictated how girls should behave in public—ladylike, demure, and asexual.

The researcher's socioeconomic status (as a graduate student at the University of Chicago) is presumably at least middle class, and as is the case with Cressey, this cultural position affects both the interview questions asked and the field notes recorded. Though we learn firsthand about the behavior and motivations of working-class girls who went to dance halls, the observations and interviews are framed by researchers in a particular way to tell a particular story. The girls' words are only slightly less edited than what might have been seen in media stories had they been interviewed at all.

Dance Hall Panic Ends but Overarching Narrative Continues

The media-generated fervor over the dance hall evil sustained a level of moral panic from 1905 through 1920, when the U.S. Senate passed the Volstead Act and began Prohibition, which shut down all public dance halls that served liquor. Some urban dance halls went underground, and girls continued to go to them for dancing and escape. The press seemed to follow prominent social reformers' objections to them even when there were fewer halls, and dance halls were rarely mentioned without a discussion about the girls who went to them.

An overarching media narrative placed the women social reformers at one end of the moral spectrum and the working-class girls who went to dance halls at the other end. In a simplistic telling, the victims were young girls who were helpless in the throes of the dance hall evil; the saviors were women portrayed as crusaders who could help them. This story was very effectively told by providing lengthy quotations, filled with moral fervor, from dance hall reformers and by simply describing the working-class girls who went to the dance halls. Reformers and researchers were allowed to tell the girls' stories and explain their motivations, but the girls themselves were rendered silent in this coverage.

Undoubtedly, they were silenced not only because they were young and female but also because they were of a lower class and sometimes immigrants or children of immigrants. Reporters from various newspapers and magazines used their own words to describe them as "big, dazed, awkward" children who lack judgment and sophistication and also as "shrill-voiced," "vulgar," and wearing too much rouge. News audiences were left with a very specific impression of the dance hall girl who was both a victim and a whore and who certainly did not perform femininity in a way consistent with upper-class social standards of the time.

The fact that most dance halls were public and the girls going to them were dancing in a public space was also problematic by the cultural standards of early twentieth-century America. This aspect of the dance hall panic was also part of its novelty to newspapers running the stories about it. Crime stories about young working-class girls who were harmed during or because of their visits to dance halls often centered on sex and violence, and all stories seemed to implicitly threaten that as the dance halls were open to the "public," any member of the public—and especially young daughters from any social class—could become dance hall victims as well. Although lower-class teen girls were perhaps more susceptible to the evil of dance halls, *any* girl, as she left her home and cavorted in the public space, could be vulnerable. The mass media of the time latched on to this, and through the storytelling devices described throughout the chapter, certainly contributed to the moral panic regarding teen girls and dance halls.

Furthermore, these narratives mask the fact that neither the young working-class girls nor the older Progressive women reformers themselves had cultural or political power in the United States at this point in history. They were not able to hold governmental office that would have influenced policy on dance halls. Until 1920 they were not even voting citizens of the United States who could elect leaders to carry out their will. Unfortunately, in provoking citizens' irrational fears about teen girls in the public recreational space of the dance hall, the social reformers might have distracted from the vital issue of women's voting rights. Stories about women's suffrage were arguably not as salacious, nor did they stir the same kind of media-generated panic as dance hall evil. In this sense the media's heavy coverage of women social reformers' crusade against dance halls' corrupting influence on teen girls (something of a frivolous pursuit, even by modern readers' standards) served to reinforce the status of women and girls, who already had limited space within public life.

But leisure and recreation also has provided teen girls with space to demonstrate strength through competition, articulate and negotiate gender and sexuality, navigate the political and social landscape, and produce their own media and cultural artifacts. In this sense, recreational space is a potential site of empowerment for teen girls. Public recreational space has also been a problematic site for girls because so many of the gender-related crises in the past century relate to it. In constructing any of these spaces as "dangerous" or "corrupting" specifically to teen girls, they become yet another excluded and exclusionary realm.

The remaining chapters provide historical case studies that demonstrate how journalists and the mass media periodically generate episodes of crises and moral panics related to teen girls' recreation, often through certain news-gathering and storytelling practices that amplify public space as dangerous for teen girls. Like the working-class girls who went to dance halls, the teen girls in these other case studies are represented in problematic ways that suggest they are sexually dangerous but also endangered and that they should be punished when they are unable to enact femininity by the standards of their contemporaries. Thus, public recreation itself becomes a consistently unstable site for teen girls. This topic continues in the next chapter, which discusses the crisis that arose after teen girls began to compete in strenuous sports, specifically track and field, from the 1920s through 1940.

CHAPTER 2

⇌

THE RISE AND FALL OF GIRLS' TRACK AND FIELD, 1920–1940

⇌

Overexertion mentally as well as physically does much
injury to the young, growing girl.

—"Girl's Athletics in Summer," *Ladies' Home Journal*

I'd have won it. I'm sure I'd have passed them because at
the end of the race I was as fresh as a daisy.

—Florence MacDonald, quoted in "Filming Florence,"
Journal of Olympic History

THE PROHIBITION ERA CARRIED ON THROUGH THE end of the 1920s and
early 1930s with the passing of the Twenty-First Amendment. The fruit of
Progressive dance hall opponents' labor was largely realized as the 1920s
progressed and an increasing number of community programs and settlement house activities promoted wholesome leisure practices for working-class girls.

As is evident in the newspapers and periodicals of the era, "girls" continued to be the popular term for any female, particularly an unmarried
one of color or lower economic status, between the ages of thirteen and
twenty-five. Much of the discussion and ensuing news coverage of these
girls' recreational practices, specifically strenuous sports such as running
and basketball, centered on this age group largely because of the problematic nature of female adolescence in general. In the early 1900s the play of
younger girls was treated much in the same way as the play of young boys,
but once girls reached adolescence, they became a problematic hybrid of
girl and woman, who (as was seen in the Progressives' concern over dance
halls) could not control their own sexual urges or the male gazes on them.

Moreover, in the question of participation in sports, they also had to worry about their own medical condition and ability to procreate in the future; many medical experts in the early twentieth century agreed that "girls" should not participate in sports while they were menstruating and should avoid physically taxing sports all together.[1] Although "teenage" was not a social category or word until the 1930s, and the word "teenager" was not used until 1941, these discussions are generally talking about teen girls but calling them girls, ladies, or young women. As such, teenage girls are the topic of this chapter, and as in the case of the earlier analysis of dance halls, are discussed based entirely on their ages (thirteen to nineteen) rather than on the historical context of their demographic. The historical and cultural construction of the teenager is explained in further depth in the next chapter.

Progressive leader Jane Addams, whose work to shutter dance halls was described in the previous chapter, called for parks and recreational sports leagues for girls and young women as early as 1908.[2] Many such urban parks and programs for the working class were built in the next twenty years, and more organizations dedicated to the betterment of the poor and minorities became influential in the realm of sports and recreation. The Playground Association of America (PAA), the Young Men's Christian Association (YMCA), the National Recreation Association (NRA), the Boy Scouts and Girl Scouts of America, and others all became forces within the promotion of sports and recreation in the United States during this period.[3] Specifically, sports and physical recreation became a more viable option as a leisure time alternative for girls, and this was not limited to the lower-income, immigrant, and African American citizens served by these organizations.

In the early 1920s, following the passage of women's suffrage, a grand narrative about independent, active, athletic women and girls emerged in the press. Almost as quickly as this notion was embraced, it dissolved, leaving in its wake questions about the appropriate performances of femininity within sports. This chapter focuses on how the arguments against competitive, strenuous sports for girls—specifically track and field—took hold. Underlying those arguments was a not-so-subtle bias against the poor and sports that would have been associated with teen girls with low socioeconomic status or teen girls of color. The chapter describes the arguments and motivations of the main moral entrepreneurs who advocated for girls to "play for play's sake" rather than for competition and examines the mass media coverage of the issue, which lead to policy and cultural changes that altered the playing field for girls' sports for decades to come.

As the press became a more professionalized industry, the issues that political Progressives campaigned for throughout the early part of the twentieth century, including Prohibition, also became more legitimized within U.S. society and were enacted as public policy and law. Newspapers were the primary means of publicity on the dance hall issue in the early 1900s, and during that era they maintained many of the journalistic conventions associated with yellow journalism and muckraking. The news-gathering and storytelling practices colored the way grand narratives about teen girls were constructed and interpreted. In the 1930s the media landscape changed, with an increased attention to professionalism and objectivity in reporting on the part of journalists, while radio broadcasts and general interest magazine audiences continued to grow. As media outlets and audiences increased, the press became an even more powerful institution in the eyes of special interest groups who wanted to gain publicity and earn public acceptance for their causes. To better understand how a pattern of marginalization based on age, race, gender, ethnicity, and class continued, it becomes important to understand media production and media audiences during this period.

Professionalism and the Press

The screaming all-caps headlines, flashy investigative first-person storytelling, and stunt reporting of the dance hall era were all but gone in a matter of a decade as journalistic norms in the United States changed drastically. A new era of ethical reporting and professionalism in newspapers displaced yellow journalism, jazz journalism, and muckraking. In 1922 the American Society of Newspaper Editors (ASNE) first published its "Code of Ethics" or "Canons of Journalism," a statement of principles about ethics, truth, accuracy, objectivity, and the social responsibility of journalists, as a response to audience demands for a press that was free of bias and transparent in its reporting practices.[4]

In the period after World War I a new era of American "objectivity" and a focus on the facts began. Media historian and sociologist Michael Schudson attributes the change in focus as a "reaction against skepticism" during a time when pessimism about political democracy was deepening and the public's desire to participate in public life appeared to be on the wane, as the Great Depression deepened and dictatorships grew in Italy and Germany. The public reaction to propaganda during World War I affected its opinion of news coverage, raising further skepticism about media messages and their powerful effect on audiences. Moreover, the public relations industry became an established and dominant (though largely disdained) source of news items for journalists in the 1920s; although reporters professed to hating public relations agents, they published information from press releases readily because it was often the only source of content from some of their more press-savvy sources, including the U.S. president.[5] To adapt to changing public attitudes as well as the changes within its own industry, the press acknowledged its subjectivity while also promoting its objectivity.

To address the former, newspapers adopted bylines beginning in the mid-1920s, and reporters became topical specialists whose names reflected greater authority within their area of expertise, including an ability to be more critical of sources. Moreover, they could provide interpretation of complicated events of the time, from the war to the Depression, and in some cases they could become expert columnists, whose personal opinions were so informed that they should be published weekly. To address the latter, the growing demand for objectivity, newspaper management demanded that reporters become educated about their craft and topical areas of coverage. Journalists acknowledged that objectivity was impossible but at the same time elevated it to an aspiration wherein reporters would attempt to set aside their own beliefs, prejudices, and convictions.[6] They began to carefully structure news stories to avoid bias while answering, "who, what, why, when, where, and how." These conventions were adopted widely, by African American newspapers as well, which had developed strong readership in several urban cities through the early part of the twentieth century.

A more professionalized press that adheres to ethical standards, objectivity, and fairness in some ways might ensure less explicit sexism, racism, and marginalization in journalism. But professionalism also can work to mask such problems. For example, in attempting to be fair and objective, journalists seek to interview people from only two sides of an issue, and in general they concentrate on authorities and government officials, even if they are part of a corrupt administration. Furthermore, relying on two sides often oversimplifies complex issues and encourages publishing only the interests of the extremes while the less quotable, moderate voices are left out of coverage. Moreover, in the early part of the century (and even to a certain extent today), authorities and officials were by and large Caucasian men with education and wealth. Women and girls were rarely quoted in news coverage in the early part of the twentieth century partly for this reason. In the nineteenth century female readers were "taken to be simple and unidimensional," writes Linda Steiner, and "women as readers, writers/ journalists, and subjects were conflated." While affluent women readers had become a somewhat more important demographic to newspapers hoping to generate department store advertising, little had changed with regard to news coverage geared toward them in the early twentieth century.[7]

Although the era of splashy, investigative muckraking had largely come to an end by the 1920s, general interest magazines, like *Collier's*, were still popular as ever and far more focused on entertainment than were newspapers at the time. *Collier's* and the *Saturday Evening Post* continued to be popular and competitive with each other, boasting a circulation of more than a million each. More focused special interest magazines, including *Ladies' Home Journal* and *Youth's Companion*, continued to flourish as well, incorporating fiction and nonfiction into their editorial pages. The third most popular magazine in the early 1930s was *Liberty*, launched in 1924 as a joint venture from the *Chicago Tribune* and the *New York Daily News*, but it was sold in 1931 to a billionaire magazine magnate who established a sensationalistic tone and geared the magazine toward the working class. News magazines *Time*, *U.S. News & World Report*, and *Newsweek* were all first published in 1933 and largely took their cues from the professionalized newspaper industry in their reporting of news and world events.[8]

Radio in the United States became available to local broadcasters in the 1920s, but radio programming was not delivered nationally until the founding of NBC in 1926 and CBS in 1927; from that time listeners could hear the same shows, broadcast coast to coast.[9] But radio stations and networks did not incorporate news into their regularly scheduled broadcasts until 1930. These reports were often based on breaking news and synopses of news events, which related primarily to political and world events. Since only historic broadcasts are available by archive now, it is difficult to know whether the issue of athleticism and girls was covered in radio broadcasts of the time, though certainly *Little Orphan Annie*, a popular radio serial that debuted in 1930, provided a fictional example of how an eleven-year-old orphan girl could be represented as resilient, outspoken, active, and independent.[10] Radio serials were incredibly popular among radio audiences, but the brief, punchy news briefs were the serials' punctuation and garnered high ratings. This early radio news format forced print journalists to rethink their own reporting methods—concentrating on a more interpretative news analysis, seeking different angles and conflicts within a story, and attempting to probe more deeply into news stories for issues to explore.[11] As the coverage of female participation in sports in this chapter demonstrates, an increased focus on conflict within the journalistic narratives might have driven some reporters to emphasize questions of gender and femininity within sports articles about girls and women.

Suffrage and the Modern Athletic Girl

Although the term "teenager" still had not entered the English language as a descriptive social category, the 1920s also brought women's suffrage and a newfound championing of the "new woman." A younger counterpart, "the new girl," also emerged and embraced her newfound independence not only by voting but by participating in all aspects of public life. Being outside the walls of the home, the domestic domain of women and girls, became more acceptable during this political and cultural shift as well. Women's and girls' participation in individual and team sports became more commonplace in the early 1920s.

More than twenty years earlier, Susan B. Anthony famously said that the bicycle had "done more to emancipate women than anything else in the world." She said, "It gives a woman a feeling of freedom and self-reliance. The moment she takes her seat she knows she can't get into harm unless she gets off her bicycle, and away she goes, the picture of free, untrammeled womanhood."[12] Bicycles were an important symbol for gender equity and also a source of controversy since they required women to straddle an object and move around alone on it in the presence of watchful others—two faux pas in an era when women were bustled into high-collared, floor-length petticoats, expected to cover themselves, refrain from flaunting their bodies in public, and generally adhere to the gendered norms of domesticity and home making. Bicycles became a symbol of the suffrage movement itself, so it is unsurprising that the ability to comfortably participate in public sports and recreation would also be an outcome of the struggle for equal rights in the late nineteenth and early twentieth centuries in the United States.

The *Minneapolis Morning Tribune* on April 25, 1920, heralded "The Sports Girl of 1920," with a bold headline accompanied by an artist's rendering of a young woman racing on horseback against a young man, losing her riding hat as the horse leaps off the page, along with smaller accompanying photographs of a Mills College high jumper, French girls playing soccer, and English girls and "young ladies" participating in a tug-of-war. The article begins, "Can you imagine what great-grandmother would have thought if anybody had confided to her that in the year 1920 her athletic great-granddaughter would be playing football on a college team instead of staying home to crochet antimacassars? Do you think it would have been possible for her to imagine a young lady winning hurdle races, breaking swimming records, and engaging in various other outdoor athletic sports, which in great-grandmother's day were all right for boys and all wrong for girls?" The author of the article, whose byline is not included, guesses that American girls' "readiness" in volunteering for service overseas during World War I might have something to do with it, though he or she does not elaborate. The article notes "young ladies" are no longer "limiting" their exercise to the relatively ladylike sports of swimming, tennis, golf, and handball and instead are "playing football, running, jumping, pole vaulting, joining a tug-of-war team, trap shooting, sculling, boxing, playing polo, and engaging in a dozen other lines of sport which call for masculinity and endurance as well as great determination and grit . . . The sports girl of 1920 is different, and also better qualified for the great outdoors by being healthier, happier, and more independent."[13] In the early 1920s young women and older girls were encouraged by media reports to exercise for their health and, as the *Minneapolis Morning Tribune* article suggests, often praised for their competitive independent spirit.[14]

Newspapers' championing of the new modern girl continued for many years in an era that some call a "golden age" of sport.[15] In a New Year's trend piece on December 31, 1922, the *Minneapolis Morning Tribune* championed "Miss 1923 = Athlete and Worker," in which the author writes, "Today girls of 18 or so are going about with complete independence. They play games with their men friends, going off by motor for a long day's golf; they lunch and dine with men in public restaurants; they come home in the early hours of the morning and let themselves into the house with their own trusty keys! As for the athletics! Some indication of what the New Year may bring forth is shown by the fact that the championships in several lines of

The Sports Girl of 1920

How a New World=wide Style in Field and Track Sports Is Being Set by American College Girls Who Are Every Bit as Athletic as Their Brothers.

French College Girls Playing Football—a Game They Learned from the Americans.

Miss Emily Baillard, a Mills College Girl, Taking the High Jump, and Below, English Girls in a Tug-of-War Contest.

"The Sports Girl of 1920": Illustration by D. Smith, *Minneapolis Morning Tribune*, April 25, 1920.

sports are already held by young sports girls." The article was accompanied by a drawing of glamorous flapper walking out of a grandfather clock at the stroke of midnight and a smaller drawing of a long-haired young woman standing in a kitchen in an apron with this caption, "Lulu McGrath, Who Typifies the Spirit of 1923 by Earning Her Way toward Fame by Her Ability as a Swimmer and Housekeeper."[16]

Independence, public recreation and sports, and working are all glamorized in pieces like these that were published in the early part of the 1920s. The *New Orleans Times-Picayune* reported that "flappers" and "sub-debs" were "following suit of their brothers and deciding on the rough-and-ready camping life as the ideal," and in the same issue, a separate article with an accompanying photo spread extolled the virtues of competitive fencing as "fine exercise" for the college girls taking part in a fencing club at Newcomb College.[17] A United Press wire article appeared in the *Trenton (N.J.) Evening Times* with a headline proclaiming, "They're Growing Heavier and Taller, So Get 'Em Now, Girls!" for a story that ascribed the average height and weight of the modern American high school–age girl increasing in part due to "the popularity of sports and physical activity among young women."[18] In a 1926 article about American tennis champions (called "Young Lionesses" in the headline), the author wrote, "time was, and not so many years ago, that vigorous out-of-door sports were supposed to be the appropriate recreation of the boys only. The young women, in their prettiest dresses, supplied the decorative frame that surrounded the area upon which the game was fought. But the girls long ago came down from their seats, donned athletic dress and began to win distinction in first one and then another test of endurance and skill."[19] Team sports were encouraged for their ability to cultivate virtue in female players. The children's magazine the *Youth's Companion* discussed team play in the classroom, linking girls' participation in athletics with an increased understanding of teamwork and increased sensitivity to others as well as to "kindness, unselfishness, and courtesy."[20]

Emma L. Wilder, a former playground worker who was the physical education director at the University of Wisconsin–La Crosse and president of the Wisconsin Physical Education Association (WPEA), reported in an annual meeting of the WPEA that public schools across her state had started to embrace team athletics for girls. Wilder suggested the increased inclusion of girls and women in the 1928 Olympic Games seemed to increase student demand for more physical activity and boosted local attendance to high school girls' basketball games and track meets.[21] Public and private junior high and high schools throughout the country responded to the increased interest in girls' sports by adding opportunities for female students to compete, and like their male counterparts they were given the opportunity to become letter winners if they succeeded.[22]

Increased Opportunity for All?

The Playground Association of America had campaigned and succeeded in bringing community team sports programs and recreational spaces to poor and working-class immigrant children between 1900 and 1920, increasing the number of playgrounds from 87 scattered through 24 cities to 3,940 in 481 cities.[23] Newspaper articles picked up on the popular sentiment that play would better the immigrant and working masses. A "jolly little 12-year-old" whose "father is dead" and whose "mother goes out to wash and scrub by the day" is described as being saved by the existence of a public playground in a 1921 *Minneapolis Morning Tribune* article:

> Little 12-year-old is housekeeper for the family. In the morning she washes up the breakfast dishes, makes the beds, cleans up the whole house, prepares lunch for herself and the younger children, and starts preparations for the night's dinner . . . She's a pretty busy little 12-year-old but she somehow manages to get through usually by 1 p.m. or thereabouts. And then—guess what she does!
>
> She washes the baby's face, and puts a clean suit of rumpers on "Buddy," and ties a pink bow on "Sister's" short curls—and carts 'em off to the playground. And they play there all afternoon. That's what keeps her such a jolly little 12-year-old.
>
> "Gee, Miss," she remarked to the supervisor the other day, wrinkling up her sunburnt nose as she spoke, "playgrounds is fun, ain't they?"[24]

Through the description of the child, including the grammatical incorrectness of her quote and the lack of remark about the child not being in school (but rather charged with caring for younger siblings), the article makes clear the child's socioeconomic status as it promotes the interests of the PAA. No equivalent stories about African American children exist;

because of national Jim Crow laws and racial segregation within public parks and buildings, only 3 percent of these playgrounds were open to children of color.[25] The Amateur Athletic Union (AAU), which had been established in 1888 as a governing body for sport competition, did not admit black athletes in the early 1900s, and the YMCA (which had a segregated division for African Americans) as well as schools and colleges for African American youth developed sports and recreation programs to accommodate them in the early part of the twentieth century.[26] Finding appropriate space for both play and competition was a constant source of aggravation for leaders seeking to sponsor youth sport events in a racially segregated America.

The number of playgrounds intended for people of color in the United States grew steadily in the 1920s. By 1925, 179 segregated playgrounds were established for the exclusive use of African American children. Established primarily through the efforts of PAA, specifically by the PAA Bureau of Colored Workers, these playgrounds hosted track-and-field competitions for neighborhood children and set up citywide competitions for the winners to compete against one another.[27]

Equal access to play areas was paramount to the mission of the PAA because its founders believed that sports held the potential to reform and raise the spirits of urban poor, many of whom were racial or ethnic minorities. This belief also propelled social organizations such as the YMCA, YWCA, and the National Recreation Association. In the late 1920s the National Recreation Association established its Division of Colored Workers, which was charged with providing opportunities for young African American boys and girls to participate in organized sports. In its monthly bulletins, youth sports and recreation leaders from across the nation would report on their successful activities with black children, often including a mix of activities such as basketball, track, baseball, volleyball, hiking, swimming, music, crafts, games, storytelling, and picnics.[28]

Sports and recreation were seen not only as a pathway to the betterment of the needy among community recreation leaders but also as a means of womanliness and beauty for young and adolescent girls in the programs. African American recreation leader Ruth Arnett, who was a YWCA secretary of Girls Work, suggested that anyone concerned with producing girls with "tomboyish" traits should rethink their own understanding of femininity; she viewed the "real man of today" as needing a vigorous, self-reliant "real woman" who had developed feminine strength as an ath-

Appropriate recreation: Girls and young women participating in the Hartley House's outdoor recreational camp, ca. 1908. (Social Welfare History Archives, University of Minnesota-Twin Cities)

letic tomboy.[29] Like the articles extolling the virtues of strong girls and women in the mainstream Caucasian-owned newspapers of the time, the black *Chicago Defender* published work professing the same, in this case through Arnett's guest editorial: "The cry today is for real women, real, live, pulsating, vital creatures, not the be-painted, be-powdered, bedecked ornamental dolls we see, for the most part, today. Let's encourage our girls to be 'tomboys.' Let them enjoy all the activities of the boys, let them enter any game of sport and recreation that the boy enters. Let's teach them to be real girls!"[30]

In addition to community programs, including those run by the NRA, YMCA, and YWCA, corporate recreation programs also offered the working girls in its forces the opportunity to participate in numerous company-sponsored sporting events, including track-and-field competitions. Although industrial recreation may be characterized as a paternalist venture, retail companies and manufacturers who sponsored corporate sports teams for employees viewed the initiatives as a chance to offset the monotony of their daily work and encourage self-betterment among the workers. Very much in line with the beliefs of the Progressive movement, physical sports and recreation were seen as another avenue to self-discipline and goodwill among employees of factories and local companies that employed working-class people.[31] Companies and large department stores from Wanamaker's and Bloomingdale's in Philadelphia and New York to Marshall Field's in Chicago and Dayton's in Minneapolis each sponsored sports teams for both male and female employees.[32]

Corporate recreation programs had an added effect for working-class teen girls who were encouraged to compete in them: they fostered one of the first generations of competitive female athletes. Although basketball, softball, and swimming were popular offerings, track and field for girls and young women was propelled to popularity in the 1920s and 1930s in part because of the fierce competition among corporate teams. These teams nurtured future Olympians, including Jessie Cross, who had quit school in 1923 at age thirteen to support her family. Along with her best friend, Loretta McNeil, she found a clerking job at the John Wanamaker Department Store in New York and joined the Wanamaker Girls track team, which trained after work hours by running through the store aisles and staircases.[33] Their races and the events sponsored by competing corporate teams often drew thousands, including a meet in which Cross participated at New York's Madison Square Garden in 1927 that hosted fifteen thousand spectators.[34] The *New York Times* published several stories recounting races and lists of the winners of the races in which the Wanamaker Girls participated. Although the young girls were never the headline or lead stories in the articles, nor were they interviewed and allowed to comment, their names were published as winners in the largest, most prestigious newspaper in the country.[35] Considering their socioeconomic status and gender, this kind of visibility was a significant achievement. Despite public arguments over regulation and boundaries regarding youth sports between corporations that sponsored teams and the National Collegiate Athletic Association (NCAA), the National Amateur Athletic Federation (NAAF), and the Amateur Athletic Union (AAU), corporate recreation programs thrived throughout the 1920s.[36]

Furthermore, AAU-sponsored track events for teen girls also were incredibly popular, and in fact Cross, McNeil, and other young working-class amateur athletes often competed on community-sponsored AAU teams in addition to their corporate teams. After a decade of training through the parks and playground systems and corporate recreation programs in urban areas, older teen girl runners found themselves becoming locally famous, as major newspapers covered their competitive feats. Lillian Copeland, a celebrated discus thrower (and future Olympic athlete) who came up through the AAU teams, was recognized in the *Los Angeles Times* for breaking the world record in discus in 1926, as was her Oakmere Girls' Athletic Club of Chicago's 220-yard relay team. The *Chicago Daily Tribune* in 1929 celebrated and ran several pictures of the "Douglas Park Girls" from Douglas Park High School who scored a record eighty points in a meet against several other high school girls' teams.[37] In 1930 ten thousand spectators crowded the stands to watch fifteen hundred athletes competing at the Central District AAU track-and-field competition in Chicago, which was not an unusual number of participants or spectators for such a regional city event at the time. Among the girls who competed at such AAU events in Chicago was Betty Robinson, who won the first Olympic gold medal for the 100-meter sprint in the 1928 Olympic Games at age seventeen.[38]

The African American press also published stories about teen girls competing in celebrated track meets. The *New York Amsterdam News* featured the headline "RACE GIRLS SHATTER AMERICAN RECORD" in a 1923 article about a black girls relay team from Meadowbrook Club in Philadelphia breaking American speed records "for the race" for track and field.[39] A similar article appeared in the *St. Louis Argus*.[40] In 1928 the *Chicago Defender* published a sports story about stand-out runner and future Olympian Mabel Jones in an article that identifies her and her teammates as "the girls' track team from Jackson playground."[41]

Despite the apparent popularity of track and field for both white and black girls in the 1920s and 1930s, it was running (and sweating, which made for an unladylike appearance) that quickly became the most controversial aspect of the new modern girls' athleticism. Although female participation in competitive, strenuous sports became increasingly scrutinized by various federations and associations, girls' track and field arguably suffered the heaviest criticism. Eventually, the participation of teen girls in track and field became a known public crisis that was covered and hardly questioned by the American mass media of the time, and the repercussions of this crisis lasted for many decades.

The criticism and scrutiny is apparent in the conferences and meetings held leading up to and beyond the 1928 and 1932 Olympic Games, but also in the media coverage of female athletes. One of the most famous and scrutinized female athletes was Babe Didrikson, whose femininity and sexuality were underlying questions throughout her years as one of the world's fastest women.

Babe Didrikson, "Phenomenal Girl Athlete"

Despite this general interest in girls' athletics, more stories were written nationally about an athletic teenage girl named Babe Didrikson than any others. Didrikson, who excelled at running, basketball, baseball, and golf—propelling herself to become one of the most famous multisport athletes—was perhaps one of the last great young women superstars of track during the 1920s and 1930s. As a teen in Texas in the 1920s, she defeated competitors on the AAU circuit, ultimately earning a spot on the United States Olympic track team in 1932 and winning two gold medals and one silver medal at age twenty-one. Earlier that year she qualified for three Olympic events after competing (and winning first place overall) in Evanston, Illinois, as a one-woman track team sponsored by the Employers Casualty Insurance Company of Dallas, competing against company teams of twelve, fifteen, even twenty-two women.[42]

Didrikson underwent constant scrutiny related to her femininity and tomboyish nature. A December 1931 sports column in the *New York Times* described controversy from the AAU's disapproving use of nicknames in promotion for the upcoming Olympic Games. The AAU cited "Babe as an example of an undesirable nickname, but Miss Didrikson has written to President Avery Brundage informing him that Babe is her given name. So that settles that. The story told at the last outdoor championships in Jersey City was that Miss Didrikson, an all-round athletic star, had walloped four home runs in a sand-lot baseball game and that then and there, she had been dubbed Babe."[43] (According to personal records, she was in fact named Mildred Ella Didrikson and in later news stories was identified as Miss Mildred "Babe" Didrikson.)[44] Moreover, in 1932 Brundage publicly sought to suspend the nineteen-year-old from the AAU and strip her of her Olympic medals after accusing her of endorsing an automobile and violating her contract as a "amateur" athlete: a Texas car dealer had run an unauthorized photo of her, according to stories in newspapers in the United States and Canada.[45]

Although the dealership owner admitted that Babe did not authorize the photo, she was still suspended from AAU competition, and in the wake of the official "clearing" of her name, rumors circulated that the "phenomenal girl athlete" would instead become professional (and perhaps marry, as she set off on a mysterious trip to Texas two weeks after the suspension).[46]

Didrikson issued a statement to the Houston, Texas, newspapers denying the wedding and saying of her suspension, "Newspapers and the public must be tired of the whole business. I know I am." Shortly thereafter, the Associated Press reported she had signed a manager and had been spotted in a downtown Chicago billiard hall "demonstrating her skill with the cue."[47] Brundage then remarked in a publicized press conference, "You know, the ancient Greeks kept women out of their athletic games. They wouldn't even let them on the sidelines. I'm not so sure but they were right."[48]

In addition to being troubled by unfair treatment from the AAU, she reportedly was also upset by accusations in the years following the Olympics that she was a lesbian or transgendered.[49] The press made much of Didrikson's tomboyish nature, including a colorful *New York Times* profile published shortly after her declaration to become professional, in which she proclaims to wish to box Babe Ruth, says she would rather coach boys than girls, and reveals that she knows little of dieting as she ordered a ham and cheese omelet from her hotel room service during the course of the interview. The reporter added, "When the interviewer met the 19-year-old girl her first request was, 'Don't ask me whether or not I'm going to get married. That is the first question women reporters ask. And that is why I hate those darn old women reporters.'"[50]

Widespread heteronormative standards mandated that a particular kind of femininity be applied to all women and girls in the era, and it seemed the mass media was eager to police these standards, even among the most elite of female athletes. Didrikson was specifically difficult to make sense of because her performance of gender did not adhere strictly to a "masculine/feminine binary," to borrow from Judith Butler's understanding of gender as a performance rather than a biological fact. "The presumption of a binary gender system implicitly retains the belief in a mimetic relation of gender to sex whereby gender mirrors sex or is otherwise restricted by it," she writes. "When the constructed status of gender is theorized as radically independent of sex, gender itself becomes a free-floating artifice, with the consequence that *man* and *masculine* might just as easily signify a female body as a male one, and *woman* and *feminine* a male body as easily as female one."[51] (The same mediated discourse that policed gender performance seemed to reappear later in the late 1970s and early 1980s in the coverage of teen girls who embraced punk rock style, a cultural episode explored in chapter 4.)

Despite her own outspoken disdain for the dominant standards of femininity, Didrikson—perhaps in an effort to acquiesce to critics who found her gender performance too inaccurate—soon after made herself over as a women's golfer who wore lipstick, dressed in a more feminine fashion, and in 1938 married a professional wrestler named George Zaharias.[52] Her new image conformed to a new image being constructed for female athletes in the 1930s—one that was part beauty pageant, part healthy participant—and fully intended to dispel concerns that female athletes were "mannish."[53] In addition to Didrikson's exit from track-and-field competition and entrance into the more accepted sport of women's golf (in which she dominated for the rest of her life) the 1930s signaled an end to the early golden age of track and field for teen girls and young women. Moreover, Didrikson was one of the last young female athletes quoted extensively in her own words in the press; in the ensuing years those who still competed in track and field rarely achieved the fame of the colorful Didrikson and therefore were rarely asked to speak for themselves in media reports.

End of the Modern Athletic Girl?

Despite the popularity of track-and-field competition among working-class urban teen girls of various races and ethnicities, the Great Depression, which began after the Wall Street crash of October 1929, led to a decrease in funding for playgrounds, parks, and public sports projects. Between 1930 and the implementation of the Works Progress Association (WPA) in the mid-1930s, cities' recreation and public works budget cuts affected the public sports and recreation programs that were so rapidly growing in the 1920s.[54] Additionally, the corporate recreation programs and sports teams that provided opportunities for working-class and minority teen girls to train and compete in track competition were largely discontinued during the Depression, and most industrial recreation initiatives never returned.[55]

Moreover, a new popular notion regarding the femininity of "modern girls" emerged during this era, gaining publicity and traction: while adolescent girls should be healthy and fit, many said, their increased participation in sports should not make them appear masculine, nor should it risk their ability to reproduce in the future. Participation in "sports of strife"—a reference to sports that appeared to require more physicality, endurance, and strength, and generally referred to basketball and track and field—became increasingly less popular in the eyes of the public, in part because of a successful campaign to change social mores as they related to athletics for both boys and girls.[56]

The financial strains on public and corporate recreation programs took away opportunities from working-class and minority competitors, but the cultural changes taking place at this time brought many high school programs to cancel girls' track-and-field teams and no longer allowed female athletes to earn letters for sports. Although girls' basketball itself continued to be played (usually using rules that made the sport less strenuous for girls), many states that started state basketball tournament championships for girls in the 1920s—for example, Kentucky and South Dakota—discontinued them by the 1930s, maintaining only boys' state competitions.[57]

This new concern was precipitated by a number of events covered by the mass media, including studies published in the popular press containing quotes from high-profile moral entrepreneurs opposed to competitive girls' sports. It resulted in a change in public attitude about teen girls' participation in track and field and other competitive sports, arguably damaging the state of girls' sports irrevocably through the decades that led to the passing of Title IX in 1972, and beyond.

The Effect of Moral Entrepreneurship in the 1930s

Despite the excitement associated with girls' sports in the 1920s, public schools were still slow to offer opportunities for girls. The inclusion of physical education classes for adolescent girls differed from state to state; however, it often was difficult for its advocates to argue even for all-girl classes where the games were noncompetitive and the activity was private. For example, the Wisconsin Association for Health and Physical Education advocated for "the equalization of physical education opportunities for all boys and girls."[58] Girls' physical education advocate Emma Wilder noted in her 1930 report, however, that their efforts were met with a "very phlegmatic attitude on the part of the general run of teachers and physical educators." She wrote, "Your committee finds it exceedingly difficult to discover individual initiative among the profession in general."[59] Likely, Wilder—who was one of few female physical education directors in the early 1930s who promoted equality for girls' and boys' sports—was meeting cultural resistance among a public that was being swayed against girls' sports by a new group of vociferous moral entrepreneurs. Ironically, they were also women directors of physical education departments at various colleges and universities nationwide. They opposed girls and women "aping" male athletics in terms of the growing commercialism associated with college and amateur sports (and performing for watching crowds), as well as the increased physicality that many felt diminished the femininity of girl athletes and made them look like "She-men" or "Amazons," disparaging comments with arguably racist undertones.

These women used their connections to and leadership positions within their universities and the NRA, PAA, Girl Scouts of America, and other recreation organizations to advance their arguments against girls' and women's competitive sports. For example, Agnes Wayman, head of the Barnard College Physical Education Department, wrote in a 1927 article titled "Play Problems for Girls" for *The Playground*—a periodical published by the Playground and Recreational Association of America—that the "modern girl" should be encouraged to take part in only "wholesome, satisfying recreation, games, and sports" that "stress the recreational side of all games, the play side" rather than the competitive side. She continued, "Teach your girls to love the race for the running of it, not just the winning; to love the game for the joy of playing it, not just to defeat an opponent. Teach them to want to win, and to play if possible the type of game that will win, not just to defeat but to have the satisfaction which comes from a thing well done." Wayman noted that competition and the "idea that winning is the principle function in our inter-scholastic contests is the root of all evil" and, moreover, "intensive competition for girls, or the making and breaking of records" should be discouraged.[60] This speech—given at a time when thousands of people were showing up at AAU-sponsored meets to watch Jessie Cross, Lillian Copeland, Mabel Jones, Babe Didrikson, and other teenage runners compete—was one of the early published arguments against competitive play for girls during the time that audiences were excited to watch them compete.

Like Wayman, numerous other college physical education directors were beginning a fight to curb the growth of competitive girls' sports just as they were at their most popular in modern history. Like most moral entrepre-

Vol. V   No. 1   PLEASE RETURN TO
DEPARTMENT OF RECREATION   April, 1911
RUSSELL SAGE FOUNDATION
NEW YORK CITY

The Playground

PUBLISHED BY

PLAYGROUND ASSOCIATION OF AMERICA

TO PROMOTE NORMAL, WHOLESOME

Play and Public Recreation

Philadelphia Playground Association

POISE

Twenty-five Cents a Copy   Two Dollars a Year

"Poise": A working-class girl prepares to throw a ball on the cover of *The Playground* 5, no. 1 (April 1911). (Social Welfare History Archives, University of Minnesota-Twin Cities)

neurs throughout history, they felt they had the best interests of society at heart. As insiders in college athletics, the women were most likely privy to the more scandalous side of college sports. Intercollegiate play in college athletics had proved to be lucrative in men's sports, but according to the Carnegie Report of 1921, their success created a system of bribery and corruption as well as a deemphasis on academics. They saw male coaches themselves as part of the problem and called for women coaches for girls; men coaching college girls' sports would only lead to the same issues happening within them, they thought. The best preventative solution, many felt, was to simply take away the competition and lower the stakes within girls' athletics. They campaigned for girls' sports that were not so competitive as to exclude girls who were not as athletically gifted, and they sought to replace competitive games with "fun" play and field days that did not privilege winning. Mass participation and a decrease in spectatorship, in their view, was an important goal.

Because of its emphasis on individual stars whose exceptional athletic ability enabled their success, female participation in track and field was particularly troubling. The enormously popular AAU track meets for girls were a major source of concern, and their existence was likely one of the precipitating reasons for the official organization of this group of women physical education directors. In spite of the AAU's general objections to girls' track and field, the organization sought to oversee and regulate the sport, most likely after realizing its popularity among both female athletes and public audiences.[61] (In a letter to famed Notre Dame football coach, Knute Rockne, AAU president Avery Brundage wrote that "regardless of how you and I feel about it, the sheer popularity of women's track and field necessitated AAU sponsorship.")[62] The AAU's takeover meant that athletes could qualify for the Olympic Games only in AAU-sponsored meets, a fact protested by a number of sports and recreation organizations.

The controversy sparked the creation of the National Amateur Athletic Federation, which was established in 1922 in part because of its members' concern about the growing power of the AAU. The NAAF, which oversaw boys' and men's athletics, objected to the increasing commercialization and corruption of college sports, as well as the increasing violence within college football. Although the women physical education directors who were concerned about the same issues in girls' athletics were present at the creation of the NAAF, the NAAF Women's Division officially was created as an outcome of a 1923 Conference on Athletics and Physical Recreation for Women and Girls in Washington, D.C. The AAU takeover of girls' track and field was a major topic of the conference.[63]

After its formal creation the NAAF Women's Division members were able to gain press coverage to draw attention to their concerns about the evils of intercollegiate competition, particularly within sports that they deemed "strenuous." Although the NAAF disbanded in 1930, the Women's Division was a strong voice within girls' and women's sports throughout the 1930s. The Women's Division's regular conferences and meetings were covered by the *New York Times*. Further, its members made speeches to social progressive groups and civic organizations and published its beliefs in periodicals such as the previously mentioned *The Playground*.

The NAAF Women's Division was organized as a federation, which meant groups and individuals from various interest groups and academic fields could join as members, but the leadership was primarily made up of women leaders of university physical education programs. In addition to Wayman, the original executive committee included Blanche Trilling, the women's PE director at the University of Wisconsin; J. Anna Norris, the women's PE director at the University of Minnesota; Helen Frost, an instructor in PE at Teachers College, Columbia University; Louise French, assistant state supervisor of PE for the state of Massachusetts; Helen McKinstry, the director of the Central School of Hygiene and Physical Education, YWCA of New York City; and Ethel Perrin, the associate director of the American Child Health and Education for the city of Detroit.[64] Moreover, its publicity prowess kept its arguments against girls' participation in sports in the media spotlight even at a time when its outlook was not likely shared by a majority of the public. The Women's Division's notoriety was certainly bolstered by electing as its president the well-known Lou Henry Hoover, the president of the Girl Scouts of America and the future American First Lady. Hoover was elected to be Girl Scouts president in 1923; at the time her husband, Herbert Hoover, was the U.S. secretary of commerce, and she retained her high-profile Girl Scouts presidency while serving as First Lady.

Women's Division members were not only concerned about the inappropriateness of girls' participation in strenuous competition on cultural and moral grounds. They felt gender difference should be emphasized over gender equality in the athletics. Lillian Schoedler, the Women's Division executive secretary, said the organization's aim was "the advancement of the girl, and not the advancement of the sport" and "to develop the sport for the girl, not the girl for the sport." Sports should allow all girls to feel healthy and confident, the members thought, and this required their sports to be inherently different from boys' sports. She explained that the Women's Division "was to be built up from the point of view of girls and women as girls and women with their special needs and conditions always in mind, not merely mimicking or imitating for girls, work and standards which had been developed for boys and men to meet an entirely different set of needs and physical equipment."[65]

The Women's Division's acknowledgment that they believed the gender differences between male and female was based on many of their professional instincts and training, and several of them had built college athletic programs with this in mind. Although the Women's Division formed partnerships with community groups often made up of "society" women who might have feared more for upper-class girls' losing their femininity, their own passion for women's physical education and fitness was rooted in professionalism.[66] This is evident in J. Anna Norris's brochure titled, "Physical Education as a Profession," which describes the job of the woman physical education teacher for any age group as "a strenuous one and long in hours" and that a key tenet to the position is having the ability to build character in her students. Femininity is an important trait for such character building, she writes: "The very first requisite is that she herself be a womanly person, so that she may radiate the kind of influence the [school] principal wants. What she is is more important than what she advises others to be . . . Honesty, sincerity, and cooperation may become habitual through her influence."[67]

Additionally, the NAAF Women's Division wished for the public to view male and female participation as distinctly different because of medical concerns that had been circulated by doctors for years. Specifically, they questioned whether strenuous sports like track and field were detrimental to the physical health—and specifically, the ability to reproduce in the future—to girls who were experiencing puberty. Even during the 1920s when newspapers were writing articles about new, modern women participating in all kinds of sports, adolescent girls who were menstruating were specifically asked not to participate in sports because of the belief perpetuated by some medical experts that it either posed a danger to their reproductive systems or needed to be respected as a time for reproductive development.

One of the most influential medical texts of the late nineteenth and early twentieth centuries, *Sex in Education; or, a Fair Chance for the Girls,* by Dr. Edward Clarke, states that "periodicity," the monthly period, was a crucial time for teen girls to pay attention to their bodies, which meant they should be free of both physical and intellectual activity that would drain and harm them. Girls between the ages of fourteen and eighteen "should not study as many hours a day as a boy" simply because their bodies needed rest from such rapid development and that "every fourth week, there should be a remission, and sometimes an intermission, of both study and exercise . . . The diminished labor, which shall give Nature an opportunity to accomplish her special periodical task and growth, is a physiological necessity for all, however robust they may seem to be."[68]

In the early twentieth century, popular women's magazine *Ladies' Home Journal* regularly published photo spreads of women's college athletic teams (including the Wellesley women's championship basketball team) and articles devoted to describing appropriate athletic attire for ladies, though some stories also questioned whether girls should be active at all. "Over-quick walking is not good for anybody, and the time to stop walking has been reached before one gets tired," one author wrote in an early piece. "Much good may come from the exercises in a gymnasium, but so many young girls overdo athletics nowadays that I almost fear advising them."[69] Another writer wrote, "Overexertion mentally as well as physically does much injury to the young, growing girl," and added later, in a passage directly written to her young female readers, seemingly drawing directly from Dr. Clarke's thoughts on exercising during menstruation, "You are not equally capable of exertion at all times, and if you do not use your judgment in this matter you may pay a severe penalty. This is applicable especially to the more vigorous games and sports. Take, for instance, tennis. There are times when you are physically incapacitated for indulging in any such exercise. Instead, you should be lying down and storing up strength for the time when your curve of health is in the ascendant."[70]

Further attention to the controversy surrounding girls' physicality and sports participation was granted by a widely reported medical study commissioned by British reformers that attested that "the girl who takes part in sports does so at the expense of herself and her children," and that the "Victorian girl made a better mother than the modern athletic woman."[71] Moreover, the study claimed that "athletic women produce female offspring mainly and seldom have sons." The New Orleans *Times Picayune*'s coverage of the 1921 study was primarily a response from New Orleans doctors and sports leaders who were skeptical of the findings, including Dr. Sara T. Mayo, identified as a medical doctor whose "other duties" included examining "hundreds of girls at the Y.W.C.A. twice a year." Mayo said, "I am an advocate of the well-directed training of women, believing that it better prepares them for mother-hood" and essentially dismissed the study.[72] The *New York Times*'s coverage of the study was also dismissive in tone, extensively quoting Vassar president Dr. Henry Noble MacCracken, who said that if anything their female students were "coddled too much" and would benefit from heartier exercise as they became mothers. Nonetheless, the *Times* also quoted MacCracken exten-sively about the harm of female athletes imitating men's athletes, drawing directly from the talking points of the NAAF Women's Division: "The stiff, intensive training necessary to develop stars is admittedly bad for girls . . . The two canons of Vassar athletics are, first, to give each girl the training she individually requires; and second, to avoid the star system, which is bad not only for the star, but for her audience, who indulge their interest in sports from the grand stand instead of participation."[73]

This quotation seemed to echo the speeches at the Women's Division's annual national conventions, which were covered in detail by the *New York Times*. In turn, members of the NAAF Women's Division were called on as sources and experts in news stories, which allowed them to further their cause on the national public stage and effectively set an agenda that decreased girls' ability to participate in competitive sports in both leagues and schools. Often, Women's Division members would suggest that girl ath-letes would be plagued by horrible medical conditions, which fed into the tabloids' need for shocking quotes. For example, Trilling told the *New York Sun* in 1927 that "evils of commercialization and exploitation of outstanding girl athletes often leads to the danger of nervous breakdowns."[74]

Women's First Official Participation in the Olympic Games

Naturally, the Women's Division voiced their protest against female partic-ipation in track and field when running events were added to the official program of the 1928 Olympic Games in Amsterdam. The addition of women's sports to the previously all-male games was done on a trial basis, and the decision was meant to be made after the conclusion of the Olympics. Thus, the

Women's Division continued to voice opposition both within the press and within reformist circles, as the International Olympic Committee weighed whether to continue women's participation in the games, specifically within strenuous sports. The IOC was not strongly in favor of female participation, particularly in track and field, but the public's enthusiasm for the competition and other countries' acceptance of female athletics likely fueled the initial decision to include girls and women. In fact, the first IOC president, Pierre de Coubertin, said he felt "women's proper role was to encourage the men and to admire male athletic achievement" and was unwavering in his disdain for female participation in the Olympics. They did not participate until after his resignation in 1925; his resignation, in fact, stemmed in part from the public support of inclusion of girls and women in the games.[75]

Furthermore, the Women's Division and other opponents of track and field were likely encouraged by a reported incident at the 800-meter race competition, a sprint twice around the track that was considered to be extremely taxing even for well-trained female Olympic athletes at the time. Although the earlier trials and heats for the race took place without incidents, journalists attending the final championship round of the race reported that girls collapsed throughout the course and at the finish line, bolstering claims that girls' and women's physicality and temperament were not suited for strenuous sprints. Official Olympic records actually show all women completing the race and an athlete from Germany winning in record time, but newspaper reports focused on the appearance of the runners and their perceived exhaustion. Under the headline, "Women Athletes Collapse—Fierce Strain of Olympic Race—Sobbing Girls," one British reporter wrote that the event "was another exhibition of sheer exhaustion by their sisters in the arena. Nine of them took part in the final of the 800 metres flat race [roughly half a mile] and it was not a pleasant sight."[76] *New York Times* correspondent Wythe Williams editorialized in his article:

> The final of the women's 800-meter run, in which Frau Lina Radke of Germany set a world's record, plainly demonstrated that even this distance makes too great a call on feminine strength. At the finish six out of the nine runners were completely exhausted and fell head-long on the ground. Several had to be carried off the track. The little American girl, Miss Florence MacDonald, who made a gallant try but was out classed, was faint for several minutes, while even the sturdy

Miss Hitomi of Japan, who finished second, needed attention before she was able to leave the field.[77]

Historians in the decades following the contentious race disputed the characterizations of the participants. The analyzed archival film footage of the race showing one Canadian athlete, Fanny "Bobbie" Rosenfeld (who claimed she had not trained for the race) slowing up just before the finish line. Seconds earlier, her seventeen-year-old teammate Jean Thompson had accidentally been struck by Japanese runner Kinue Hitomi's swinging arms and began to fall while still sprinting. Canadian Olympic reports, which suggest the incident demonstrated amazing sportsmanship, stated that Rosenfeld "placed her arm on Thompson's shoulder in comfort," and after taking a few steps across the finish line consoled her as Thompson dropped down in tears.[78]

None of the athletes themselves were interviewed after the race (which is not surprising considering the absence of teen girls' voices in the mass media in general), but Florence MacDonald, described by the *New York Times* as the "little American girl" and who was eighteen when she competed, disputed the media reports, saying in an oral history interview seventy-three years later: "This collapsing business was a lot of nonsense." In a spirit that would have provoked the anti-champion Women's Division, she also expressed regret that she had not won: "I was too dumb. I'd have won it," she said. "I'm sure I'd have passed them because at the end of the race I was as fresh as a daisy."[79] After the spectacle of the women's 800-meter flat, the press heavily covered the argument over allowing women to compete in track-and-field events at future Olympic Games at all, sometimes referring to the reports of the contentious race.[80] In its final vote on the inclusion of female participants in future games, the American delegation of the International Amateur Athletic Federation (IAAF) voted against the inclusion of nearly all track events (including the broad jump, shot-put, 200-meter flat, the 100-meter flat, the 800-meter flat, the 400-meter relay, the high jump, the discus throw, the javelin, and the 80-meter hurdle race), but it was outvoted by other countries on most events. Nonetheless, the women's 800-meter race was canceled for the 1932 Olympic Games and considered so dangerous to girls' health that it did not reappear in competition until the 1960 Olympic Games.

Despite the international vote that mostly upheld female participation, the Women's Division was able to keep their opposition to girls' and wom-

en's participation in the Olympic Games in the news well after their conclusion. In fact, the *New York Times* reported the division's official protest
of the 1932 Olympic Games' inclusion of women while covering its 1929
convention. "The making and breaking of records has become so tied up
with the athletics that play for play's sake has been quite lost sight of," the
article quoted Ethel Perrin's speech. "We can set ourselves as opposed to
an American women's team and we could go forth to do battle against it as
crusaders, with the hope of having it abolished in 1932."[81]

Furthermore, the Women's Division members were able to garner support
among some prominent sports journalists. Most notable among them was
John Tunis, a famous sports reporter and author who began writing sports
columns in 1925 and contributed to the *New Yorker, Reader's Digest, Esquire,*
and the *Saturday Evening Post* and in 1934 broadcast the first Wimbledon
match to air in the United States.[82] Tunis was a speaker at the NAAF Women's
Division convention in 1928, and he published some of the most critical stories about the harms of strenuous competition for girls and young women.[83]

In the July 1929 issue of *Harper's Monthly Magazine* Tunis wrote an
article lamenting how "women in many branches of sport have begun to
ape the athletics of men." As an example, he reported hearing about a high
school girls' basketball tournament in which girls were "utterly exhausted"
and even as the play continued had to be "removed from the floor in faint-
ing and hysterical condition."[84] The referee was described as an "ogre"
and the audience "grew wilder and wilder, all excited" in a "wild frenzy."
Susan K. Cahn, the author of *Coming on Strong,* surmises that his source,
the "director of women's physical education at a Midwestern university,"
who witnessed the scene, was most likely outspoken Women's Division
member Blanche Trilling, based on Trilling's records in which she notes
having conversed with him about the matter of female athletics that year.[85]
The reporter-source relationship between the two continued into the 1930s,
as evidenced by Trilling's archived letters.[86]

When the NAAF Women's Division made a final plea in 1938 to prohibit
girls under age sixteen from competing in the 1940 Olympic Games, IOC
president Count Henri Baillet-Latour of Belgium responded, without hiding his disdain for female participation: "Unfortunately, the majority is in
favor of participation of women in track and field events, and the question
of the right age for participation is in the hands of the 'International Federations.'"[87] The games in 1940 and 1944 were canceled due to World War II,

and when the summer Olympics resumed in London in 1948, the Women's Division—having accomplished many of their goals related to diminishing competitive aspects of girls' sports—had disbanded.

Race and Class Differences among Girl Athletes

As the competitive landscape began to change for girls in the 1930s, differences in the perceptions of African American and Caucasian teen girl athletes also began to emerge. As media coverage of young white female athletes decreased along with their participation in competition, coverage of young black female track athletes remained consistent, at least within the black press. A *Chicago Defender* article typical of this kind of positive coverage of girls track, "High School Girl Breaks Jump Record: Pennsylvania Lass Shatters American Mark," celebrated Marion Gibson breaking the official American record in standing broad jump. "Marion Gibson, stout little athlete, led Media high school to victory in the ninth annual Delaware county girls track and field championship at Wayne," read the article's lead. "Miss Gibson hung up an official American record in the standing broad jump with an effort of 8 feet 5 inches." A later *Defender* piece, "Chicago Girl Track Stars Have Eyes on Olympic Team Berths," reported that the Chicago Comets Track and Field Club's girls' team had intensified their training efforts in preparation for Olympic track and field tryouts.[88] None of the articles about girls' track and field in the African American press made special note of gender or femininity in its coverage (and in Gibbs's case, described her in specifically unfeminine terms—"stout little athlete"), offering a sharp contrast with the descriptions of young white female athletes in earlier coverage that often noted their beauty.

Historically black colleges continued to allow young women to compete in interscholastic track-and-field competitions after most other colleges and universities banned them in the 1930s. African American newspapers nationwide celebrated the girls track team at the Tuskegee Institute in Alabama, a private, historically black college that was founded in the late nineteenth century.[89]

Moreover, girls who participated in the YMCA (the YWCA did not sponsor girls' athletic competitions) track-and-field contests and playground contests received favorable coverage newspapers in large cities, such as Chicago, where the playground movement's legacy was especially strong among the poor and working-class youth.[90] Since many of the girls competing were African American, the *Chicago Defender* also covered the YMCA competitions, highlighting the accomplishments of the black girl athletes.[91] In the 1940s and early 1950s, however, their events also were largely limited to individual throwing and jumping field events or short sprints (like the fifty-yard dash) rather than longer sprints or hurdle relays.

The Aftermath of the Women's Division

A *New York Times* feature piece in 1933, written much in the vein of articles from the previous decade about how far the "modern" girl had advanced, looked at colleges throughout the United States and discussed how college girls' lives had changed over the past several years. It reported that many schools had become coeducational, smoking lounges were installed and young women allowed to smoke in public, and although curfews were still enforced in girls' dormitories, they were allowed to socialize with men in the lounges until curfew. The article also pointed out that competitive sports on campus for both sexes (specifically, football for boys but all competitive team sports for girls) were on the decline. The following passage nicely demonstrates how the work of the NAAF Women's Division and the media coverage of their views effectively stamped out competitive sports for girls: "As for the girls' campus heroine, the one-time supremacy of the [women's] basketball captain has apparently gone for good. At several colleges the girls with whom I talked just could not remember who was on the class basketball team anyway. Except for a few traditional events like Rally Day at Smith College and the girls' so-called 'Yale-Princeton' basketball game at Oberlin, there is none of the cheering and singing for class teams that in 'big games' used to amount to a frenzy."[92]

Blanche Trilling herself, who was still the women's physical education director at the University of Wisconsin when the article was written (and who was not credited with working in the Women's Division), was called on to comment about how the lack of sports heroes on campus—for both the male and female students—had transformed campus culture, in her viewpoint for the better:

> "There has been a complete change in the past decade," said Professor Blanche Trilling of the physical education department at the

University of Wisconsin, "from emphasis on team sports to that on individual sports. Girls nowadays are getting team games out of their systems in high schools. In college, while they still have house and class hockey and basketball matches, they are mainly looking for a chance to improve their skill in individual sports which they can use the rest of their lives. A girl today who can't swim and play tennis is considered a dub."

The director of girls' physical education at Bryn Mawr College later confirmed that while the students are required to pass a swimming test to graduate, that "dancing of the right kind will be the essence of physical education in the future."[93]

Indeed, the 1930s press coverage in general was far less celebratory of "new" women's independence and robust, competitive spirit and more enthusiastic about how new women were embracing femininity (for example, becoming great ballroom swing dancers with male partners) than the 1920s coverage. In fact, some media backlash against the sporting women idealized in the 1920s is evident. In 1931 Wolcott Gibbs in the *North American Review* (America's oldest literary magazine) drolly opines in his opening paragraph: "Since I was sixteen I have been bored to insanity with articles about the Modern Young Woman, who, it develops, is an enigma, a clear-eyed rebel against something or other, an alcoholic with no morals worth mentioning, a girl very like my grandmother, only brighter, and a lot of other things I am far too tired to remember." The rest of the article is about the author's annoyance that "ladies" had become an "economic factor, or menace" because of opening their own shops or attending college, "where they had absorbed a great deal of dubious information about sex equality—fundamentally women were as brave, as bright, as strong as men, and they meant to do something about it." He laments in the conclusion, "women, God knows, have managed to get over being feminine."[94]

Although teen girls certainly continued to participate in athletics on a less formalized basis in their communities (and girls in rural communities still participated specifically in six-on-six girls' basketball), the decline in athletic participation and visibility was noticeable. A simple online search for media stories about girls' track-and-field events from major historical newspapers yields only a few stories between the years of 1931 and 1960, and none of these are private or public junior high or high school teams but rather club teams for young working-class girls or YMCA (and in the later years, YWCA) teams. Not until the 1960s and early 1970s do stories begin to appear again about teen girls who wished to participate in competitive track and field in school.[95] Equality had again become a national topic of conversation in the United States, following the passing of the Civil Rights Act in 1964. Although the act was written to stop discrimination against people based on their race, ethnicity, national origin, or religion, the National Organization for Women organized and persuaded President Lyndon B. Johnson to include women in executive orders and clarifications to the act in 1967. The executive clarifications dealt primarily with sex discrimination in hiring, but they were an important piece of the second-wave women's movement in the 1960s. Public support for further legislation for women's rights eventually led to a call to pass the Title IX amendment, which was originally an equal education provision that was part of the Higher Education Act of 1965.

Title IX was passed as a law on June 23, 1972, and although it did not specifically address athletics in its language, in its enforcement and interpretation in the following years it mandated that any school receiving public funds had to treat male and female athletes equally in terms of treatment, benefits, and opportunities to use facilities; equally accommodate the interests and abilities of male and female students; and receive federal assistance based on a proportional basis to the number of male and female participants in the institution's athletic programs. Finally, Title IX mandated that "institutions must provide both the opportunity for individuals of each sex to participate in intercollegiate competition, and for athletes of each sex to have competitive team schedules which equally reflect their abilities," which could mean providing sports opportunities in proportion to the student enrollment, demonstrating a continued expansion of athletic opportunities for the underrepresented sex, or accommodating the interest and ability of the underrepresented sex.[96]

In the 1960s and early 1970s, the years leading up to the passage and enforcement of gender equity in sports as a result of Title IX, a new gendered crisis emerged and was covered by the mass media regarding teen girls' participation in sports like track and basketball. The new panic was focused primarily on economic issues associated with the inclusion of athletics and often took the form of stories about small-town high schools that would have to "give up" boys' sports teams to pay for new girls' sports teams. (Although girls' participation in sports increased by 450 percent between the passing of Title IX and 2006, research did not demonstrate a decrease in boys' sports.)[97] Echoes of the arguments from the Women's Division still lingered within this resurgent discussion of teen girls' participation in strenuous sports.

For example, Kathryn Pierce, head of the girls' physical education department at Maine Township High School South in Park Ridge, Illinois, was quoted in the *Chicago Tribune* in 1971 questioning the wisdom of girls competing against boys since it would provide opportunities only for a few exceptional girls (though she also noted it might discourage schools from opening programs open to all girls, which is a tenet of Title IX in sports). "I wonder whether these efforts to avoid discrimination wouldn't result in much greater discrimination?" she said.[98] A 1978 article about increased girls' sports participation in the *Minneapolis Star* included a quote from a young high jumper's father, concerned about his daughter's ability to have children in the future: "When she jumps," he asked, "won't some things come out of place?"[99]

The African American press, which covered girls' track and field throughout the 1960s and 1970s, also reacted to the renewed interest, but it did not question the ramifications of Title IX. An opinion piece from Negro Press International and prominent black sports columnist A. S. "Doc" Young in 1964 noted that the recent Olympic competition with the Russians seemed to ignite enthusiasm for young female track-and-field athletes once again. In the column he jabs at how "most" Americans so recently "frowned on girls' track and field with a tigerish twisting of their faces" and "gnashed their teeth at the thought of it." He continues, "The frowning was, perhaps, more official than unofficial, for countless educational leaders spoke verbosely and eloquently in speeches which, boiled down, simply said, 'Nuts to girls on the track.' The claim was that track and field was detrimental to femininity. Track and field, said the critics, made girls muscle-bound. The sport wasn't wholesome and it wasn't healthy for girls, others said. The more outspoken hinted (hinted, did I say?) that there was something queer about a girl who liked to run or jump in competition."[100]

He then pointed out how African American girls continued to compete in track and field at historically black colleges and in city programs geared toward serving youth of color, while Caucasian track-and-field competition for girls was almost universally canceled. This propelled the top African

American track athletes to compete and dominate in the Olympic Games over the previous several decades. "Not a living soul complained because Negro girls were carrying the banner for America, the torch for America. And for a while there, the Negro girls saturated and dominated the field," he wrote.[101]

Concluding Thoughts on the Rise and Fall of Girls' Track and Field

This chapter demonstrates how a social issue related to gender can so quickly turn from progressive to regressive in a short period in part because of the advocacy of savvy moral entrepreneurs and their coverage by the news media. By drawing attention to American female athletes' lack of femininity just as these athletes were gaining media attention and popularity, the Women's Division was able to manufacture a crisis related to both gender and youth that effectively upset the status quo (especially with regard to girls' potential ability to reproduce). The mass media, primarily through newspaper and periodical coverage of the issue as it was hashed out in "official" meetings of various organizations, legitimized the crisis and created a public narrative about girls' participation in strenuous sports like running. The coverage also validated the dominant understanding of femininity as in binary opposition to masculinity and associated femininity with weakness and victimhood in the thinking that girl athletes must be prevented (by official organizations, parents, and other cultural authorities) from participating in strenuous sports like running to preserve their ability to have children. Moreover, this narrative reified the patriarchal notion that girls and women were intended to remain in the private, domestic sphere rather than enjoy themselves publicly in a manner that defied feminine gendered norms. Perhaps it also brought comfort and normalcy in a time when the world was in disarray, as World War II raged on. This particular need to adhere to traditional gender roles became even stronger in the 1950s, as the next chapter explains.

Much like the analysis within the rest of this book, this crisis describes issues related not only to gender and youth but to class and youth. Track and field and basketball were coded as "lower-class" sports. Upper-class sports, such as the ones that Blanche Trilling described as "individual sports"—tennis, swimming, and riding—were individual achievement-oriented sports seen as superior to the strenuous team sports popularized by the PAA and YMCA. In this way, Trilling and the Women's Division were moral entrepreneurs who policed not only appropriate femininity but also the boundaries of appropriate sports for women of higher socioeconomic status. These voices then became amplified in the context of a press that sought to garner attention and prestige among the wealthy classes. Although their voices were female, they might have been well suited to the news frames that the prestige press, including the *New York Times* but also the larger regional papers, wanted to adopt at the time to rise to prominence among its preferred audiences (including the women news readers who they hoped would see their department store advertisements).

African American and lower-income teen girls were largely excluded from any of the negative, panicked news coverage about track and field, but the legislative actions of the IOC and public schools affected them nonetheless. Because part of the narrative depended on the belief that girls should not engage in competition in front of spectators, both for medical and moral reasons, they were excluded from participation in any athletics deemed too competitive or too strenuous. This also effectively kept them out of the public sphere and limited their social and cultural power.

Finally, this historical episode proved to have lasting consequences for athletics, but it also has consequences for how we consider teen girls in the public sphere. Adolescent girls were discouraged from participating in sports—a recreational space where they could be progressive and show off leadership skills in the same way that boys could—and instead encouraged to participate in recreation and clubs that prized domestic and social skills, like Girl Reserves and Hi-Yi Princesses, where their leadership skills were limited to the domain of housewives, including organizing charity drives and planning dances. Although these were socially acceptable leisure choices in the 1940s and 1950s, they were also viewed as trivial and having nothing to do with intellectual or political power. Furthermore, such domestic skills were not commercially valued in a capitalistic society, although they were believed to be valuable social capital for the American teenage girl—specifically, as she was constructed as a cultural and social category throughout the 1940s and into the 1950s, a construction explored in more depth in chapter 3's discussion of teenage Elvis Presley fans.

CHAPTER 3

~≺

THE ELVIS PROBLEM, 1956–1959

~≺

They shrieked. They screamed. They jumped up in their seats. And they gazed at their idol as though transported into a state of ecstatic bliss.

— "Elvis Makes 'Em Shriek," *Orlando Sentinel Star*

He had a great beat, he had a lot of melody, and the music had tremendous feeling.

— Judy Healey, recounting an Elvis Presley concert she attended in 1956, personal interview

THE YEARS UP TO THE END OF World War II and the following postwar years saw cultural shifts that are crucial to understanding the contextualization of both the state of youth and the state of femininity. Connecting femininity, domesticity, and the home had increasingly become politically and culturally important to Americans in the years after the Women's Division's successful attack on strenuous sports for females, and in essence girls and women had been successfully relegated to the role of homemaker by the 1950s.

Elaine Tyler May refers to the period between 1945 and 1965 as an era of "domestic containment," in which it became important to tie the domestic sphere and family to stability in the wake of a postwar world fearing the Cold War and nuclear weapons. In that postwar period, Americans of all ethnicities and social classes retreated to a suburban life in which the wife and mother's role of full-time homemaker was viewed as both a representation of a family's social status and a contrast to communist nations' championship of women in the workplace. "The yearning for family stability gained momentum after the war, but the potential for restructuring the family withered as the powerful ideology of domesticity was imprinted on everyday life," May writes. "Ironically, traditional gender roles became a central feature of the 'modern' middle-class home." In her analysis of popular postwar teen girl icons, Ilana Nash attributes the shift to an overall postwar "crisis in masculinity" as returning servicemen sought to regain their literal and symbolic place in American culture. Furthermore, Susan J. Douglas, in her media criticism of popular communication messages directed at teen girls, recounts how the "warring messages—'be an American': no, no, be a girl—one softer and occasional, one louder and insistent, were amplified, repeated, and dramatized" in all facets of teen girls' lives in the 1950s. This was especially evident in the ever-prevalent discourses about domesticity perpetuated in entertainment television programming.[1]

Concurrently, a rise in media attention to youth started in the late World War II years and into the 1950s, emphasizing the rise of a new demographic that could be of great value to marketers and advertisers. The social constructions of childhood and adolescence changed drastically from the early postindustrial age in the United States, as increasingly over a period of forty years young people no longer had to support themselves and their families by laboring in urban factories and rural fields.[2] Even the term "adolescent" was applied only to young people who attended high school.[3]

Between 1900 and 1930 a number of pivotal changes in the United States worked to challenge the cultural understanding of the definition of childhood, which eventually led to the development of the teenager as a new cultural category.[4] First, public education was institutionalized, and an increased percentage of both working-class and middle-class youth stayed in schools longer. In this period high school attendance increased from 10 to 50 percent of eligible youth (aged fourteen to seventeen). By 1936, 65 percent were high school students, the highest proportion to date in U.S. history, and it reached 85 percent by 1960.[5] Second, youngsters became the focus of scientific research, as exemplified in the work of G. Stanley Hall, who coined the term "adolescence" in his 1904 book of the same name. Third, as was seen through the formal adoption of Progressive policy and the establishment of government-supported interest groups, the promotion and protection of children's welfare (especially poor and working-class children) became socially accepted. Moreover, formal government policies were passed into law to "protect" children (e.g., child labor laws, mandatory schooling laws).[6] Finally, as Ellen Wartella and Sharon Mazzarella point out, children—newly defined as innocent and in need of protection—were meant to be cared for and molded by adults (specifically mothers), and as a result, the sales of child-care advice manuals flourished and parenting experts became regular fixtures in media and society.[7]

Popular Science magazine is often credited with first using the label "teenager" in a 1941 issue on the topic, but according to Kelly Schrum, "teen," "teener," "teen-age," and "teen-ager" were used at times during the late nineteenth and early twentieth centuries.[8] But not until 1944 did "teenager" become "the accepted way to describe this new definition of youth as a discrete, mass market."[9] Indeed, during the 1940s and 1950s teenagers—particularly teenage girls and especially "bobby soxers"—were primarily considered consumers. Schrum describes the decades preceding the 1950s as "the formative years" of teenagers "as high school students, consumers, and trendsetters." She contends that by 1938 teenage girls' culture was identifiable, even if it was not a "single, unified teenage girls' culture," as such a statement would imply that culture itself is a "static, coherent system of symbols and meanings" rather than "fluid, impermanent, and loosely defined."[10] Nonetheless, certain aspects of the varying teenage girl cultures at this time overlapped, particularly in the realm of recreation and fashion. "Dancing the Lindy Hop, the Suzie Q., or the Big Apple (and showing a little too much thigh and enthusiasm for adult comfort), high school students gained national fame as 'bobby soxers,' the popular name bestowed on sing-crazed fans who were developing a new teenage style," writes Grace Palladino. "In their saddle shoes, skirts, and sweaters, they became the new symbol of high school life, one that was identified with music, fads, and fun."[11]

Mary Celeste Kearney ties the rise of the teenager directly to both the pre- and postwar baby booms and the "transformation of adolescents' public roles," precipitated in part by returning vets displacing young people from the workforce and leading them to enter or return to high school.[12] This time also marked a period of increased production and availability of varied consumer goods, and along with the boom in manufacturing came an increase in advertising spending.[13] Early teenagers were increasingly viewed as a highly lucrative and influential consumer demographic sought after by a multitude of corporate clients, and teenage consumption of popular culture and products soon became more of an accepted part of American culture.[14]

Even the "rise of the teenager" and visibility of "bobby soxers" was largely constructed through media representation of a particular type of American teenager—the white, middle- and upper-class "subdeb" who was featured prominently in *Life* magazine throughout the 1940s and 1950s.[15] This new American teen girl provided an example of the dominant hegemonic understanding of what acceptable feminine gender performance entailed: wearing feminine clothing, like full skirts with crinolines; demurring to adults and boys; quietly pursuing a life where she might stay home as a housewife and mother. The image was silently conveyed in those pages of *Life* and *Look*. And although postwar prosperity had opened doors to minority and working-class teenagers who began to attend high school and even college, these teenagers were not the ones represented sipping milkshakes and swooning over Frank Sinatra (or their own musical idols) in magazines and newspapers.[16]

The Cultural Construction of the Teenage Girl

Teenage girls themselves are a site of crisis because of the cultural perception of their innocent sexuality and positionality between childhood and adulthood. As the cultural construction of the teenage girl became more pronounced as a social and marketing category in the 1940s and 1950s, the crisis became all the more articulated through mass media portrayals. Nash describes the phenomenon in *American Sweethearts:* "From the moment of their earliest proliferation in the 1930s, representations of teenage girls as heroines of mass-culture comic entertainments rapidly coalesced into a limited range of interpretive options: either the girl was a quasi-angelic creature, praised for her bubbly charm, her obedience to authority, and her chastity, or else she was an exasperating agent of chaos who challenged the boundaries and hierarchies of a patriarchally-organized society (one that protects the social, economic, sexual, and political privileges of mature males)."[17]

Angela McRobbie and Jenny Garber note that cultural studies scholars have written extensively about the culture of teddy boys or teds (a British subculture of teen boys in the 1950s who dressed in old-fashioned Edwardian style that eventually moved to the United States and became strongly associated with rock and roll music) without spending time analyzing the girls who hung out with them, perhaps because the girls' excessive loitering in the scene in the 1950s was viewed as a potential invitation for sex by others. They argue that the 1950s double standard was reproduced in the ethnographic research of the time because of the girls' literal public invisibility, which was predicated on maintaining a good reputation by staying at home. "The difficulty in obtaining effective contraception, the few opportunities to spend time unsupervised with members of the opposite sex, the financial dependency of the working-class woman on her husband, meant that a good reputation mattered above everything else," they write. "As countless novels of the moment record, neighbourhoods flourished on rumours and gossip and girls who spent too much time on the street were assumed to be promiscuous."[18]

Although the portrayals of teenage girls in popular media in the late 1940s and early 1950s focused on the coming-of-age debutante who was preparing to marry, an undercurrent of worry and crisis surrounding teenage girl juvenile delinquents resonated within news media and public policy circles. Rachel Devlin argues that in the postwar years, juvenile crime committed by females was interpreted as a new crisis that stemmed "from the dynamics of a girls' relationship with her father, both as a parent and authority figure," in a time and place "where girlhood was increasingly marked by social and sexual precocity and where female juvenile crime was visibility and dramatically on the rise."[19] Indeed, this concern about good girls being corrupted fueled an American crisis of sorts when rock and roll music emerged in the 1950s as a rebellious style that flouted the standards of white adults, and this crisis was most articulated through the widespread mass media coverage of teenage girls' adulation of Elvis Presley, coverage that started in 1956 when Elvis's first record debuted and he appeared on television for the first time, and lasted through 1958, when he departed for a stint overseas in the U.S. Army.

Midcentury Mass Media, Rock and Roll, and Elvis

Although girls' studies scholars' arguments that American teen girl culture was established long before the 1950s, the mid-1950s was indeed a significant cultural moment in the permanent establishment of youth culture. As Gil Rodman writes,

> Far from being natural, the articulation between "rock 'n' roll" and "youth" that came about in the mid-1950s (e.g. that link that made it reasonable to describe someone as 'too old' for rock 'n' roll was forged by a variety of historical agents and social forces; teenagers trying to

mark off a portion of the cultural terrain as their own, parents (and other 'concerned' adults) in the midst of a moral panic over a number of perceived threats to traditional middle class values, shrewd (or perhaps merely cynical) musicians and industry executives who recognized that catering to engaging the emerging youth culture was profitable, and so on.[20]

One of the main perceived threats in 1956 was embodied in a twenty-year-old man named Elvis Presley. When Presley's first record hit the airwaves in January 1956, the sound of his hybrid mix of rhythm and blues, rockabilly, and country sung in a clipped vocal style that most critics seemed to loathe, he was merely portrayed as a southern country boy (or hillbilly, in the more derogatory news stories) who was likely the latest music trend. But his televised and live appearances—in which he showcased a trademark hip swivel that was distinct and markedly read as sexual—caused the stir that likely propelled him to superstardom among a generation of teenagers. Although the young males in audience were portrayed as identifying with his rebellious, raucous musical performance style, the girls were inevitably portrayed as weak in the knees, screaming and crying, and out-of-control over his mere appearance.[21] Both newspaper stories and television reports focused very specifically on this teenage girl audience, which at once was seen as making a public spectacle of itself in its screaming acceptance of Elvis's performances and also as a source of victimhood. After all, these seemingly naive girls could be influenced by Elvis's sexually charged brand of rock and roll in a way that could lead them to delinquency and (for many in the 1950s, worse) promiscuity.

Teen girls' screaming over popular musical idols was not a new phenomenon at this time in U.S. history. In the 1940s the original "bobby soxers" quite famously fawned over then teen idol Frank Sinatra. Schrum points out that critics chastised Sinatra and his handlers for constructing an image specifically to cater to teenage girls, from a slightly askew front lock of hair to a boyish frailty demonstrated by the way he clung to his microphone, shyly crooning to them.[22] Contrast this to Elvis Presley: strumming his guitar so loudly that he routinely broke strings (which was fairly uncommon in the pre–rock and roll days), employing howls and hiccups as he swung his hips around with the microphone. Unlike Sinatra, Elvis didn't provoke a motherly swooning reaction from fans; he seemed to provoke visceral, out-of-control screams. In the 1940s and early 1950s adults preferred to understand teenage girls as both innocent and asexual; Palladino sees this denial of the sexual nature of girls as linked to the same middle-class denial of rock and roll music's African American origins.[23]

But to better understand the rise of Elvis Presley as a rock and roll star and his intrinsic connection to the screams of teenage girls (a connection mentioned in nearly every newspaper article written about him in the 1950s), we must first understand how the media landscape had changed since the period covered in the previous chapter in this book, when newspapers and magazines were widely read, radio broadcasting was primarily limited to dramatic entertainment and family programming, and popular media like film were still disparaged by many cultural critics. Commercial television in the United States made its grand debut in 1947, and although television sets themselves were still too expensive for purchase by some American families, children and teenagers in particular often befriended schoolmates with TV sets so they could join them to watch their favorite programs after school.

In addition to an acute cultural fear of juvenile delinquency, especially female juvenile delinquency, there developed an even more distinct fear of the corrupting effects of television.[24] In her analysis of American television in the 1950s, Karal Ann Marling contends that scholars, cultural critics, and average citizens alike all expressed concern over the dangers of television, especially for young people:

> Fraudulent by nature, the illusory presentness of the moving image was one of several factors that made TV dangerous, especially to the young. From mid-decade on, the baleful effects of television on American life became a national obsession. Polls, surveys, and experts all agreed that something terrible was happening. People stayed in the house more and read good books less. Kids were glued to the set for three or four hours a day. The content of programming aroused "morbid emotions in children," stirred up "domestic quarrel . . . loosed morals and made people lazy and sodden."[25]

About half of U.S. households contained a television set by 1955. Nonetheless, and in spite of more serious news shows such as *See It Now* by respected journalist Edward R. Murrow, television was still viewed by many as a low-brow medium—made for less serious content than either newspaper or radio. Looking back on the social history of television in the 1970s, Raymond Williams suggested that TV broadcasting was a "new and powerful form of social integration and control." "Many of its main uses can be seen as socially, commercially and at times politically manipulative," he wrote. "Moreover, this viewpoint is rationalised by its description as 'mass communication,' a phrase used by almost all its agents and advisers as well as, curiously, by most of its radical critics." After all, he wrote, " 'masses' had been the new nineteenth- century term of contempt for what was formerly described as 'the mob.' "[26]

This view of the television audience of the mid-1950s as "the masses" is very clear in some of the print criticism of Presley's television appearances; for example, *New York Times*'s TV critic Jack Gould's comparison of his moves to those of a burlesque performer following his second appearance on the *Milton Berle Show* in June 1956.[27] After Elvis's controversial appearances on the *Milton Berle Show,* Steve Allen booked him for his own prime-time Sunday evening variety program, *The Steve Allen Show,* for a July 1, 1956, performance. The news dismayed Associated Press columnist Charles Mercer so that he published an "Open Letter to Steve Allen," criticizing the decision. The underlying presumption that television had the power to propel Presley's career and influence youth is clear:

> Dear Steve:
>
> Word comes to this department that you're planning to book Elvis Presley, the hysterical shouter of rock 'n' roll, for your second regular weekly NBC-TV show Sunday evening, July 1. Why?
>
> Until now I've refrained from joining in the chorus of public and critical condemnation of Presley's primitive exhibition on the Milton Berle show a couple of weeks ago. My theory is that characters like Presley thrive on bad press. The more they're condemned, the more people are aroused to watch and listen to them. Obviously, however, my thinking that something unpleasant would go away if ignored was wishful and foolish. For now, so soon, you apparently plan to bring Elvis the Pelvis back to a national television network to titillate teenage girls and cause numbskull boys to imitate him.[28]

Allen might have won back the admiration of Mercer by dressing Presley in formal tuxedo with tails singing, ludicrously and unenthusiastically, to a live basset hound.[29] Not all media writers were amused by this satirical stunt. John Lardner of *Newsweek* wrote, "Allen's ethics were questionable from the start. He fouled Presley, a fair-minded judge would say, by dressing him like a corpse, in white tie and tails. This is a costume often seen on star performers at funerals, but only when the deceased has specifically requested it in his will. Elvis had made no such request—or, for that matter, no will. He was framed."[30] The ratings boost for Allen's show was so pronounced, however, that the news soon broke that Ed Sullivan had booked Presley for a three-show engagement beginning in September 1956. By some estimates, more than sixty million viewers, or 82.6 percent of Americans with access to a TV, saw Elvis's first appearance on the *Ed Sullivan Show*.[31] In the first appearance Sullivan himself was recuperating from a car accident, so actor Charles Laughton introduced Presley. He performed "Don't Be Cruel" and "Love Me Tender," and his entire body was shot, including his infamous gyrations; girls screamed in the background.[32]

Marling suggests the combination of Presley's perceived hypersexuality and television's perceived ill effects on audiences made his early appearances all the more salacious; with the increase in the masses watching television, worry about Presley's effect on young people was widespread.[33] Indeed, Pat Strodt, who was fourteen at the time of Elvis's performance on the *Ed Sullivan Show,* said that even in her own home, she screamed and "carried on" for Elvis, much to the embarrassment of her sister (though her "liberal" parents seemed more amused than anything). Still, she was surprised by the outcry of some adults and media accounts about his performances. "I didn't know what the big deal was at all—it seemed so ridiculous," she remembered. "It's not like he was doing something pornographic or really even suggestive. He was dancing."[34]

In addition to a general cultural preoccupation with teens' susceptibility to juvenile delinquency and promiscuity, Hollywood film in the mid-1950s followed suit and began to portray teenagers' rebellion and disaffection through such popular movies as *Rebel without a Cause*. Marling argues that the representation of rebellion through both rock and roll music (and specifically Elvis Presley) and these new films were "watersheds through which the teenager became once again, a massive preoccupation for Americans."[35] After Elvis's second performance on Sullivan's show, the *New York Times*'s Jack Gould again was highly critical both of Presley and the TV industry, in a column titled, "Elvis Presley: Lack of Responsibility Is Shown by TV in Exploiting Teen-Agers," in which he suggests that the strong effects of Presley's performance would negatively influence the youth audience.[36]

From 1950 to 1953 radio was still very popular among American youth, who listened to serials in the late afternoon after school (especially younger kids) and music and comedy shows any time of the day. Television cut the young audience for radio in half by 1955, as young viewers watched upward of four hours of TV daily on average.[37] Most shows were created for general audiences, though as if to further supplement young people's affection for popular music, televised music and dance shows were developed at both a regional and national level. These shows were generally shown in the late afternoons and on Saturdays. Colorado teens watched Denver-based *Teenage Dance Party,* Richmond teens watched *Top Ten Dance Party,* and Philadelphia teens watched Dick Clark's *Bandstand,* which became the national *American Bandstand* in August 1957. Alan Freed's *The Big Beat* debuted a month earlier, but Freed lost his show after a cameraman accidentally showed black teenage singer Frankie Lymon dancing with a white partner.[38]

Rock and roll music and Elvis Presley in particular presented the mostly Caucasian middle- and upper-class American radio and television audiences with a musical form rooted in southern black culture in a time of racial inequity and segregation. Despite racism apparent both on television and in daily life in the mid-1950s, Presley's early music and its hybridity spoke to interracial audiences, Rodman argues.[39] This is evidenced in a newspaper column written by Memphis WDIA radio personality Nat D. Williams: "A thousand black, brown and beige teenage girls in that audience blended their alto and soprano voices in one wild crescendo of sound that rent the rafters and took off like scalded cats in the direction of Elvis."[40] The reaction of the African American press to Elvis is explored later in this chapter but suffice it to say, his hybrid music was also the most pronounced version of the "threat" that the new genre of rock and roll would provoke "cultural miscegenation (i.e., the blurring of the line between black and white cultures)," a concern that subtly made its way into the news coverage of his concerts and TV appearances.[41]

Moreover, Presley's style and fashion choices made himself a target of the mass media, in some ways connecting his own predilection for hot pink, black velvet, and gold lamé suits both to "Negro" fashion (Marling points out that he shopped at Memphis's Lanksy Brothers, "where white kids rarely ventured") as well as to femininity. With his pink suits and eyeliner juxtaposed with pelvic thrusts, his performance of gender did not fit into the masculine/feminine binary referred to by Judith Butler.[42]

Stories ultimately suggested that Elvis was not only a bit like a girl but strictly for girls. In a rare, mostly strong concert review, Walt Christie wrote for the *Honolulu Star Bulletin* that Presley is "strictly for the girls," and his "male audience, for the most part, was far more reserved, or at least, stoic."[43] By relegating Presley's music as important only to female audiences, critics in effect further marginalized and feminized Presley himself too.

Heteronormativity abounds in the media coverage of teen girls' fascination with Elvis. In many cases his own sexuality is subtly questioned in critics' descriptions of his style and dancing; in other cases the girls themselves are treated with something of a raised eyebrow as they got haircuts like Elvis, donning faux sideburns and slicking back bangs except for a "lank hank" on the forehead.[44] Sinatra's female fans also were known to dress like their idol, whose style at the time centered on bowties and sweaters, which also provoked concern from their parents. Schrum notes that music then (and always) "provided the teenage girls with an avenue for exploring sexuality and romantic fantasy as well as the opportunity to experiment with gender boundaries."[45]

But even the fact that Elvis Presley was so widely covered by all facets of the mass media did not have to do entirely with Elvis himself but with a newfound realization that the acknowledgment of teenagers and youth culture in general was big business. Beginning in 1950 American teens spent billions every year of the decade, topping out at $10 billion in 1959.[46] The press and broadcasters were keenly aware that as a new consumer demographic, teenagers—many of whom for the first time in history had their own cash to spend on themselves rather than support their families—were crucial to attract advertisers.

Eugene Gilbert, a market research guru who studied teenagers, was a crucial part of this new interpretation of teenagers as consumers with valuable insight. Gilbert wrote in the style of a journalist who knew how to translate social scientific data into everyday terms by using direct quotations from teenagers and interpreting trends. His company employed young surveyors who could relate to young people, and this data was later sold to advertisers, but he gained the most visibility by turning his data into news columns that ran in newspapers nationwide discussing the various trends and whims associated with the teenage population. Several articles were about the popularity of Elvis and rock and roll music among teenagers. His columns positioned him as an expert who could speak for and translate the language of teenage girls and boys.[47]

In the years following World War II, mass media was not only acknowledging the existence of the demographic in its coverage but also increasingly gearing itself toward teenagers in the form of teen magazines.[48] *Seventeen* magazine debuted in September 1944 with broader teen appeal. Circulation exceeded one million copies by February 1947 and two and a half million by July 1949. Despite the predominantly white, middle-class audience, *Seventeen* reached many more teens than *Calling All Girls* or subdeb columns. In the 1950s gossip magazines, such as *Teen Parade* and *Hep Cats,* sought working-class readers, while *Seventeen* emphasized fashion, dating, and early marriage.[49] A cheaper new breed of magazines geared toward teens, and specifically teen girls, proliferated beginning in 1955, including *Dig, Flip, Confidential Teen Romances, Hollywood Teenagers, Modern Teen, Sixteen, Teen Screen, Teen Time,* and *Teen Today.* The writers employed by these magazines were youthful, and much of the content revolved around appearance and popularity, with the occasional celebrity profile.[50]

Even newspapers tried to emulate the style of these early teen magazines through such ongoing features as "Teentime Turntable" by Phyllis Battelle, a well-known witty journalist who served as the women's editor for the International News Service. Although her stories, which ran in newspapers throughout the United States, were written with a light tone, her stories on Elvis very nicely captured the spirit of a burgeoning youth culture and a nation's reaction that was at once amused and panicked. An article headlined "Cold-Eyed, Hot-Voiced Elvis Is King of Teens" begins with the note, "This is the second of four articles to appear on 'Teentime Turntable' reporting on a nationwide survey of educators, clergymen, parents and teen-agers on the controversial Rock 'n' Roll Craze."[51] Battelle's article, with an extended feature-like lead, perfectly encapsulates both the attitude of teenagers—specifically female teenagers—toward Elvis and the cultural backlash against Elvis and against the teens' adulation of him in rather eye-rolling, tongue-in-cheek sentences:

> Elvis Presley is a 21-year-young man who makes more than $40,000 a week for rockin' from his heels and rollin' his suggestive songs off his animated larynx.

He is the almighty king of millions of rock 'n' roll fans around America, and he puts on the kind of show that makes young girls violently excited, and adults violently angry.

"He ought to be banned!" is a frequent suggestion among shocked members of the older generation who have observed the seductive, undulating gestures that accompany his stage and TV vocals.

But no steps have been taken to ban Mr. Presley because rock 'n' roll is the hottest fad to strike the musical frenzy since the Charleston. It is big business. The kids love it. And youth, as usual, will be served.

Rock 'n' roll music (though "beat" is a more apt word than "music") might conceivably have died of monotony in 1955 after two years of bouncing prosperity had not Elvis come along.

Within the article appears the many tropes that seemed to belong in media coverage of Elvis—the screaming girls, a description of his flash and sexuality, the questioning of rock and roll as a genre, and the acknowledgment that teenagers are a valuable demographic that "will be served" by whatever it demands of the culture industry. These themes become all the more pronounced within the other mass media coverage of the day, whether in magazines, radio, television, or newspapers. Furthermore, the gendered nature of this coverage is noted, as is explored in the next section.

Teenage Girls and Public Expression of Sexuality

Nearly every newspaper and magazine article or television broadcast that discussed Elvis Presley in any way—from biographical feature to news brief to concerned review—contains a mention of screaming girls. Teen girls in decades past were known to swoon and squeal for Frank Sinatra (and were infamous for screaming and crying over the Beatles less than a decade later), but the screams for Elvis Presley were characterized differently, as a public sexual reaction to his own public display of sexuality through movement. Some journalists acknowledged this difference: "Presley's fans scream with more agitation than the girls did a decade ago for Frankie-boy Sinatra. In San Diego they stormed the stage. Elsewhere they wait outside the stage door and tear buttons off his shirt," wrote one in a June 1956 article. "They shrieked. They screamed. They jumped up in their seats," wrote another reporter about an August 1956 concert in Orlando.

"And they gazed at their idol as though transported into a state of ecstatic bliss." In another, "Elvis Presley—the stuff of which some teen-age dreams are made—swept Buffalo like a whirlwind Monday evening. Behind him he left more than 10,000 hoarse throats and about the same number of emotionally wrung-out psyches."[52]

Many tied the screams directly to Elvis's performance. For example, "Elvis Presley, young bump-and-grind artist, turned a rainy Sunday afternoon into an orgy of squealing in St. Paul auditorium," wrote a *Minneapolis Tribune* reporter in May 1956. "He vibrated his hips so much, and the 3,000 customers squealed so insistently at the vibrations, it was impossible to hear him sing. None of the smitten seemed to care."[53]

Often, the reporters' language describing the teenagers makes them sound orgasmic, which in the domestically contained 1950s was not an attractive trait in a teenage girl. In a large spread titled "Elvis, a Different Kind of Idol," *Life* magazine published a photo of crying adolescent girls with the cutline, "The girls out front go into their screams and seizures. From then on most of them do not hear what Elvis sings as he flings about, bringing his susceptible audience to the breaking point."[54] The fans are in such a state of "bliss" that they are out of control, which certainly fuels the fear of both juvenile promiscuity and delinquency already pervasive in 1950s America.

Despite the hints of "crisis" within many of the reports on girls screaming for Elvis Presley, some reporters simply made fun of the screams and occasionally admonished the audience for not listening more closely. In a November 1957 concert review, Bob Krauss of the *Honolulu Advertiser* wrote of his concert experience:

> One girl behind me kept screaming with the shrill intensity of hysteria. Between screams she gasped, "Oh Elvis, you're killing me. I can't stand it. I can't stand it."
>
> It was difficult to judge Presley's performance as a singer on the basis of yesterday afternoon's concert. The screams drowned out his voice a great portion of the time. This apparently didn't bother his teenage fans, who seemed to recognize each melody from the opening word. "Don't Be Cruel" and "Hound Dog" drew the maximum decibels of admiration.
>
> Oddly enough, there was very little clapping after each number.

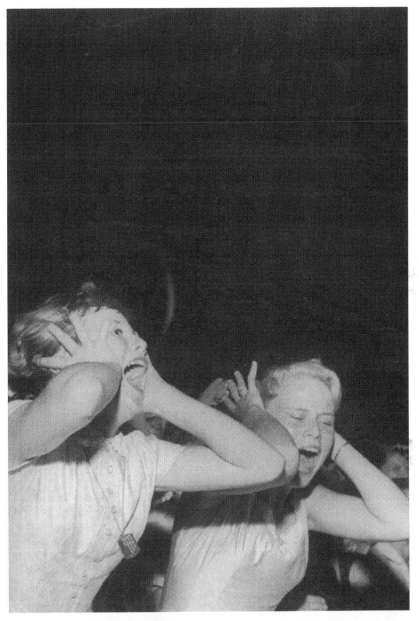

"Happy Screechers": Elvis fans in Jacksonville, Florida, photographed by Robert W. Kelley, for "Elvis: A Different Kind of Idol," *Life,* August 27, 1956. (Getty Images)

But Presley had only to say, "Thank you, thank you very much," and the audience would scream. He'd scratch his nose; another scream. He'd laugh; another scream.[55]

Indeed, the news articles reinforced a notion that was becoming more common in terms of the cultural understanding of the teenage girl—that she was silly, that she enjoyed triviality, and that she did not have particularly good taste or judgment. This creation of a cultural stereotype that started arguably with bobby soxers in the late 1940s became more pronounced as the teenager itself became a cultural archetype in the 1950s.

Not only was it common for most mainstream media coverage of Elvis Presley to note teen girls' sexuality on display through their screaming and carrying on, but it was also common to dismiss their passion for rock and roll and Elvis's music. Critics were not kind to Elvis in these early years, calling his vocal style "hiccupping," and worse. Following Elvis's second appearance on the *Milton Berle Show, New York Times* TV columnist Jack Gould wrote, "Mr. Presley has no discernable singing ability. His specialty is rhythm songs which he renders in an undistinguished whine; his phrasing, if it can be called that, consists of stereotyped variations that go with a beginner's aria in a bathtub." Gould noted his only strength was "an accented movement of the body that heretofore has been primarily identified with the repertoire of the blonde bombshells of the burlesque runway." A Florida critic in 1956 called his performance an "old fashioned bump and grind routine," and dozens of articles referred to Elvis as "The Pelvis."[56] The fans, and especially the teen girls fans, were most often chastised for their poor taste in music, which has led in part to this crisis. They were called "tin eared," and one reporter wrote, "It's a toss up which was worse, Elvis or his fans."[57]

In the years before Helen Gurley Brown changed the emphasis of *Cosmopolitan* magazine's content to sex and the single girl, it was a more general interest magazine geared toward the urbane, which would explain its commissioning jazz musician Eddie Condon to write a piece titled "What Is an Elvis Presley?" for its December 1956 issue. He opines about his thirteen-year-old daughter, Maggie, who "went stark, raving cuckoo over Elvis. The house resounded to the beat of 'Hound Dog,' causing our own hound dog, a beagle named Punchy, to creep under furniture in terror. Maggie began wearing an Elvis Presley charm bracelet and she refused to go to sleep unless she was surrounded by her enormous collection of pictures of his delinquent-like map. She also started an E. P. scrapbook, which she generously offered to show me. 'Make sure there's a fireplace handy,' I growled." Later in the article, he describes Elvis's voice as a "wheezing grunt" and notes that he has combined "moonshine, hillbilly songs, backwoods bawls and goat calls, and has come up with something that sells."[58]

Many objections to teen girls' fascination were tied not only to Elvis's public displays of sexuality, and the question of his own masculinity and links to black culture, but also to his socioeconomic status, which is perceived as poor "hillbilly," though the Presley family was probably closer to lower middle class. This is clear in Condon's commentary and myriad other pieces in which reporters quote Presley verbatim, writing phonetically in a southern drawl and leaving in all improper grammar.

The 1950s marked the first point in history where young people, and teen girls in particular, were regularly interviewed and quoted within print media stories. In the previous chapter, which focused on the rise and fall of girls' and women's track and field between 1920 and 1940, the only young females quoted within news stories were famous Olympic athletes (and even then only the flamboyant Babe Didrikson was quoted often). In those pieces, as well as in earlier stories about teen girls' dance hall attendance, mostly more "legitimate" sources—authorities, academic and cultural experts, government and political officials, and commission members—were called on to lend color and credibility to stories about teen girls. The postwar era privileged expertise even more so than previous decades, especially those with scientific expertise—be it social or physical science.[59] Unsurprisingly, the media's practice of including quotations from experts to lend legitimacy to stories continued in the early coverage of Elvis Presley. In fact, experts abound within the news coverage—from psychologists to clergymen to experts on teens and pop culture (such as Eugene Gilbert and Phyllis Battelle).

For the first time in media history, actual teens' voices were included in the majority of the stories about Elvis. But these voices—much like the voice of Elvis himself in his "hillbilly"-accented southern drawl—were added seemingly to lend comic relief and alert the reader that even though "youth, as usual, will be served" (in the words of Battelle), readers should not take their opinions too seriously. In one, the author notes that a critic who gave Presley a scathing review received letters calling her "an old stinkin' rat!" and a "so-and-so old bag!"[60] The exaggerated language and slang are common in media stories, as the following quotes demonstrate:

> "LIKE him?" she says to the reporter. "We LOVE him! Because he's so neat, I guess. He's the most."[61]
> "I think he's the coolest cat on earth."[62]
> "I sat through 'Love Me Tender' three times in one afternoon," another girl bubbled. "I was in a happy daze for a week afterward."[63]

But often these quotes could be interpreted as representing the teen girl as a creature not to be trusted because she is so stupid and naive. Although reporters probably would argue they were simply recounting direct quotes and showing the girls' cuteness, in many cases, it is clear that the audience is supposed to read the teen girl as dumb. For example, a *New York Times* critic printed a letter from a preteen including an egregious spelling error: "I am an Elvis Presley fan but my father is not. My father and I made a deal. He said that I could only see 'Love Me Tender' if your review was recommend for 10-year-old girls. Please kinsider [*sic*] your review before condemning Elvis."[64]

In the following story the reporter clearly conveys the breathless, irrational nature of teen girls who believed that when they called a woman working at a Memphis store, Elvis was there in the store:

> I called this girl, her name is _____, in Memphis, Tenn.—and he was there, he was THERE! RIGHT THERE WHILE I WAS TALKING TO HER! She wouldn't let us talk to him, though. She said she couldn't cuz too many kids call all the time. It's hard to talk to her because we get so excited we cry. I told her, I said, "I bet you think we're silly for crying," and she said, "No, I think you're sweet." Another girl said once she sent Elvis a teddy bear that cost her $14, and Janice said she sent him two shirts.[65]

This means of representing the adolescent female Elvis Presley fan uses language and selected quotations to diminish their opinions and further marginalize their status within a patriarchal culture. They are described as screaming and having "seizures" and as part of an out-of-control mob. The media narratives also position cultural experts—music and TV critics and "credible" musicians themselves—against teen girls, who are specifically shown as having poor taste and judgment. It is hardly a stretch to see that poor taste and judgment are also connected to the girls' perceived vulnerability and potential victimhood.

Teen Girl Elvis Fans as Victims

Douglas reminds us that the "legacy of the 1950s was that no 'nice' girl ever, ever went all the way before marriage, and no nice woman ever really liked sex."[66] People who were wary of Elvis's gyrations in concerts and on television worried primarily that teen girls who felt comfortable enough to scream and carry on hysterically in public would also be more apt to stray morally in their private lives. In other words, public articulation of sexuality might also signal private articulation of sexuality, which in the 1950s meant that a girl was promiscuous and ruined for marriage.

Television personality Drew Pearson in 1956 titled one program "Drew Pearson Tackles the Elvis Controversy" on *Drew Pearson's Washington Merry-Go-Round,* asking in the introduction, "What effect does he really have on juvenile delinquency and who's to blame?"[67] He immediately made clear that the delinquency he referred to was sexual promiscuity and specifically promiscuity of teen girls: "The main source of the controversy is that he's become sort of a sex symbol for teen-age girls. They go wild over him," he says in the manner of a serious television news anchor. "Presley doesn't smoke or drink, but he does like girls. And they're prone literally to throw themselves at him." Pearson makes clear that he does not believe that Elvis himself should be blamed for his sudden "influence over girls." Instead he blames "the big music companies, the TV MCs, and the business managers who are looking for profits and high ratings." In his view, the teen girl fans are helpless in the throes of the corporate Elvis machine.

In her article "The Presley Crush: The Teenage Declaration of Independence," Ruth Millett, a correspondent for the Newspaper Enterprise Association (NEA) news wire service quoted an "unnamed practicing psychologist," saying, "Because he is a grown-up who doesn't have to behave like a grown-up, teenage girls find it easy to fit him into their dream world."[68] Experts (who also remained unnamed) in psychology and social work who served as sources for a *New York Daily Mirror* story, "Girls Identify Elvis as Lover," blamed teen girls' hormones for their potential victimization. The reporters summarized, "When a teenager on the threshold of womanhood watches or listens to Elvis Presley, there is only one thing on her mind— sex. She may deny this. She may not even believe it herself. But that's what it is, according to specialists." An unnamed specialist points out that while teen girls in the not-so-distant past swooned over Sinatra and Johnny Ray, they felt a sweet, romantic attachment, but "there is nothing sweet" about a young girl going crazy for Elvis.[69] The article suggested that Elvis was a "primitive man" (another subtle connection to race and sexuality, perhaps) and that girls would be unable to control themselves in his presence.

Although the *Daily Mirror* arguably tended to print salacious stories that suited its tabloid style, Canadian music critics in an article about his performance in Vancouver, British Columbia, in September 1957 seemed just as descriptive in their concern for Elvis's effect on youth. They suggested that Elvis Presley employed specific and deliberate tactics to send impressionable teen girls into a frenzy. Various writers and critics were called on to comment in this article, which was picked up by several U.S. newspapers:

> Feature writer Ben Metcalfe said: "A gang moved into OUR town to exploit 22,000 pre-conditioned adolescents, hired OUR policemen to stop anybody who wanted to get too close, then left with the loot and let the police and the kids fight it out for what was left—nothing." Dr. Ida Halpern, music critic, said the performance "had not even the quality of a true obscenity: merely an artificial and unhealthy exploitation of the enthusiasm of youth's body and mind. One could call it subsidized sex."
>
> Wrote entertainment editor Les Wedman: "It was disgraceful, the whole mess. It was planned artificially at its best and the gullible and truly worshipful Elvis fans bit." Policemen, ushers at Empire Stadium and air cadets failed to hold the first mob which rushed the stage. "The kids moved back," Metcalfe wrote. "A girl, her dress torn, was carried screaming in very real hysteria off the field. Presley came forward, winking gleefully at his cronies, and started it again . . . On stage, Presley winked again for his cronies to move into another wiggling song. It was obvious he was enjoying himself."[70]

Even jazz musician Condon in his *Cosmopolitan* magazine article discussed the "curse" of Elvis's "bumps and grinds": "These gyrations have to concern parents—unless we're the kind of parents who approve of kids going around stealing hubcaps, indulging in promiscuity, and generally behaving like delinquents," he wrote. "I don't think for a minute that my thirteen-year-old Maggie is going to become delinquent because she's batty over Elvis. But I think that if she were older, and not as strictly supervised as she is now by the nuns and her parents, I might be a trifle worried."[71] In 1957 a *Time* magazine writer declared him a "sexhibitionist" who thrived on impressionable teen girls' attention.[72]

Parents were indeed worried. In the *San Antonio Express,* the "Teen Editor" wrote a story titled "Piggy Banks and Boy Friends Shelling Out to Take Presley Fans to Sunday's Shows." According to one teenage source who was trying to convince her boyfriend to take her to an upcoming Presley concert, rock and roll shows are "pretty wild," and most mothers would prefer their daughters be escorted to them—especially to an Elvis Presley concert.[73]

School officials also worried. In 1957 a group of high school principals at the conference for the National Association of Secondary School Principals declared their schools to be free of Elvis Presley records in cafeteria juke-boxes. Many also banned Elvis-style haircuts and sideburns as well as blue jeans in their schools, according to an Associated Press story titled "High School Principals Wince at Presley, Blue Jeans, Ducktails."[74] Newspapers across the United States also ran a story about female students in a Chicago high school being forbidden in 1958 from wearing Elvis Presley dog tag jewelry to class, in protest of the singer's drafting into the U.S. Army that year. "I've forbidden the girls to wear the dog tags. If they keep on, I'll simply have to dismiss them from school," their principal said. "It's too frivolous and silly. They're at an impressionable age."[75]

Even law enforcement in this period seemed affected by the suspicion over all things Elvis Presley. A national wire story about two sisters found murdered in Chicago, the Grimes sisters, noted in various versions of the story that the girls had disappeared after leaving home to see an Elvis Presley movie and were last seen with a boy with Elvis Presley–type sideburns and a ducktail haircut.[76]

Of all the moral entrepreneurs who fretted about Elvis Presley's effect on teenage girls, some members of the Christian clergy certainly were most vocal and active in their opposition. The media, from television to newspapers to magazines, covered the stories of both Baptist preachers and Catholic priests who vehemently protested the existence of Presley, both his live appearances and media coverage.

Life magazine ran a feature photo spread about how Presley's concert in Jacksonville, Florida, sparked both excitement and revilement across the city. A Jacksonville judge prepared an arrest warrant for Presley, charging him with impairing the morals of minors in the event that Elvis swiveled his hips at the show, but photos of young people dancing to his music abound throughout the spread. It also included a photo with a dozen young girls dancing with an older man, their minister, in a church hall, with the caption, "ANTIDOTE TO ELVIS was a church social at Murray Hill Methodist church two nights after Presley left. Before dance, group heard Presley denounced in sermon on 'Hotrods, Reefers, and Rock 'n' Roll.'" Next to this is an iconic photo of Rev. Robert Gray from Trinity Baptist Church, standing at the pulpit clutching a promotional poster for the Presley concert, and beneath it a larger photo of young people bowing their heads in prayer, titled "PRAYER FOR PRESLEY." Reverend Gray was quoted saying that Elvis "achieved a new low in spiritual degeneracy. If he were offered his salvation tonight, he would probably say, 'No thanks. I'm on the top.'"[77]

The editor of the newspaper published by the Catholic Archdiocese of La Crosse, Wisconsin, perhaps took his offense at Elvis the furthest of all by writing a letter to J. Edgar Hoover, the powerful director of the Federal Bureau of Investigation, to report his "conviction that Presley is a definite danger to the security of the United States." He noted in his letter that he sent two reporters to cover the show but also heard from other media workers and community members "that it was the filthiest and most harmful production that ever came to La Crosse for exhibition to teenagers": "Eyewitnesses have told me that Presley's actions and motions were such as to rouse the sexual passions of teenaged youth. One eye-witness described his actions as 'sexual self-gratification on the stage'—another as 'a striptease with clothes on.'" Although police and auxiliaries were there, the show went on. Perhaps the hardened police did not get the import of his motions and gestures, like those of masturbation or riding a microphone.[78]

Although the archdiocese noted that the local police captain and assistant district attorney who attended the show did not find any reason to halt the show for obscenity, he then did say that he had heard "gossip" that the Presley fan clubs "degenerate into sex orgies" and that he firmly believed Elvis was a sexual pervert and a drug addict and that he was "convinced that juvenile crimes of lust and perversion will follow his show here in La Crosse." He wrote that eyewitnesses assured him that "Presley's actions and motions were such as to rouse the sexual passions of teenaged youth."[79]

The editor's letter was published in his own local newspaper, but *America*, a weekly national Jesuit magazine devoted to "Catholic Scholarship," picked up the La Crosse story and published its own reaction under the headline, "Beware Elvis Presley." In it, the writer noted that the reader might not have heard of him, but that his or her children have, noting "If his 'entertainment' could be confined to records, it might not be too bad an influence on the young, but unfortunately Presley makes personal appearances." It then quotes what it calls "the La Crosse paper" (the Catholic Diocese newspaper and not the *La Crosse Tribune*, the nonsecular local newspaper) that described the show as a "strip-tease with clothes on" and "youngsters . . . rolling in the aisles." The piece went on: "Citizens groups of La Crosse were so concerned that Lyons Associates, who had billed Presley, said they would never again bring him or anyone like him to town. Yet the National Broadcasting Company wasn't loathe to bring Presley into the living-rooms of the nation on the evening of June 5 . . . If the agencies (TV and other) would stop handling such nauseating stuff, all the Presleys of our land would soon be swallowed up in the oblivion they deserve."[80]

The Associated Press many months later wrote a wire story, "Elvis Presley Likened to Golden Calf," in which Rev. W. Carter Merbreier, pastor of St. Matthew's Lutheran Church in Philadelphia and "observer" for the police department's juvenile aid bureau described a local audience at a concert as "screaming, falling to their knees as if in prayer, stretching rigidly and wriggling into a supreme effort of ecstasy."[81] Unlike the Catholic and Baptist detractors who received publicity for their criticism of Elvis, Merbreier did not blame Elvis himself but rather the "victims"—the "idiotic parents" who allowed their "nervous giggling girls" to attend the show. "Even though the gesticulations of Elvis Presley are unquestionably suggestive and possibly even immoral, the condemnation must lie with those who have by their adoration made him the golden image," he told the AP reporter.

One of the "screaming" girls who attended the La Crosse concert, Judy Healey, many years later recalled the screaming (though she herself said she did not participate in the described histrionics nor did she remember girls at the concert being as out of control as described in any of the media coverage) but not the obscenity. Healey, herself a seventeen-year-old Catholic school girl at the time, attended the show with her boyfriend. "I considered myself 'older' than the girls who were displaying themselves at the concert at La Crosse, and it really seemed sort of wild, but I loved the music," she said. "What I think this media coverage missed and what the Catholic Church and a lot of older people missed was the rhythm and the music—he had a great beat, he had a lot of melody, and the music had tremendous feeling. Everything he was saying was coming in with rock and roll—boom, boom, boom, 'don't you step on my blue suede shoes'—and the ballads that he sang were really lovely. He had some very haunting ballads. These people were missing that." She then hinted at the heteronormativity that pervades so much of the discussion of Elvis and his fans. "All they were doing was looking at this guy swinging his hips around, and you know, men don't do that."[82]

A Noticeable Lack of Panic

In many ways it makes sense to emphasize the screaming girls and their lack of judgment since that did appear to be the main, most important story within most mainstream media. Among the almost-entirely adult, Caucasian reporters covering Presley's music and concerts, this was the most noteworthy point to make about a performer believed to be of low class, poor taste, and marked by gender, sexuality, race, and class. But the African American press took a different approach in its coverage of Elvis Presley. Returning to Palladino's statement that "black teenagers were largely invisible" at this point in history, it is perhaps surprising at how expansive the black press's coverage of Presley—truly a phenomenon of 1950s youth culture—actually was.[83] About three hundred stories that mention Elvis Presley ran in the *Chicago Defender* and *Daily Defender* between January 1, 1956, and January 1, 1959, and dozens ran in other African American newspapers at the time. Although many of these were pop culture or news briefs that mention Presley filming a movie or dating a movie star, the lengthier stories that focus on him tend to have a very different tone than the stories that ran in the mainstream white press.

First, none of the stories disparage (and few even note) the teen girls who screamed about Elvis. Like many of the white newspaper critics, many stories and reviews did criticize his music specifically and surmised Presley was a passing fad, but these stories also made some important connections to Presley's co-optation of traditional American black music, especially the blues. Although Elvis was rumored to have made racist statements that circulated in the 1950s and 1960s, the earliest stories about him in the black press do not suggest the writers are concerned about racism.[84]

On the contrary, *Chicago Defender* Hollywood reporter Hazel Washington wrote many stories and briefs about various aspects of Presley's early career, including a glowing interview feature with him that mentions how wonderful and humble he is. The story ran on March 16, 1957, with a photo of Elvis at rehearsal with Dudley Scott, an African American pianist. "It has probably been rather apparent to you, that I have had a great deal of admiration for a young singer named Elvis Presley," she writes in the lead. "I know that I have told you so, many times, that this newcomer to our town is one of my favorite people." She goes on: "Here is a clean-cut, sincere, honest youngster, who knows that he is in the limelight, but as yet is unspoiled. From the moment that I met him and looked into his deep dark blue eyes and then felt his firm warm handshake, I knew that I had been 'so right' about him."[85]

Baker E. Morton wrote in the *Defender* about "this young upstart with the embarrassing body contortions hailing from Tupelo, Miss." He was convinced by all he had heard and read to clean his own blue suede shoes and see him live when he played in Chicago. Although Morton mentions the girls, it is in a different manner than the other stories—not hysterical or screaming but rather as authorities on what is attractive in a man: "Described by certain elements of the female sex as a combination of Marlon Brando and the late James Dean, the young man . . ."[86]

Most of the articles related to Elvis discuss his reliance on Delta blues as an undercurrent within his music. Some stories note that this is simply in homage to great bluesmen, and it is unsurprising that the style is good. In a *Chicago Defender* story titled "Arrival of Elvis Presley, No Puzzle to T-Bone Fans," the story—a general interest feature about Elvis playing a show in Miami with many of the "usual" conventions, including making fun of his accent, calling him "The Pelvis," and mentioning teen girls' fondness of him—begins with this headnote in bold type "Editor's note: He's playing the type of music and in the style introduced by the late Lonnie Johnson and T-Bone Walker that the latter pair have been unable to take before the nation's jitterbugs on a mass scale. Neither T-Bone nor Lonnie could have

appeared in this hall, before same jam, because of bias."[87] By acknowledging "bias," or racism, this brief introduction (not written by the reporter
himself) sets an entirely different tone for the reader from the one the original story conveyed.

Race is also an underlying theme of the *Daily Defender*'s story, "Dixiecrats Even Like Rock 'n' Roll by Elvis." After a dateline of Tupelo, Mississippi, the author wrote, "Dixiecrats and members of White Citizens Council
closed their eyes, or did they, since many of them were present, as this town
honored a nature son, Rock'n'roll star Elvis Presley. The above group aren't
supposed to like that style of music you know."[88] And in another *Defender*
story headlined, "B. B. King Hears How Presley Copied Style," the author
wrote, "Elvis Presley may be the King of Rock and Roll act and make a million dollars at it. But down on Beale Street here it's common knowledge that
without bandleader B. B. King the world may have never heard of Elvis the
Pelvis." The article then goes on to say that they do "give the sideburned
kid credit for" readily admitting that he "patterned his style after B. B.
King, whom he used to watch perform when he was a $20 weekly truck-
driver." The article notes that Elvis has copied King's mannerisms, including using a guitar to accompany himself as he sings, but that he still was
grateful to King for lending to his own musical style: "Recently, at a local
radio station's charity show he showed up unheralded and without any
urging went on stage with King to join him in a duet. Backstage pandemo-
nium broke out when both of them catered to autograph seekers. To all who
were in earshot Presley was heard telling King, 'thanks man for the early
lessons you gave me.' Arthur Godfrey would surely call that 'humility.'"[89]

A number of articles, however, still demonstrated concern over Elvis
Presley's influence over teens and in some ways made fun of the teen girls
who admired him. At least two of these articles, interestingly, were written
primarily by Phyllis Battelle, the well-known (Caucasian) popular culture
and teen columnist for the International News Service.[90] Others mirrored
the popular and more general fear of the spread of juvenile delinquency.
One article, without a byline, referenced concern that juvenile delinquents
might be swayed into a life of crime (specifically assault and mugging rather
than promiscuity) because "somebody has told them it's cute just like rock
'n' roll and Elvis Presley."[91] Another that ran in the *Atlanta Daily World*
simply quotes from Eddie Condon's *Cosmopolitan* magazine piece on Elvis.[92]

Both were answered by reporter Hilda See's "Fanaticism over Blues, Rock 'n' Roll Is 'Old Hat,'" in which she wrote: "How has rock 'n' roll influenced youngsters is a question being asked the world over with no truly accept-able answer. Charges range from contributing to juvenile delinquency to just plain batty, which may or may not be acceptable in all corners. Particularly when rock 'n' roll is blamed for it all. Pessimists claim rhythmic terror arrived with rock 'n' roll saying the batty demonstrations were unknown prior to the scene years ago—long before the Elvis Presleys and others were famous." But she points out that previous crises and moral panics related to the effect of music on youth existed in the early years of ragtime and the blues.[93]

Further, the African American press's coverage of Elvis Presley as less of a threat to teen girls and more of a problematic figure within music is apparent in many of the articles, though often it comes in the form of pok-ing some fun at Presley as a musician and celebrity. For example, in the *Daily Defender*'s Housewives' Corner column titled "If Music Be the Food of Love, Play On!," the author wrote, "We found the nicest way to do light exercises. You sit down (natch). Play the record machine and wiggle any part of you that you can in time to some 'Elvis Presley.' If there is a teenager around, you are sure to have one of these hi-class recordings. If you can't work up enough disgust at the music to shake—rattle and roll, then just get disgusted at that fat roll around your middle." Subtle resistance to the Presley media juggernaut can also be seen through dismissive headlines such as "Presley Film Did Okay in Chicago" (in which the story notes his new film was the top box office earner even though it did not have a lot of competition) and only days later, "Ed Sullivan Praises the Presley Guy."[94]

In general, though, the African American press's resistance to Presley had little to do with his perceived morality and effect on young girls. Perhaps this could be attributed to the fact that the United States was still a largely segregated society in the early and middle 1950s and a relatively small number of black teenage girls attended Elvis's live shows. In the South, where Jim Crow laws were still in place, Elvis performed at segregated concert halls and venues with "Negro Only" sections, but he also did make a point of playing on "Colored Night" at the amusement park in Memphis and attending all-black charity events—occurrences that were likely not deemed worthy enough for coverage in the mainstream white newspapers of the time.[95] In addition to radio personality Nat D. Williams's reference to "a thousand black, brown and beige teenage girls" in his audience, there is other evidence that Elvis had teenage fans in the black community. For example, one famous photo by Alfred Wertheimer shows three African American teen girls at the Hudson Theatre in New York City, reaching out to touch or get an autograph of their idol after his *Steve Allen Show* performance on July 1, 1957. "I don't know why, but I just loved his voice. His sound just did something to me," said Ilva Price, an African American woman who years later recalled first hearing Elvis on her dad's car radio as a ten-year-old.[96]

Perhaps some of the lack of African American teen fans might be attributed to a widely circulated rumor that Elvis was a racist who had disparaged African Americans in a quote to the press. *Jet* magazine in 1957 researched and wrote a story discounting the racism and noting that he genuinely respected black people and their music, but the rumor persisted and some African American parents forbade their daughters from being Elvis fans as a result. Price recalled that immediately after her epiphany that she loved Elvis's voice, her father turned off the radio and became angry, later saying Elvis had stolen his style from black musicians and then disparaged them.[97]

The civil rights movement was still in its fledgling stage at this point in U.S. history, and racialized codes of public conduct existed in the same way that gendered codes of public conduct existed. For example, the press coverage in this chapter suggests that middle-class white youth in many ways seemed almost expected to rebel and act out in public over their rock and roll music idols even at the same that they were being represented as a crisis. Black teens, regardless of social class, were hardly afforded the same tolerance; in an extreme example, fourteen-year-old Emmett Till of Chicago was brutally murdered in 1955 for reportedly flirting with a Caucasian woman while visiting relatives in Mississippi. Moreover, bell hooks and Amalia Mesa-Bains note the racialized sexual hierarchy of girls and women of color make the representation of them all the more problematic, both now and certainly in the historical context of postwar America: "Part of the racialized sexism wants everyone to think that a 15-year-old Mexican is not a girl, she's a woman. We know she's a girl. We can never emphasize this enough, because this is the fate of colored girls globally right now: the denial of their girlhood, the denial of their childhood, and the constant state of risk and danger that they are living in."[98] Indeed, the proper performance of gender and femininity was all the more crucial for teen girls of color in segregated midcentury America. In many ways, their livelihoods and ability to enact freedom depended on it, which might explain why black girls were so often left out of the conversation about the advent of rock and roll in the 1950s.

A Socioeconomic Shift

Like all the other historical moments analyzed in this book, socioeconomic status is an important point of discussion. The moral entrepreneurs in the dance hall chapter were concerned with the largely working-class or poor girls going out to dance halls (though a fear existed that upper-class, wealthy girls could access the halls as well, which was a real source of panic for many of the news audiences). The moral entrepreneurs in the chapter about track and field were concerned with policing both femininity and class boundaries in their denouncement of strenuous sports. In the arguments against teen girls' adulation of Elvis, it was the middle- and upper-class teen girls who were seemingly losing their minds and virtuousness in public. In this case, it seems that the panic related to class had come true and a force had indeed corrupted daughters of well-heeled families. This intersection of gender and class continues to be prominent in the cases of moral panic in the following two chapters as well.

This chapter has explored yet another brief cultural moment within U.S. history in which teen girls were the focal point of a crisis that painted them as either oversexed or victimized by a central aspect of their public recreational activities, in this case, their enjoyment of Elvis Presley and his music. The proper performance of femininity was central to the cultural understanding of the female teenybopper—particularly in the context of a historical period marked by its "yearning" for stability, family life, and dependence on traditional gender roles.[99] Although teen girl Elvis fans were marginalized for a lack of seriousness and intelligence and placed in the dual position of victim and whore, they could at least be counted on to enact a gender performance that was acceptable within the confines of 1950s America's cultural norms.

This was hardly the case of the teen girl punk rockers whose preference for masculine, outlandish fashion and loud, violent music provoked popular media outcry that placed them on the far margins for their problematic gender performance. Although the chapter again concerns music, teen girl punk rockers were treated far more like track-and-field athletes because of the concern about their lack of femininity (particularly in their appearance) in a growingly conservative U.S. political atmosphere.

CHAPTER 4

PUNK ROCK AND A CRISIS OF FEMININITY, 1976–1986

I believe that the music I heard is a killer. It's a killer of hope. It's a killer of spirit.

—Dr. Quincy, "Next Stop, Nowhere," *Quincy, M.E.*

I just can't handle being like everyone else just because that's what everyone else wants, you know?

—Daryth Morrissey, guest on *The Phil Donahue Show*, February 3, 1982

IN EARLY 1982, *THE PHIL DONAHUE SHOW* took a look at the punk rock movement. The conversation between Donahue and his guests, four punk rockers and two mothers went like this:

"I don't have to tell you that most parents would be extremely depressed if their daughter came home one day looking like this. Was your first reaction shock, anger, depression, what was it?" Donahue asks Mrs. Anne Morrissey, whose daughter sits in a chair next to her, wearing two different sizes of earrings in each of her ears. She has a short haircut and wears a leather biker cap, lavender t-shirt, black vest and make-up that is far from outlandish, even by 1980s' standards.

"I was extremely angry, really went bananas," she says.

"How old was she when this happened?" Donahue asks.

"Probably 13, 14 years old."

"We're talking like it's a disease," laughs Donahue, looking to the camera and the audience.

"Through counseling, and through Serena [Dank, founder of the Parents of Punkers support group, who is also appearing on the show], I can understand it better."

"What do you understand?" he asks.

"That she doesn't want to be like everyone else, and she wants to be her own person, and through the dress code and her lifestyle, she's expressing this. It doesn't conform with our rules, but we're learning to cope. It's a very, very difficult thing," the mother says close to tears.

The camera repeatedly flashes to her daughter through entire clip. She smiles, looks concerned, looks like she loves her mom and like Donahue is an alien. He doesn't ask her anything until a few minutes into the interview:

"Daryth, let's let you speak for yourself . . . Perhaps we should let you say why you're a . . . punker."

She laughs quietly, says under her breath, "why I'm a punker . . ." and then, "I really wouldn't consider myself a quote, unquote, punker, but I just can't handle being like everyone else just because that's what everyone else wants, you know? Just because somebody else does something does not mean that I have to do it. I have my own morals and ideals, and I go by them," she says.

"Mmmmm, hmmm," Donahue says. "Are you drug-free, Daryth?"

"Yes, I am," she answers clearly.

"Uh, is this a political statement then? Do you have some misgiving about society?" he asks.

"Yeah, there are a lot of problems, you know . . . The rich, the poor, the people starving, the wars . . . Why can't everyone just get along and live their life?"

And then, Donahue returns to his main complaint:

"How does this dress and this lifestyle correct the grievances that you see?"

"It doesn't really correct it," she answers. "I don't think dressing is going to correct the problems that we have, but this is my statement. It's a way of getting recognized for my beliefs."[1]

This episode of the popular 1980s television talk show focused on a group of teenagers who identified with the punk rock movement in some way—through music, dress, or worldview—and how their parents coped with this newfound aspect of their identity. Donahue's audience, peppered with punkily dressed young people, quietly listened to the host question both the teens and their parents almost entirely about their style of dress and hairstyle. He seemed most troubled by the adolescent girls assembled in the panel onstage, including Daryth, whose conservatively dressed mother was distraught by her daughter's appearance. Although she did not have a Mohawk, dyed hair, facial piercings, or clothing being held together by safety pins, she looked somewhat unfeminine, even within the popular fashion standards in America at the time (which were not exactly conservative among most young people). Additionally, her rebellious attitude, deep concern for social issues (income disparities and war), and punky looks also were not grounded within the dominant cultural norms of femininity.

Donahue, one of the most famous figures in 1980s popular media, was a professional broadcast journalist, but he was most famous for hosting his own daytime talk show, which often focused on controversial topics, including abortion and civil rights. His show featured guests arguing with one another as Donahue himself moved through the audience with a microphone seeking their comments and questions. Nonetheless, he was seen as an authoritative source with his audiences, and his show was the precursor to the myriad of TV talk shows that followed in the 1980s and beyond, including *The Oprah Winfrey Show* and *Jerry Springer*. As a well-known fixture in the 1980s media landscape, Phil Donahue was able to use his show to explore current media topics and help to shape cultural opinion about those topics among a large daytime viewing audience. In this case, he conveyed a tone of "crisis" as it related to teenage girls who had embraced the punk style, much to their parents' displeasure.

The chapters in this book so far have not provided exhaustive histories of each of the historical moments that they represent but rather analysis of how teen girls were represented through dominant media discourses that often tended to portray them as both (to borrow from Lynne Edwards's wording) victims or vixens—often calling into question their intelligence, taste, sexuality, and heteronormativity.[2] This is apparent in the example of Daryth on *The Phil Donahue Show,* and indicative of the way teen girls who dressed like punks were represented within various media of the late 1970s and early 1980s. Like the teen girls who participated in competitive running in the 1920s–40s, their femininity was called into question by public moral entrepreneurs and mass media practitioners, and they were policed in many ways for their improper performance of gender (among them, being questioned about whether they abused drugs).

The punk rock movement itself has a murky history, with some argument about when and where it officially began (for example, different sources argue about whether it was born in the United Kingdom or whether it began with the early performances of the Velvet Underground and Patti Smith in New York), but this chapter can offer some basic factual background to provide context. The American punk scene began in New York in the 1970s and migrated several years later to Los Angeles, but popular cultural concern over punk corrupting teenagers was not prevalent until after the punk music scene itself was established and "punk" and "new wave" were terms with which even typical Midwestern parents were familiar. This likely had to do with news stories covering violence that broke out at concerts as well as the popular media's depictions of the punk scene through both television talk shows and prime-time television shows. Although the underground music press and rock critics documented punk's early roots in these years (and earlier), the mainstream media truly picked up on punk after that, with news stories and programming concentrating more on the hairstyles and clothing favored by punks as well as the violence and drug use associated with the punk movement. This explains my decision to use the years 1976 to 1986 to bookend the punk stories analyzed for a cultural snapshot of teen girls and punk rock.

Subculture, Teen Girls, and Punk Rock

Cultural studies scholars have written famously and extensively about music and subculture, and punk is certainly one of the most discussed subcultures of the twentieth century, especially as it developed in the United States and Europe.[3] The introduction of this book explicates moral panic as it was developed by Stanley Cohen in his own study of rockers, a subculture of motorcyclists who embraced 1950s leather jackets and pompadours and served as a precursor to the British punks of the 1970s. The media in the United Kingdom ran heavy coverage of the rockers' violent riots in southern England with mods (another subculture with an entirely different aesthetic), in which Cohen noted both mods and rockers were represented as folk devils, or deviants—much in the way that the media considered punks to be deviant several years later.[4] In *Subculture: The Meaning of Style,* Dick Hebdige explored the lives of British punks (as well as mods, teddy boys, rockers, and skinheads) as they established a subversive, radical sense of fashion and living—such as wearing safety pins as facial piercings.[5]

Cohen's understanding of moral panic, however, focuses on a masculine, male-dominated subculture, and Hebdige's analysis also ignores gender difference and the participation of girls and women in the punk subculture. Angela McRobbie and Jenny Garber lament the invisibility of girls within subcultures in general, wondering whether girls were truly not present or whether it is "something in the way this kind of research is carried out that renders them invisible?" When girls are acknowledged in the literature, they note, it tends to focus on their degree of sexual attractiveness or attachment to the males in the subcultural groups. Furthermore, they point out that this general invisibility was in fact, "cemented by the social reaction to the more extreme manifestations of youth subcultures," as popular press and media focused on the sensational incidents associated with each subculture. It makes particular sense in the case of the punk movement that teen girls be excluded from scholarly analysis as well as from popular media representation, they say, because the narratives focused primarily on the crisis of violence incited by punks: "One direct consequence of the fact that it is always the violent aspects of a phenomenon which qualify as newsworthy is that these are precisely the areas of subcultural activity from which women have tended to be excluded. The objective and popular image of a subculture is likely to be one which emphasizes male membership, male focal concerns and masculine values. When women appear within the broad framework of a moral panic it is usually in more innocuous roles."[6]

Even the women and girls who were musicians in punk bands endured patronizing critiques of their playing, notes Helen Reddington, who found reviews published in 1977 about the Adverts' bassist Gaye Advert that both noted her "sultry, tempting eyes" and one critic's opinion that she looked mostly at her bass (instead of the audience) because she barely knew how to play it; another review that Advert "graduated from her initially fearful and delicate finger placement to an adequately ballsy attack" seemed positive but was truly a backhanded compliment praising her for transcending the weakness of her gender. Considering that punk is a genre known (and loved) for its musical simplicity, critique of musicianship at all might seem somewhat frivolous, but Reddington notes it is found specifically in reviews of the female punk bands. Furthermore, this diminishment of the feminine with punk rock creates the notion of a "subculturette" (much in the way that early punk band critics would call female punk rockers "punkettes"), Reddington jokes, noting the masculine "subculture" is discursively normalized and naturalized.[7]

Simon Frith and McRobbie argue that the antidomesticity of punk and rock and roll in general inspires an antifemale ideology and privileging of masculinity, which could account for much of the underlying sexism inherent in the genre.[8] Lawrence Grossberg, however, disagrees with their characterization, saying the antidomesticity is rather "an attack on the place in which its own youth is constructed." He continues, "It is a resistance to the very disciplinization, which is, paradoxically, constitutive of its 'youth.' Such resistance is a crucial aspect of the rock and roll apparatus. But what if rock and roll begins to succeed in challenging the control of the hegemony over the category of youth? For example, if youth is defined in part by its ambiguous and risky relation to sexual practice (especially intercourse), what happens to it when that relationship is fundamentally changed?" Grossberg argues that rock and roll exists within youth cultures in a way that cannot be defined "solely in musical terms" but rather by the definitions that different audiences impose on the genre, as different audiences are "differentially capable of listening to, and finding 'pleasure' in, different forms of rock and roll."[9]

Given the obvious framing of teen girl punks by the news and popular media as deviant, unfeminine, and victims, I argue the genre must be understood through both the ideological lens of gender and resistance to disciplinization more generally. Moreover, while sexism within the punk community certainly matters, the mass media's stereotypical and sexist representation of teen girl punks is lasting. Media and popular culture imagery of teen girl punks as a specifically problematic population are still easily available on YouTube and in digital archives. They are still viewed as evidence of the "crisis" posed by youth in the socially conservative early 1980s.

While keeping in mind gender, racial, and class differences in the punk audience from 1976 to 1986, in this chapter I seek to understand how one part of that audience—teen girls—were represented as they found pleasure in punk and to make sense of the mediated crisis that seemed to stem from this representation. Arguably, some of the audiences' enjoyment might have been rooted partly in the growingly conservative political and mass media climate surrounding it, especially for middle-class female audiences in the early part of the 1980s after the election of U.S. president Ronald Reagan. Grossberg argues for locating punk in "this broader context (which was made to appear to correspond to a particular class formation as much by hegemonic media practices as anything else makes it a set of strategies for living in the face of the collapse of meaning and increasing paranoia."[10] This work attempts to do so.

Much of the popular discussion about crisis and female teen punks, Elvis fans, competitive runners, and dance hall goers ties to their use of public space for personal recreation. McRobbie reminds us that it "has always been on the street that most subcultural activity takes place (save perhaps for the more middle-class oriented hippies): it both proclaims the publicization of the group and at the same time ensures its male dominance." Yet, she says, the street remains taboo for women, noting the "unambiguous connotations of the term 'street-walker.'" Much of this sexist relegation of the feminine to the closed domestic space can be tied directly to socioeconomic status, McRobbie explains. In writing about British working-class girls in the 1970s and early 1980s, she notes that societal concern about their public leisure often related to class: "Few working class girls can afford flats and so for them going out means either a date—an escort and a place to go—or else a disco, dance-hall or pub. Younger girls tend to stay indoors or to congregate in youth clubs; those with literally nowhere else to go but the street frequently become pregnant within a year and disappear back into the home to be absorbed by child-care and domestic labour."[11]

American teen girl punks were seen as out of control and, specifically, out of their families' control. Parents could not get them to dress in a more conforming manner, for example, or adhere to norms of femininity. This criticism can be connected to class markers as well. Families who could not control their daughters' dress might have been seen as less involved in their lives because they were busy working outside the home, leaving children to fend for themselves as "latchkey kids"—a term that gained popularity in the 1980s and indicated that the increase in working mothers *required* a term for children who were not greeted by them when they arrived home from school. Moreover, like the girls who went to dance halls in the early 1900s and those who participated in competitive team sports in the 1930s, they were not seen as part of the status quo because they chose to exist within a culture filled with men. And like the teen girls studied in those historical moments, teen girl punks in the 1980s were viewed as vulnerable within an established masculinized culture. They might have been corrupted or convinced to move into a life of crime (prostitution is mentioned as a possibility both for girls who frequent dance halls and for girls who frequent punk rock clubs). Neither adhered to the feminine, heteronormative standards of public appearance for teen girls of their time. The runners were said to look like "she-men" and "Amazons" as they became more muscular and fit; the punkers wore Mohawks or short hair and adorned themselves with piercings and tattoos. Both groups did so to the consternation of various moral entrepreneurs who supposedly had their best interests in mind in their attempts to prevent them from looking this way in public.

How it is possible that such different examples over a century's time could be tied together in this way? In 1905 no women were allowed to legally vote in the United States, and in the 1970s and 1980s the nation was still in the throes of "Women's Lib"—a movement of second-wave feminists who campaigned loudly for equality. The ideals of the punk movement starkly contrasted with the political, economic, and cultural realities of the 1980s, and this landscape is an important aspect of how the narrative of teen girls as a "crisis" population carried on throughout the twentieth century and into the twenty-first century.

Morality and Mass Media in the Early 1980s

Although U.S. president Jimmy Carter, a Democrat, was defeated after one term in the White House by Republican Ronald Reagan in the 1980 election, the political and cultural atmosphere of the nation had already started to lean toward conservatism in the late 1970s, particularly with the establishment of the Moral Majority. This political action group, founded by evangelical preacher and televangelist Rev. Jerry Falwell in June 1979, began in the South but had extended to eighteen states by 1980. Its primary goal was to support political candidates who believed Christianity and moral law should be intrinsically connected to law and public policy. With a membership in the millions, it became one of the largest conservative lobby groups in the United States, and when it disbanded formally in 1989, it did so with Falwell saying the group had achieved its goals. (Most contemporary Americans would recognize at the beginning of the twenty-first century that the Moral Majority had become the new Christian Right—a movement that some believe was the early spark for the eventual election of evangelical Christian Republican George W. Bush to the presidency in 2000 and 2004.)[12]

In the early 1980s its influence on American culture and politics was evident both in social policy and attitudes (for example, its lobbying efforts helped defeat the Equal Rights Amendment to constitutionally offer equal rights to women), but in its attempts to punish media content that it deemed antifamily, the Moral Majority was perhaps most visible and closest organized group that could be classified as moral entrepreneurs of their time. For example, on the local level, the *St. Petersburg Times* reported Dade County citizens identifying themselves as members of "the Moral Majority" had pressured convenience store owners to stop selling *Playboy* magazine and had removed sex education books from local libraries.[13] At the national level it organized a boycott of advertisers who were featured on some of the most popular network television shows of the time, including popular programs like *Hill Street Blues, Dukes of Hazzard,* and *M*A*S*H,* because the group found their content of sex and violence to be offensive.[14] Although the moral entrepreneurship of the Moral Majority was limited (the group was viewed as an outlier for its targeting of Jews and non-Christians for conversion to Christianity as well as its extreme views on sexuality), the conservative influence of President Reagan was more apparent.

Although Reagan was more socially liberal than members of the Moral Majority, his fiscal conservatism and belief in free market propelled his administration's promotion of the deregulation of media, which had a strong effect on the media landscape that has continued into contemporary times. In 1981 the Federal Communications Commission (under the leadership of chair Mark Fowler, a Reagan appointee) extended the length a media corporation could hold a television broadcast license and expanded the number of broadcast stations any single media conglomerate could own, among other changes.[15] Deregulation is significant because it creates the opportunity for corporate media conglomerates to form. Corporate media conglomerates, in using corporate synergies among their newspapers, magazines, and radio and television stations, tend to broadcast or print much of the same content across their holdings—often resulting in one uniform message or one distinct ideology that may be reflective of the corporate media owner's beliefs. Consolidation of media began in the Reagan administration, but it remained the trend in the next few decades, leaving only five to ten massive media conglomerates to own and control all global media through the present time.[16]

In the 1980s newspapers and both news and general interest magazines proliferated, but network television (made up of CBS, NBC, and ABC) was a dominant medium among audiences. At the end of the 1970s, 90 percent of the prime-time viewing audience on a given night was tuned to one of the three major networks.[17] Cable television was an option for those able to subscribe to it beginning in the 1970s, but by 1980 only about 20 percent of American households subscribed to cable. Cable offerings were still fairly sparse in the early 1980s, though CNN had launched in 1980 and, more pertinent to this chapter's topic, MTV launched in 1981.

MTV itself could have been a catalyst of sorts in the moral panics that revolved around the punk movement. Although punk and new wave music had largely been underground, subcultural movements in the late 1970s, MTV provided audiences with audial and visual understanding of the style and sound of bands like Blondie, the Go Go's, and the Clash. Although most hardcore punk bands resisted producing videos for a corporate media entity like MTV (which is owned by Viacom, one of the global mass media conglomerates), punk's influence was evident even in the more mainstream rock bands in the MTV stable, like the Police or Joan Jett and the Black-hearts. The music channel was, in Jerry Falwell's view, a moral corruptor of youth. As Charles Acland points out, youth was "a central component and defining feature of the contemporary American scene and the particu-lar hegemonic project of the New Right" in the 1980s, and music offered a specific site of contestation.[18]

Although the Moral Majority did not take specific steps to protest MTV, punk, or rock music in the early 1980s, the group did align itself with Ted Turner, founder and president of CNN and TBS, when in 1983 he began a music video program block on weekends on TBS called *Night Tracks*.[19] Intended to focus on more light top forty hits, it later blossomed into its own music channel, Cable Music Channel (CMC), but the money-losing channel lasted only five weeks on the air before Turner pulled the plug.[20] Nonetheless, this exemplifies the tension between conservative influence on the mass media and audience preferences that seem to counter those influences. Although the Moral Majority did not insert itself directly or particularly publicly in the battle against punk rock, its political and finan-cial influence—particularly within big media—Falwell and the group's moral entrepreneurship did influence media content and, among its mem-bers and followers, did instill a sense of fear about youth listening to music the group deemed harmful or evil.

The punk community itself was well aware of the moral entrepreneurs of the time. Reagan himself functioned as an icon to punkers who viewed his presidency as a sign that the U.S. government was becoming a fascist regime. "Sure, you can scoff and say that cops, parents, and the Man were the main fuel to the fire of all things fast, loud and out of control in the Me Decade," writes Craig Hlavaty for the alternative weekly *Houston Press,* "but it was Reagan who incited more vitriol and angst, and made it onto more flyers and album art then any one woman could." One of the best-known punk rock songs of the day was written by DRI (which stood for Dirty Rotten Imbeciles) and repeats the phrase, "Reaganonmics killing me, Reaganonmics killing me, Reaganomics killing me, Reaganomics kill-ing you" as the song's only lyrics. A New York punk band called Reagan Youth considered themselves to be political anarchists as well as musicians, and the Dead Kennedys in 1981 released "Moral Majority" with lyrics that clearly demonstrated their disdain for the political views of both religious and political figures of the time:

> Blow it out your ass, Jerry Falwell
> Blow it out your ass, Jesse Helms
> Blow it out your ass, Ronald Reagan
> What's wrong with a mind of my own?
> You don't want abortions, you want battered children
> You want to ban the pill as if that solves the problem
> Now you wanna force us to pray in school
> God must be dead if you're such a fool[21]

Despite punkers' disdain for Reaganomics, Jerry Falwell, and Jesse Helms, there is little record of any formal acknowledgment of the punk scene at all. When the Parents Music Resource Center (PMRC) was founded in 1985, a committee of several U.S. senators' wives lobbied for the Recording Industry Association of America to label rock albums containing "offensive" lyrics with "Parental Advisory" stickers, and they sought legislation requiring the labeling system to work in the same way that movies were rated. They were backed by Reverend Falwell and a conservative Congress, but their campaign—which was successful in that the RIAA voluntarily added the labels even without a federal law—was targeted against hard rock and heavy metal of the late 1980s rather than punk music, which most certainly would have been just as offensive to them.

Why? Perhaps this was simply because they had never heard actual punk music. In this era before the Internet was available to the public and long before peer-to-peer music file sharing existed, hardcore punk bands were hardly known to mass audiences, and therefore their shock value was limited to the audiences who sought out their records and live performances. They maintained an underground, noncommercial mentality that kept them off the radar of many of the radical conservative groups.

Mainstream media did, however, report on punk rock in its articles and broadcasts about the issues associated with punk (specifically, violence at live shows and the shocking fashion choices made by punks, as was exemplified in the *Donahue* transcript at the beginning of this chapter). Moreover, even prime-time network television—which, in the early 1980s still had a very large viewing audience—attempted to represent punk rock and the "crisis" that seemed to surround it. For example, an *ABC After-School Special* in 1987 titled "The Day My Kid Went Punk" depicted a mother coping with her son's sudden transformation, as he spiked his hair, pierced his ear, and bought a leather jacket.[22]

The popular NBC television show *CHiPs* addressed the punk crisis in a 1983 episode titled "Battle of the Bands." The show was a comedy and crime drama that aired from 1977 to 1983 and followed the lives of two California Highway Patrol officers. Partners Ponch and Jon navigate massive freeway pileups and try to help troubled youth, who in the punk episode, are punk band rivals—Snow Pink, led by a young, seemingly naive female vocalist with pink hair, whose guitars were stolen and van vandalized by another band called Pain, the clear villains of the episode. The members of Pain, young Mohawk-sporting guys with names like "Trasher" and "Potato Head," trash bathrooms and incite a riot at the club where they perform in addition to stealing guitars. They later lock the police out of a riotous rock club and attempt to blow up Ponch with gasoline and a lighter.[23] Despite its campy style, the episode presents its viewers with a representation of punk rock that exaggerates the violence and style of the punks and likely makes them fear for their safety when punk rockers are nearby. Moreover, the episode's victim was a young female punk who, after dying her hair and starting a punk band, became victimized by the more hardcore members of the punk scene; thus, audiences could see that the punk scene was no place for a girl.

The late punk-inspired indie filmmaker Sarah G. Jacobson (*I Was a Teen-age Serial Killer*) called the depiction of punk rockers on the 1980s crime show *Quincy, M.E.* one of the most detrimental representations of punk to mainstream America.[24] The sentiment in the episode, titled "Next Stop, Nowhere," echoes Acland's understanding of a "structural crisis of youth in the United States throughout the 1980s" that "escalated rapidly to a point that is now commonly recognized as one of unprecedented social strife and disparity between social factions . . . now part of the popular common sense that something has gone wrong with today's youth."[25] The role of gender is notable in this TV episode, which aired December 1, 1982. In it, medical examiner Dr. Quincy (played by Jack Klugman) investigates the death of a young man stabbed with an ice pick while slam dancing at a live punk concert. In the process he learns about a teenage girl who was at the club that night whose parents say she has begun burning herself with cigarettes, shredding her clothes, and "locking herself in her room listening to that violent oriented punk rock music that does nothing but reinforce all those bad feelings." Quincy believes she witnessed the murder and is in danger of being lured to overdose on codeine by the killer, but she has disappeared.

In an attempt to find her Quincy visits the club and takes the stage at closing time, pleading with the audience of young, heavily made-up, nihilistic youths to give any information they might have about her whereabouts. They respond by yelling, "Why should we tell you?!" "If I did know anything about that girl, I sure wouldn't tell a cop! Cause that's all you are—a dog without a uniform!" "You think we're all zombie killers!" (they are, in fact, seemingly made up to resemble zombies), and "Sorry, man. Who the hell cares?" The episode also features Quincy appearing on a *Donahue*-like talk show, where he says, "The music I heard said that life is cheap—that murder and suicide are okay." (This program aired two years before Phil Donahue did his show on punks and parents.)

Both the *Quincy, M.E.* and *CHiPs* episodes demonstrate how female youth who enjoyed punk rock were a particular focus of crisis within media representation of teens and punk. McRobbie points out that it is "important to separate popular public images and stereotypes from lived experience, the range of ideological representations we come across daily from empirical observation and sociological data," which is an essential reminder when contrasting the lived experiences of teen girls and the media representations of them. But, she continues, "in practice the two sides feed off each other. Everyday life becomes at least partly comprehensible within the very terms and images offered by the media, popular culture, education and the arts, just as material life creates the preconditions for ideological and cultural representation."[26] The *CHiPs* and *Quincy, M.E.* depictions fed into the narratives about teen girl punks that questioned their ability to properly perform gender, and this carried over into the news media coverage that suggested teen girls and punk rock were specifically problematic.

Shaved Heads, Mohawks, Green Hair

Although teen girl punk fans engaged in many public behaviors that were most likely not considered to be feminine—for example, slam dancing— they were most criticized within popular culture and media for looking unfeminine. Teenage girls who dressed like punks did not adhere to the dominant gender norms of 1970s and 1980s culture, but they often were also represented as a distraction or disruption, words that suggests that even appearing in public rather than in the gendered space of the home was problematic. Many of the news accounts and features about punk rock described the fans as "youth" and in nongendered terms, which might have related to the androgynous punk fashion aesthetic in which the boys wore makeup and piercings, and girls shaved their heads and wore leather. Nonetheless, the narratives that single out punk girls as problematic make clear that girls are even further on the edges than boys, since rock itself was a masculine domain. Norma Coates says that women and girls in this male-dominated culture were constantly questioned for their authenticity (especially as performers), asserting, "Such violations of the invisible yet potent rules of power in rock result in the mobilization of tropes of 'traditional' femininity to keep women firmly in their marginal place in rock."[27]

An example of the way that news media covered teen girl punks as a crisis because of their appearances can be found in an Associated Press story titled, "Hair Wild, Girl 'Pleasant,'" which was carried in newspapers throughout the United States on August 25, 1984. It told the story of a "teenager who transferred high schools rather than give up her punk and black mohawk hairstyle," noting in the lead that she is a "'pleasant young lady' who has caused no problems since entering her new classes." The news focused on Lory Marques, a sixteen-year-old sophomore from Cobb County, Georgia, who was sent home from high school after her principal objected to her hairstyle. "We try to be pretty liberal and not get involved with short hair or long hair, but when they dye it purple or pink and it's sticking straight up in the air, it creates a real problem," the principal, Roger Russel, said in a quote to the AP. Marques was quoted as saying, "none of the teachers minded and none of the students minded. In the dress code, it didn't say anything about hair. In all my classes, nobody even paid any attention to me." But she was told if she did not change her hair, she would be expelled. Instead, she transferred to an alternative high school, where her new principal attested that neither Marques nor her hair were a "problem" or "disruption."[28]

In a popular local daytime television show in Minneapolis, *Twin Cities Live,* journalist Eric Rump hosted a program about punk rock teens in July 1985 during which, like Phil Donahue and the Georgia principal, he seemed to buy into the notion that a girl with punk style must be troubled. After spending a few minutes chatting with a green-Mohawked teen named Amy, he turned to sixteen-year-old Rachel Weber with ratted, black hair, and heavy makeup and spent several minutes talking to her about her hairstyle and the many colors it had been before she settled recently on black. "How do you do that?" he asked awkwardly.

"How do I dye my hair?" she clarified, with only a small sound of amusement in her voice.

"I mean, where do you get the stuff to do that?" he asked.

"It's different stuff," she answered. "Sometimes it's mixing a clothing dye with a regular hair dye."

"This is like, work," he replied, "to get it to do what you want to do, isn't it?"

She answered astutely, "It kind of is, but it's really not any more than all the girls who have [hair] flips who wake up in the morning and spend an hour and a half with a curling iron . . . I just rat it. It only takes a couple of minutes."

After asking where she bought her clothing and noting with humor it likely was not from local department store Dayton's, Weber countered that, indeed, her black top was from Dayton's. Giving up his line of questioning, the host moved on to fifteen-year-old Brian, whom he asked whether he was ever in Boy Scouts and if not, why, rather than ask about his spiked hair and clothing. The host focused on his rebelliousness and relationship with his parents, and he asked what he would like to be when he grew up—again, a very different line of questioning than from the female punk on the show. Three of the five interviewees were teen girls, and the questions directed toward all three of them were entirely about their outward appearance.[29]

The dominant cultural narrative surrounding young female fans of punk fashion also focused on the decidedly unladylike attitude that people imagined the girls to have because of their unconventional appearance. In an article about the genre "positive punk" that ran in the *Los Angeles Times* on December 23, 1983, writer Robert Hilburn interviewed three teenage girls at a club awaiting a punk band's performance, one of whom told him, "Positive Punk isn't really positive at all." He wrote,

> The music performed by bands with such incendiary names as Sex Gang Children and Southern Death Cult is characterized by gloomy, Gothic tales of death and despair.
>
> Gloomy? Death? Despair?
>
> "Yeah," one girl said, her eyes twinkling. "It's a lot of fun . . ."[30]

Readers cannot tell whether the girl was being somewhat facetious because her eyes were "twinkling," but that does not seem to matter to the reporter. He is more interested in the juxtaposition of a teen girl having fun listening to bands that peddle gloominess, death, and despair—the antithesis of what teenybopper girl culture was *supposed* to enjoy. Teenybopper culture has always been focused around being indoors—in the bedroom, listening to music, or attending chaperoned concerts that end early on a weeknight, McRobbie notes.[31]

In a seven-and-a-half-minute segment from NBC's *Today Show* on the Sex Pistols making their American debut in 1978, reporter Jack Perkins spent most of the segment deriding the band for their lack of musical talent and manners. After their show, a teen girl was interviewed and remarked, "They weren't half as hard core as people really expected. I mean, America was so scared to let them into the States—there's nothing to be scared about. I mean, it's just another band." Like her, none of the people interviewed were actually dressed in a punk style (the camera, early in the segment, recorded a few of the more outlandish-looking attendees, but they are not interviewed). Perkins and later *Today* hosts Jane Pauley and Tom Brokaw commented about the Sex Pistols being a short-lived fad of a band that was attempting to get media attention rather than make good music.[32] Although the girl interviewed seemed somewhat articulate in her fandom, the tone of the rest of the report discounts any credibility she or any other fans might have had.

A local TV news reporter in San Francisco employed a similar storytelling technique in a piece about a governors' task force for the state of California cracking down on punk rock music and punk rockers as "subversives who should be treated as such." The story's first shot was a close-up of a young woman with a shaved head wearing a leather jacket and nose ring, and the reporter (off camera) asking her, "Are you a good person or a bad person?" She answered defiantly, "I'm a great person! I'm a [bleeped-out expletive] great person." The lighthearted news segment pointed out that youth historically have attempted to shock parents (including examples of flappers, Elvis fans, and hippies engaging in love-ins) but ended with the bald girl swearing, saying the governor can "shove it up his [bleep] sideways."[33] The teen girl punk again proved to be a more shocking and novel image than even the teen boy punk. Considering that novelty is a news value, it is little wonder that so many news stories turned their cameras to the young female punks.

Teen punk girls, with their refusal to adhere to feminine norms of any kind, were certainly a marginalized section of the larger punk subculture. When teen girls identify themselves within a subculture, like punk rock, they are already on the margins of the subculture, McRobbie says, since so much of the shock of punk behavior can be defused because they can be seen as "boys having fun" or sowing their wild oats—"a privilege rarely accorded to young women." She continues, referring specifically to the Sex Pistols, the punk band that the *Today* show journalists found so distasteful, "if the Sex Pistols had been an all-female band spitting and swearing their way into the limelight, the response would have been more heated, the condemnation less tempered by indulgence. Such an event would have been greeted in the popular press as evidence of a major moral breakdown and not just as a fairly common, if shocking, occurrence."[34] But the popular press did not have to focus on female punk performances as "evidence of a major moral breakdown." The media was often able to do so without much evidence at all because of a narrative that was easily perpetuated, suggesting that teen girl punk rock aficionados could be delinquents who were potentially violent and promiscuous—a narrative explored in further depth in the next part of the chapter.

Corruptible, Corrupting, and Violent Punk Rock Girls

As was the case in the 1950s, a cultural preoccupation with youth becoming corrupted reemerged in the 1980s. Acland states that the structural crisis of youth in the 1980s was historically unique because of the broad acceptance of the description of "youth in crisis"; this characterization of youth became "part of the popular common sense that something has gone wrong with today's youth," he writes.[35] Moreover, the crisis can be linked specifically to the mass media landscape of the 1980s: "This is the context in which American youth came under scrutiny in the 1980s. And 'youth in crisis' took many forms. Whether it was *The Oprah Winfrey Show* on 'Teens in Crisis,' Tipper Gore's book *Raising PG Kids in an X-Rated Society* (1987), an NBC prime-time news special entitled 'Bad Girls,' or a Cinemax documentary called 'Why Did Johnny Kill?,' there was definitely a vociferous public debate concerning the nature of contemporary youth."[36]

Acland sees the infamous case involving teen girl mass murderer Brenda Spencer as an important turning point in the public acknowledgment that youth were in crisis. In 1979 the sixteen-year-old Spencer carried out a shooting spree at an elementary school playground across from her home in San Diego. Her remorseless explanation at the time was "I don't like Mondays; this livens up the day." Acland writes, "The frankness and banality of this explanation—who, after all, would disagree?—were a terrible contrast to the image of her spraying bullets into a schoolyard. How could sense be made of this?" From this instance, where a teenage girl, the least likely cultural figure to carry out a mass murder in many people's view, becomes the villain and signifies a true crisis.[37] This "crisis" becomes all the more clear in stories that link punk rock—even subtly—to abhorrent behavior.

It is unsurprising that Phil Donahue in his show on punk and teens pointedly asked Daryth if she was "drug-free," even though she showed no signs of a person who abused any kind of substance in his interview; she seemed articulate, in the moment, and clear eyed. Indeed, the early New York punk scene was riddled with stories about punk musicians and fans who abused drugs as well as teen girls and young women in the scene who turned to prostitution or crime to fund their drug habits. Nancy Spungeon, a groupie within the punk scene, who was reportedly murdered by boyfriend Sex Pistol Sid Vicious— who died of an overdose himself before being tried for the murder—is the most infamous case.[38] The cultural narrative of punks held that they abused drugs and alcohol, so considering Donahue felt she had an outlandish appearance, it followed that she might also abuse drugs. (Interestingly, by the time the Donahue episode aired, many U.S. punks had moved to a straight-edge lifestyle that encouraged veganism and discouraged alcohol and drugs.)

Looking back on her own punk style in the early 1980s, Kathleen Hallinan remembered having a "wave of bordeaux" across the top of her head when she was eighteen, which she felt was "not too crazy at the time," but her mother (with whom she had a good relationship) was "concerned."[39] She said the style was more of an articulation of individuality for her than any kind of affiliation with punk music or ideals. When she participated in a study-abroad program in England in 1984 as a college student, she said she became more experimental with her look since it was easy to purchase commercial-grade hair dyes at street markets. She recalled, with her long "tails" of hair in the back colored fuchsia, that a number of students in her program were afraid to approach her because of her radical look. A few months later, she had "steps" shaved up the side of her head and colored them yellow and orange, she said. "I was curious to find out later how many students in the program weren't willing to approach me based on my appearance. They expressed surprise that I was friendly and funny," she said. "That was really interesting. Again, I wasn't an angry youth. It was creative expression and not part of a movement in my mind." Looking like a punk, however, was a signal to many that a girl was troubled.

An article in the *Omaha World-Herald* in July 1984, "Teen Delinquency Control a Growth Industry," an adolescent violence specialist listed "punk rock" among the four main factors spawning adolescent violence (along with the growing rate of substance abuse, counterfeit religious movements and cults, and family disintegrations). Stories about "wolfpacks" of teens terrorizing shoppers at malls circulated as well, illustrating Acland's point that a new fear of juvenile delinquency (much like the one in post–World War II America) appeared to be on the rise.[40]

New stories also arose connecting girls' interest in punk rock to delinquency and violence. For example, in 1983 a seventeen-year-old girl in Texas was charged with assisting her boyfriend in committing suicide by encouraging her boyfriend to shoot himself. Although a minute detail, all stories mentioned that the girl "wanted to attend Kretsinger's funeral and play punk rock music as a memorial but the victim's family did not allow it." Again, the subtle link to punk rock seems intended to explain where part of her deviance lies—in punk rock music.[41] This particular news story is reminiscent of the story in the previous chapter in which the teen Grimes sisters' interest in Elvis might have led them to be murdered by a drifter with Elvis-style sideburns.

Out of Control, Under Some Other Control

Acland's understanding of 1980s youth in crisis is no more apparent in any news report than in one published in the *Modesto Bee* in 1981, titled "The Children of Milpitas," an editorial that lamented the murder of a four-teen-year-old girl whose body was seen by at least thirteen other teenagers before anyone reported it to the police: "The shock is the shock of the encounter with icy indifference, the indifference of the kids in the first instance but, much more importantly, of the culture that produced them. How did we lose them in this void of television and electronic games and punk rock and violence in which they seem to live? The depersonalization did not begin yesterday; it is not unique to this moment, yet it seems more complete—and they seem more alienated and isolated—than what we have ever known before."[42] The article suggests that uncontrollable social forces might be responsible for their actions and that adults cannot know the extent of the problem. This theme—the idea of blaming media and technology for the actions of some youth—was apparent in the 1950s fear of television's effects and is even more apparent in the more contemporary fear that the Internet leads young people to trouble.

This is the same theme of the infamous *Quincy* episode described earlier in the chapter, which reached millions more audience members than any news editorial might have: a teen girl falls in with the wrong kind of crowd (punk rockers, specifically) and begins hanging out in the wrong kind of place (a rock club where punk bands perform), and suddenly she becomes implicated in a murder, and after she is cleared of wrongdoing, nearly becomes a victim of drugs and murder herself. Not only is she out of control, but she also is under the control of other punks and, potentially, drugs. The outlandish and exaggerated representations of punk rock music and culture in the episode are beside the point. The message—that teens, especially vulnerable female teens who are not expected to go out to raucous clubs at night, will be harmed and corrupted by their enjoyment of punk rock music. A quote from the doctor himself in the *Quincy* episode makes the sentiment clear: "I believe that the music I heard is a killer," he said on the fictional talk show about young punk rockers. "It's a killer of hope. It's a killer of spirit."

Moreover, like in other historical news coverage of teen girls and public recreation, the girls are portrayed as stupid or naive. In a *Chicago Tribune* story where a male reporter writes a first-person story about going to the "netherworld of punk" with a group of teen boys, his encounter with the teen punk girls sounds more like a description of the teen girls at Elvis shows in the 1950s:

> I ask a group of gawking, giggling girls why they are here. What is it about this music? Profound thought does not come naturally to them.
>
> "It's fun," says Zowie.
>
> "The difference between this and rock and roll is just rock and roll," says Davie C. . . .
>
> My hearing and voice are gone. Michele Black comes over and prints in my notebook: "I think their music is powerful! It has a wonderful approach! I'm totally against nuclear power, and Naked Raygun [the band playing at the club] is, too! That's why they really show energy toward nuclear power!"[43]

Between the reporter's description of "gawking, giggling girls," the note that they are incapable of profound thought, and the inclusion of exclamation points, it is clear that he does not necessarily respect the opinions of his young interviewees.

Teen Punks and People of Color

Much as teen girls were represented problematically as members of the punk audience, people of color were not mentioned at all nor were they included in any of the mainstream pop culture portrayals of punks. With the exception of the "wolfpack" articles mentioned previously in the chapter, which sometimes noted that the crowd was mostly black, the race of the troubled youth almost seems presumed to be white. There are myriad reasons for this. Although Latino, Asian, and African American teens were afforded the same civil rights as white teens in the 1970s and 1980s in the United States (unlike the previous decades examined in this book), they were still largely invisible on prime-time television's mainstream crime shows in the 1980s (including *Quincy, M.E.*), unless they were committing crimes. This era of television followed a relatively progressive one in the 1970s, where working-class blackness was celebrated; although some of those shows survived into the early 1980s, less positive depictions of racial minorities were prevalent on crime dramas.[44]

As was the case with Elvis, the black press seemed far less panicked over the emergence of the new genre of punk and its effect on young people. Moreover, a common thread in the black press focused on how punk rock was at odds with black culture and not embraced by black youth. Many punk rockers did, in fact, wear Nazi signs on their clothing (though many acknowledged they did not really understand the symbolism of the act at the time they were doing it), and the NAACP gained media attention for protesting the performance of a group called Jehovah's Sickness in 1987 because of its reputation for using racist lyrics.[45] Certainly many of the early British punk bands were viewed by many as racists—a reference made by journalist Major Robinson in a *New York Amsterdam News* story from 1978 titled "Why Punk Rock and Blacks Don't Mix":

> Loud, rowdy, undisciplined and lacking a danceable beat, punk rock will never have an appeal for Blacks, is the opinion of Black musical experts.
>
> A phenomenon born in England a few years ago, this musical import "turns off" Black teenagers who've heard it. A trio of 18-year-olds in Bobby Robinson's record store on West 125th Street asked their opinion, rejected punk as being "junk, not punk."
>
> Primitive in sound, the music reminds one of a group of musicians tuning up their instruments before they go on stage. It bears no relationship to groups such as Earth, Wind and Fire, the Tramps, or even such exciting white groups as the Bee Gees or the Average White Band—both big favorites among Black record buyers.
>
> Punk rockers onstage manners include vile lyrics, insulting the audience and even vomiting. They often enrage their audiences by pitching rubber rats at them. Characteristics of the genre are names like the Stomach Pumps, The Accidents and Rear Ends.

Robinson also suggests that punk's "racist origins" prevent black audiences from truly taking the genre to heart. He wrote, "Its progenitors are the same English youths who protest against and assault London's West Indian, East Indian and other dark-skinned residents, screaming that they should be deported." Moreover, he criticizes the lack of "groove" in punk and takes issue with "suggestive body movements and weird costumes."[46]

The acknowledgment of a suspicion of racism is an underlying feature of punk as a genre, and in this piece it can be argued that Robinson is creating a discussion of what Catherine Squires has called a "black public sphere," which builds on the idea of "marginalized counterpublics"—a particular strategy that marginalized publics may employ while producing debate internally, as in the pages of a historically black newspaper.[47] This debate can also move into the wider public sphere through legal and political action, like lawsuits and formalized protests, or even simply through media critique, which is clearly being employed here. Considering that the black public sphere might have rejected the punk movement because of its racist origins, a panic over black female youths' involvement within punk rock did not even warrant conversation.

Girls and Women in Punk: Absent from Discussion

Like audiences of color, girls were still mostly left out of any discussion of punk as a musical genre. Until at least a decade later with the advent of the riot grrrl movement, which placed feminist teen girls and young women specifically at the center of that scene, teen girls did not produce their own media (in the form of zines or home videos) to speak for themselves as teen punks. Although much of riot grrrl music and culture certainly roots from some of the earliest female punk bands, the same outspoken, political ethic did not seem to apply within the mainstream media's representation of the punk movement, especially in the early 1980s. Rather, in accounts and oral histories of the early American punk scene, teen girls and young women were portrayed as groupies whose goal was to have sex with punk band members or rowdy girlfriends who picked fights with one another and abused drugs.[48]

Moreover, Blondie's Deborah Harry, Patti Smith, Siouxsie and the Banshees, X's Exene Cervenka, the Au Pairs, the Runaways, and the Slits were all pioneers of the genre—many of them teen girls at the time that they started playing punk rock—but these women are hardly referenced in mass media accounts of punk rock in the late 1970s through the mid-1980s. Again, because of their playing and appearance, which did not fall into the dominant norms of femininity at this point in history, they were represented as a problematic population and a crisis in need of illumination.

The teen girls who embraced punk style, however, were even more problematic. News and popular media accounts never broached teen girls' involvement with politics or the environment movement (even the scholarship on subculture tended to ignore this aspect of young women's involvement with punk); for example, when Daryth Morrissey mentioned her outrage with regard to income inequality on his talk show, Phil Donahue turned the conversation back to her appearance. Because they were viewed for not conforming to dominant standards of femininity in late 1970s and early 1980s, there was also fear that they would be corrupted by the music itself.

Furthermore, the media coverage of teen girl punks seemed in many ways to work in the same way that the coverage of working girls and dance halls in the early 1900s did—it reinforced the lower-class position of the punks themselves and put fear into affluent readers that their own children might be susceptible. In many ways, this type of reporting, even as it made fun of teen punk girls, also fear mongered and sold papers and advertising. The media coverage fed a quieter cultural fear that teen girls who embraced punk would not be able to ever live up to the expectations associated with young womanhood—to go to college, find a job, find a husband, and have children. Although the 1980s was different from the 1950s, the conversations on both daytime talk shows discussed in this chapter demonstrated fear that the girls' nonconformist appearances would prohibit them from ever having "normal" lives. This type of discourse seems almost preposterous in contemporary times, when a large percentage of middle-class American moms have tattoos and piercings, but at the time of the punk rock crisis, looking so punk was viewed by many as such a failure of feminine performance that it would potentially impede their futures. It stands to wonder whether in twenty or thirty years, people will look back on the media discourses presented in the next chapter and find them ridiculous as well. In those, teen girls are a subject of broad cultural concern because of the use of the Internet and digital media.

CHAPTER 5

≥⋦

POLICING TEEN GIRLS ONLINE,
2004–2010

≥⋦

Many of the teens' Web profiles include photos of them drinking or smoking or posed provocatively in revealing clothes. Many also provide their full name, high school, hometown and other identifying information. As if the world's sickos needed help finding prey.

—"Parents Warned of Teens' Use of MySpace," *Cleveland Plain Dealer,*
December 18, 2005

It was an artistic self-portrait that revealed my arms and legs behind a guitar but was not necessarily sexy other than the fact that it alluded to me being naked. . . . I found it to be a work of art rather than a cry for attention.

—"Nicole," recalling a photo she posted of herself on MySpace

IT IS DIFFICULT TO VIEW A CHAPTER looking at the way teen girls have been using the Internet in the twenty-first century as history. In fact, given the quickly changing nature of the online landscape, much of the research and analysis might read more like outdated scholarship than a historical snapshot. Already, in the years following the official end of this case study, the news media has seized on new technologies—most recently, mobile apps that allow users to take and send photos that self-destruct within seconds and wearable digital video recorders that could invade privacy—and how these technologies might be used for deviant purposes. Headlines such as "Be Careful Sexting with Snapchat!," "Snapchat: Sexting Tool . . . ?," and "Will Google Glass Destroy Your Life?" abound; a recent story about a Swedish teen girl who reportedly caused riots after posting Instagram photos of her "slutty" peers made international news.[1] As this chapter demonstrates, the Internet became yet another public space where teen girls would be scrutinized for the various ways they interact within a public space. These headlines are only a few in a long line of news stories that started in the mid-1990s and increased in number (and fervor) over the following decade or so. This chapter focuses on a period of particularly fervent media coverage of girls and the Internet—at the time that social-networking sites, like Facebook and MySpace, first became popular with teenagers.

The period leading up to panic-laden coverage of social-networking sites was a time of rapid technological change. Between 1986 and 2004, the year that provides the starting point for this chapter, the entire media landscape shifted in a way that affected how mass media produced and released content, how teen girls were represented by the mass media in their daily recreation, and ultimately how teen girls could finally represent themselves very easily and cheaply through new media opportunities. The popularization of the Internet caused this massive shift.

Although Americans were getting online through Internet platforms such as Compuserv and AOL in the late 1980s and early 1990s, mass adoption did not occur until after the World Wide Web launched in 1995 and browsers like Mosaic, Netscape, and Explorer made it easy to navigate one's way through the Web. Newspapers and broadcast media organizations followed suit and began publishing content on websites they developed where anyone with Internet access, anywhere in the world, could read their stories for free. With this new platform, news stories were more widely available. Furthermore, with the advent of Web 2.0—a term first used in 2004 to describe online interfaces designed to allow audiences to collaborate, share media and information, generate their own content, and in general advance the use of social media—the online audience was able to take a more active, participatory role in media production. As both computers and mobile technologies in the United States became more available and affordable during this period, that audience grew exponentially. Some of the earliest adopters and heaviest Web users were American teens. Despite widespread belief that boys were "natural" users of technology, teen girls showed even in these early years of the Web that they could create their own sites and communicate with one another quite naturally online through a process of cultural production that often has been both social and creative.[2]

In the early years of the new millennium, young people demonstrated exactly how quickly they could master the swiftly developing technologies on the computer screen and mobile devices. Many used the Internet to communicate and navigate their social spaces in the privacy of their own homes.[3] Parents worried about children's and teens' use of Instant Messaging, or IM, which would often keep them glued to their computers for hours on end after school as they chatted with one another, often carrying on several different conversations with several different people at one time. IM proved to be an exciting new space where adolescents could negotiate identity and control their social lives while seemingly out of the watchful eyes of parents, teachers, and even other peers.[4] In her research on adolescents, Sonia Livingstone showed how the Internet was a space where they felt a stronger sense of intimacy with their peers and yet often had a false sense of privacy there. My own research on adolescent girls' use of IM explained how many would cut and paste supposedly private conversations into other conversations, and sometimes these snippets would be passed along among hundreds of peers.[5] Adults and authorities had serious worries about the new media at this time, ranging from concern that kids' use of slang and abbreviations would be detrimental to their everyday use of grammar and language to outright panic that they might use IM to enter an online chatroom where a sexual predator was lurking.

When American cell phone companies first began to market the idea of mobile-to-mobile texting to teens in the early 2000s, most adolescents were already comfortable with instant messaging by computer, making a similar mode of communication more comfortable for them. But similar concerns about language and sexual predators emerged early on. After mobile phone companies deployed phones with cameras several years later, a sense of cultural crisis elevated, as stories about adolescents "sexting" (or sending nude or seminude photos of themselves to others via cell phone) emerged.[6]

The most intense concern about girls' use of technology has centered on the Web's social-networking sites, which can be basically defined as sites that enable users to easily share content and communicate with a network of "friends." Although early social-networking sites existed at the time that IM was extremely popular, roughly in 2000 to 2004, the first wildly popular social-networking site was MySpace, which launched in 2003. At its height of popularity in 2006 MySpace surpassed Google, Yahoo, and EBay as the most visited website in the United States.[7] Although its own audience steadily declined after Facebook's launch in 2004, and it was quickly overtaken in popularity, it received more visitors than any of its social-networking counterparts—including Friendster, Bebo, Xanga, and even Facebook in its early years.

MySpace was able to tap into the Millennial Generation's apparent need to communicate and connect in a virtual space, possibly also because of its ability to attract media attention. Acquired by Rupert Murdoch's NewsCorp in July 2005, MySpace flourished in terms of number of users (reportedly 240,000 new registrations every day) and in its presence in the news.[8] Although the minimum age requirement to create a personal page on MySpace was fourteen, many younger users simply lied about their ages (which entailed checking a box online to say they were fourteen or older) and became avid users of the site.

In the United States, where the site was first established, MySpace was brought into the cultural consciousness partly because of the famous (or infamous) news-oriented television program, *Dateline: To Catch a Predator,* in which a reporter would masquerade as a child or teenager to lure would-be sexual predators to a place where they could be captured on camera and then by authorities. Combining elements of television drama, entertainment, and journalism, *To Catch a Predator* was in the tradition of both Phil Donahue and TV news programming such as *60 Minutes* that rose to popularity with their "gotcha" reports reminiscent of the early muckraking journalists discussed in chapter 1 regarding the investigative stories about dance halls. MySpace was often used by the journalists on *To Catch a Predator* to find and trap the predators.

Thus, for many Americans—especially the older ones who did not use or understand the site—MySpace was synonymous with danger. Cultural panics over technology are not new and in fact flourished at the time the telegraph was invented and resurfaced to an extent every time a new technology has been introduced.[9] Panic and crisis, however, are discursively linked to the Internet in a way that is quite gendered, particularly in terms of journalistic coverage. The media attached itself to the idea that MySpace was dangerous for young people in various ways, creating a specific narrative of crisis around the teen girls who embraced it. Although this message carried through into teen girls' use of Facebook, Twitter, YouTube, and other sites where users can create, upload, and share their own content (and very likely will carry through into whatever new social media becomes popular in the coming years), it was remarkably visible in the early years of social networking and specifically in MySpace.

Despite MySpace's massive early success as a social-networking site, Facebook overtook MySpace in user numbers and popularity shortly after

MySpace's peak, especially when Facebook opened its membership to the general population. In Facebook's early years, users could have an account only if they had an address with an "edu" extension—first, exclusively college students, then in 2005 high school students and in 2006 anyone over age thirteen who had a valid e-mail address. According to *Social Media Today,* an estimated 41.6 percent of the U.S. population had a Facebook account by April 2010. In June 2011 Facebook became the most visited website in the world, with a trillion page views that month; and later that month NewsCorp sold MySpace for a fraction of what it paid because it proved unprofitable.[10] Because of its impact and prevalence in American culture, especially as a primary social space for teen girls in the twenty-first century, the media coverage of Facebook is also important in any analysis of girls online.

The Internet as a Public Recreational Space

How might the Internet, and social-networking sites in particular, function as a recreational space for teen girls in the same way that music, dance, and sports did in the past century in the United States? To the millions of adolescents who use the Internet every day, their time online is simply an extension of their everyday lives.[11] They do not think about their lives or personas online as any different from the ones that they engage in face-to-face (although they may employ different ways of speaking, writing, and communicating or say something online that they might not say in person).[12] As danah boyd attests, "a cultural artifact, the Internet exists within the broader cultural context in which people live" and should be understood as such, particularly in the lives of teens who have grown up using digital media.[13]

This understanding of how the Internet works in the lives of twenty-first century teens is quite different from the way scholars conceptualized it, specifically as a "playground" or "lab" for identity experimentation.[14] Although anonymity is still possible online, it has become more difficult as the Internet has become a more visual space where one can "Google" an image of anything or anyone and usually find a corresponding photo. Lynn Schofield Clark describes this teen demographic as the "Constant Contact Generation."[15] Sharing personal aspects of their lives (from listing hobbies and random thoughts throughout the day to uploading photos and videos shot from their own phones) is such a normalized part of the teenage online experience that it would be quite difficult to separate off-line lives from online lives. A full 93 percent of teens (aged twelve to seventeen) in the United States regularly used the Internet as of 2013, and it has become a primary mode of communication, work, socialization, creativity, and recreation for most teens.[16]

It is increasingly difficult to dispute the public nature of online communication. While conversations through any of the current popular online chat applications (Facebook and Google had two of the more popular applications at the time this book was published) seem to be private, the ability to copy and paste, or even archive and later print or e-mail, a conversation exists for all users, and the corporations that own the proprietary technologies used to communicate have access to everything that users share online. Moreover, a status update on a Facebook or MySpace wall or on Twitter implies the poster has an audience. In fact, that is the main attraction for most people who use the sites. There are many ways for audiences to validate and acknowledge the posting, too—by hitting a "like" button on Facebook or retweeting a status on Twitter, for example—and this process, which takes place in the eyes of any other person in the users' network and is decidedly public, is often acknowledged by both adults and young people as the most gratifying aspect of using a social network.[17]

Social-networking sites can serve as a space of identity articulation and creativity. Its users generate much of the sites' content through a pastiche of their biographies ("blurbs"), interests, blogs, list of friends, and posted media in many forms; one of a site's primary goals is for its users to form as many interconnections among themselves as technologically possible. In essence, media creation and constant communication can take place at a grassroots level and where people from different worlds converge and represent themselves. Individual users' pages may change as often as they like. They may post photos and videos of their friends, bands they discover, stories that they write or others' stories that they wish to share, and more. Still, questions linger about blurring the line between public and private, and producer and audience, and how to navigate socially mediated publicness as social networks evolve online.[18] Digital media must be treated as emergent and rapidly moving, and even when they are considered as such, researchers still might not fully capture their meaning to audiences and producers.

Even so, this intersection of media representation and media creation is an important theme within this chapter. Although the American mass media has portrayed, framed, and represented teen girls in ways that are often problematic throughout the twentieth century and beyond, the tools of new media technology have empowered many teen girls to produce and publish their own content. More than ever before, they are able to represent themselves and question the hegemonic representations of femininity and masculinity that persistently followed teen girls throughout media narratives in this book. Even with this unprecedented power shift, though, the mass media narratives sometimes prove to be so strong as to limit the cultural and social power of adolescent girls, particularly as they represent girls using social networks.

Traditional Mass Media versus New Digital Media

From children to older teens, girls often perform gender based on the mass media's images of what they feel a modern girl is supposed to be. This is not new. In the 1920s accounts of the "New Modern Girl" analyzed in chapter 2, girls emulated the fashion choices and active lifestyles that "modern" girls and women were touted to embrace in the new era. In the 1950s they styled themselves within the dominant paradigms of beauty of the time, which usually meant wearing full skirts with crinolines and coifing their hair with hairspray. In contemporary times teen girls learn to perform their gender by the dominant cultural norms set through popular culture and media, for example, from the impossibly rich and thin New York fashionistas of *Gossip Girl* (a TV show that aired from 2007 to 2012, on the WB and CW networks) or their real-life California counterparts in the reality TV show *Keeping Up with the Kardashians* (which debuted in 2007 on E!) and its many spin-off shows about members of the family. These types of mediated images of girls project unrealistic portrayals of gender, which can make such performances impossible for young women to fulfill.[19] Adolescent girlhood in the twenty-first century is more complicated than popular media representations suggest.

New media offers a new opportunity for girls to represent themselves to a mass audience rather than simply be represented, effectively making them cultural producers in their own right.[20] Furthermore, this ability to create their own media online affords girls a larger arsenal than ever to fight mass culture's stereotypical constructions of commercialized femininity and sexuality, and many do just that.[21] According to the Pew Internet and American Life Project, 64 percent of online U.S. teenagers ages twelve to seventeen engage in at least one type of content creation—writing a blog, creating online videos, posting photos and other visual content—and adolescent girls are far more likely to participate in content creation online than boys.[22] But this creative, resistant, and occasionally politically active girl online is not the one the media most often portrays. Moreover, teen girls often play part of a hegemonic process that imitates and validates images, often those of a sexualized girl, as she represents herself in a way that is consistent with dominant cultural norms of beauty and fashion.[23]

Most often, contemporary dominant media discourses, particularly those from news media, tend to focus on the Internet as a dangerous space where sexuality runs amok. As many girls themselves will acknowledge, the Internet is an easy place to enact sexuality, and this sexuality may be played out in various ways online, sometimes through relationships with boyfriends or girlfriends and sometimes with an imagined audience.[24] This seemingly new, progressive—and often aggressive—sexuality has been explored in recent literature about adolescent girls as they negotiate identity off-line and online.[25] Girls' practices of public gender negotiation are consistent with the early new media studies literature that sees the Internet as a space where identities can be constructed, cast off, and reconstructed.[26] The negotiation taking place also somewhat defies adolescents' own assertion that they express a more truthful sense of self online than they do in other aspects of their lives.[27] This could mean healthy conversations about sexuality, but it could also mean observing pornography that represents sexuality in a way that is patriarchal and sexist and places the girl as a sexualized object of desire rather than a participant in a healthy sexual relationship. This sexualization has become increasingly rampant in the mass media depiction of younger and younger teen girls, and it has pervaded all aspects of media, including the Internet.[28] Still, while the negotiation of sexual identity is important to how many teen girls use the Internet, it is only one aspect of girls' use of the online realm.

Mass media audiences in the early twenty-first century might be led to believe that teen girls use the Internet *primarily* to articulate their sexuality and that they are especially vulnerable as a result. Much like the media coverage of dance halls in the early 1900s, news-gathering and storytelling devices often emphasize their sexuality and potential victimization. And much like in the case of girls and dance halls more than a century earlier, a panic has ensued partly as a result of the large amounts of media coverage devoted to the topic.

"Young Girls . . . Are Setting Themselves Up for Disaster"

In the early twenty-first century an overwhelming number of stories in the news media focused on how teen girls using social-networking sites were prey for older male sexual predators. This line of news reporting was bolstered by (and often rooted in) the United States Justice Department reports warning of the prevalence of sexual predators in online spaces inhabited by young people. For example, in a New Orleans *Times-Picayune* story in 2007, the reporter quotes a U.S. Justice Department official who said in a press conference that "pedophiles are finding new ways and new opportunities to network with each other on how to exploit children," especially through Facebook and MySpace. "Young girls who are innocently posting very personal information, or their identities, on these sites are setting themselves up for disaster."[29] The reporter does not question the statistical prevalence of sexual predators' attacks on girls who use social-networking sites. She also quotes (word-for-word) the Justice Department's press conference statement, which was released as part of its public service campaign devoted to Internet safety, and she does not quote any other sources who might provide a counterpoint.

Although the U.S. Justice Department might be viewed by some reporters as a reliable enough source to function as the lone source for a story, it actually spread misleading information in this case. The statistics it released were later proved to be incorrect or overblown because of both the study methodology and the way the information was worded. In fact, Justine Cassell and Meg Cramer pointed out "the percentage of single offender crimes against girls where the offender was an adult and a stranger had declined, not increased, since 1994—concurrent with the rise of Internet use."[30] Most of the cases in the Justice Department's data set involved a minor involved in a consensual relationship with a person she already knew off-line; often, this was a slightly older peer who was a legal adult.[31] Certainly these cases were problematic in that the minor probably was often not in a position to negotiate sex and often the sex was coerced. But the actualities about cases of online sexual predation were quite different from the media's narrative of an unknown predator stalking and attacking a young naive victim. In actuality, the majority of children and teens reported they had never been approached by a stranger online to engage in illicit, inappropriate, or illegal behavior, even though many parents report their biggest fear to be kids being stalked online.[32] Sarah Wright, Henry Jenkins and danah boyd surmised that it was the publicness of social-networking sites that fueled the crisis in many ways, noting political and mediated discourse that emphasized how "openness puts youth at risk, making them particularly vulnerable to predators and pedophiles."[33]

Still, these misleading U.S. Justice Department statistics were used for years as proof that the Internet put young people at risk. By making the message as uncomplicated as possible, though, it fulfilled its own aims in, borrowing from Stuart Hall, "policing the crisis": it sent a clear, effective message that a crisis (and one specifically mentioning "young girls") was at hand. In turn, this simple, unnuanced message helped the press craft a strong narrative about the dangers of the Internet, which induces fear in the public and often, moral panic. Fear makes it easier to exercise social control, to enforce a law, sway juries in the prosecution's favor because of anxiety about a perceived threat, and support public policy that continues to help create and enforce laws through the justice system.[34] The media overrepresents these numbers in its coverage, perpetuating other troubling ideologies about contemporary girls as victims, often portraying them as passive and almost inhuman.[35] For example, the following excerpts from typical newspaper stories about sexual assaults through MySpace say very little about the girls themselves:

> A 22-year-old youth soccer coach who allegedly raped a 14-year-old girl he met through the MySpace.com Website was arrested earlier this week, San Rafael police said.[36]

> A convicted sex offender who admitted having sex with a 15-year-old St. Paul girl he met at Myspace.com has pleaded guilty to third-degree criminal sexual conduct.[37]

> Police said this case shows the potential dangers when children and teens meet strangers on social networking sites.
> "This case involves young girls meeting and communicating with someone on Facebook. As a result, they were seduced and enticed to

meet with an individual, and the sexual assaults occurred," said Gary Stansill, who supervised the investigation and the Sex Crimes Unit before retiring from the Tulsa Police Department on Friday. Stansill said when youths are "enticed across state lines, it often makes big news. But this occurred locally. This can happen right under your nose in your own town."[38]

Stories also portrayed girls as naive victims who met predatory strangers out of a sense of romance (romance being a silly, frivolous construct historically associated with teen girls). For example, in 2006 a sixteen-year-old from Michigan named Katherine Lester was reported to have "tricked her parents into getting her a passport" so she could fly to the Middle East to meet a twenty-year-old man she met on MySpace. Broadcast, print, and online media all ran versions of the story, and in most the girl was represented as helplessly stranded in a foreign land needing the help of parents and law enforcement to bring her back. The FBI reportedly tracked her flight to Tel Aviv and brought her home before she was able to meet the man. In the statement that Lester "tricked" her parents, she was portrayed as manipulative. But according to Fox News, Lester was a "straight A student" whose father said she had "never given me a day's trouble" until the incident.[39] This statement somewhat counteracted the idea that Lester might be conniving, overly sexual, and out of control and reinforced her usual adherence to feminine norms (after all, she sounds like a nice girl). But this statement lends weight to the idea that the Internet was at least partly to blame for causing her to act so foolishly (in much the same way that the dance halls were to blame for causing working-class girls to act foolishly or Elvis Presley was to blame for causing 1950s teenyboppers to act overtly sexual). This storytelling technique basically told parents that any girl, even a straight A student who was not a troublemaker, could be at risk. This fear mongering is more subtle, and it certainly could help television news ratings in the same way that such stories used to sell newspapers and magazines.

In this media narrative Lester was ultimately a victim of her own foolishness and stupidity. In a concluding statement to his report on the story for CBS News, Larry Magid, who was identified as a "CBS News technology analyst," said, "This is almost a stereotypical example of how kids become compliant victims. Internet predators don't abduct their victims; they persuade them. And as is apparently the case in this story, it's not uncommon for the child to know that she's dealing with an adult. Aside from the distance involved, this is a pretty typical case. The most vulnerable kids are teenage girls who willingly get together with adult men they meet on the Internet."[40] Magid acted as an authoritative source for the news organization and was even given an official title (other than reporter or correspondent) for the report. As a result, viewers were led to believe his opinion, which suggested teenage girls were vulnerable and easily persuaded to do wrong. As it turns out, Magid was also the founder of SafeKids.com and codirector of ConnectSafely.org and served as an advocate of Internet safety in his work as a syndicated columnist, journalist, and author of books about the Internet. Even though he probably believed in safety for children online, he also had a stake in perpetuating this narrative as it might lead to more consulting work and book sales. Even in his work as a journalist, Magid might also have been functioning like a moral entrepreneur. The line has increasingly blurred between expert and journalist in contemporary media.

The various media reports on Katherine Lester also seemed to connect femininity to weakness (for example, predators "con," "persuade," or "groom" girls). Conversely, they also suggest that girls are completely out of control—of their parents and even law enforcement, as in the case of Lester when she secretly flew to the Middle East. The real story about Lester was probably far more complicated, and meeting a strange older man in the Middle East was very likely not in her best interest, but this was not the narrative that journalists seized on at the time the story was prominent.

Stories about girls meeting men online are often more complicated. Looking back ten years, twenty-four-year-old Kara remembered being an almost fourteen-year-old in small-town North Dakota when she met a twenty-five-year-old theater grad student on an online message board for discussion about the film *Moulin Rouge*. For many months she carried on an online relationship with the man, who disclosed his name and the fact that he attended Stanford, until her friend's mother learned about it, called a dean at Stanford about the guy, and alerted Kara's parents. They monitored her computer time from then on out. "I guess I knew it was inappropriate, but I was from this very small town where people just didn't really 'get' me—I was so far ahead of my classmates in terms of maturity and school—and so it was really nice for me to find this connection," she said. "So, we started talking on the phone, and then it got serious, though I never met him in person, but I lied about it like crazy to my parents. I normally don't lie to my parents, but I did." In hindsight, she noted it was "creepy," but she (and her friends, who she would also put on the line with him) "thought it was cool to talk to a real, grown-up man." Although she never spoke to him again and heard that he had "either left or was expelled from" Stanford as a result of the incident, she made the point that this online relationship was hardly similar to the alarmist news stories she read or saw on *To Catch a Predator,* and she said, "This was also totally my fault and my friends' fault."[41] Most adults would find Kara's story troubling, and the situation being "totally her fault" is truly debatable and probably untrue, considering the older man should have known an off-line relationship with her would be illegal. But there was something powerful in hearing her tell this story in her own words. Perhaps this is because in news stories about older men meeting minors online, teen girl "victims'" stories are never told.

Moreover, many news reports on teen girls and the Internet reinforced the idea that they were unaware of the consequences of being online, even when they were not actually being victimized. Myriad stories in broadcast and print emphasized the problem of posting private or personal information that might harm teen girls, either immediately or in their future. In a 2009 *CBS Evening News* report from Kelly Wallace titled "The Secret Lives of Teens Online," which was a feature story on two seemingly average, middle-class teen girls from New Jersey, noted they both admit they had "posted things online they have later come to regret."[42] In a more pointed example, TV journalist Rondrell Moore for WTHI-TV 10 in Terra Haute, Indiana, used his own Facebook profile to track down personal phone numbers of "friends of friends" on Facebook; he called one, who sounded like a college-aged woman, to chastise her for posting such personal information and ask whether she could understand how this posting could be dangerous. "All your friends can find you with only a few clicks, but police warn, so can complete strangers," he said in the segment. "They say information as basic as your birthday could be all a stalker needs."[43] Moreover, the reporter suggested that her disclosure (of information that the majority of both male and female Facebook users post on their profile pages) might be a reason for her to be attacked. In this case, the reporter himself, much like the journalists reporting on the "dance hall evil," used his own authoritative voice to reinforce social-networking sites as dangerous public spaces for girls and women.

Sexy Teen Girls Can't Help but Attract Predators

Through its ability to connect young people with similar backgrounds, interests, and needs, the Internet has proven to be an important and safe space for
many teens who in the recent past had no safe off-line space to discuss gender
identity and sexuality. Today, adolescent girls are able to use anonymous
forums or private online conversations to discuss sex or their bodies without worrying about being labeled a slut, and LGBT teens are able to connect
with one another online to discuss issues and feelings when they feel unable
to do so safely in a physical space.[44] Often, in using online space, teens use
language that they view as "sexy" or adult, and post photos that they realize
are sexually provocative as a means for this negotiation. Often this type of
production is done by appropriating patriarchal language and imagery of
pornography—imagery that places girls directly within the male gaze.[45] That
teen girls should appropriate male-oriented pornographic discourse to make
sense of sexuality is hardly surprising, given contemporary culture's sexualization of younger and younger girls and given that the bulk of pornography
that can be found online is created for the male audience. Teen girls are able
to negotiate sexual identity like this on social-networking sites and by texting sexually provocative images to others (images that are often shared with
more than their intended viewer). The publicness of this process of negotiation, however, is a source of much consternation in American culture, and it
appears to be an ongoing source of media crisis.

One of the most enduring media narratives about the Internet focuses on
how girls portray themselves as "sexy" online, usually through the photos
and videos they post of themselves but also through what they write. One
example discussed the U.S. House of Representatives' proposed legislation
to "do something about" MySpace. The reporter wrote, "A recent flurry of
news stories about sexual predators lurking on social-networking sites such
as MySpace.com and scantily dressed teens depicted in videos on other sites
have resulted in congressional hearings about the dangers of the Internet."[46]
The "scantily dressed teens" in this story (which probably does not refer to
male teens) codes the girls linked with MySpace not only as inappropriately
sexy but also as sexually promiscuous. A reporter leads with a sentence
that invokes both scantily clad women and cyberstalkers in this *Philadelphia Inquirer* article about a school presentation on the "dangers" of the
World Wide Web: "Marty Howe sat a little unnerved after being exposed

to websites with scantily clad women and the prospect that one of these photos could serve as a disguise for a cyber stalker. The Havertown father has a son, 6, and a daughter, 3. 'I'm so conscious of predators now,' Howe said immediately after a 90-minute presentation, 'A Cyber World of Trouble,' at Haverford High School Monday night. 'It's certainly an eye-opener. I'll try not to throw the computer out when I get home.' "[47]

In a 2006 issue of the *Boston Globe* magazine, a journalist used frank language and editorial license to tell the story of a driver's education instructor who was accused and acquitted of raping one of his teenage students. His word choice casts the girl as shallow, pretty, and undeniably slutty. The story was about how the charge of rape ruined the life of the man she accused:

> THE GIRL WAS BEAUTIFUL. Still is. And she's hardly shy about it. That much is obvious from her Web page on MySpace.com, which appeared less than three weeks after the trial ended. On her page, the girl, who is now 19, says "shopping is one of my favorite things to do" and "i ALSO LOVE TO LOOK HOT AND SEXY for myself and anyone who cares." Beneath one of the pinup shots she has posted of herself is the caption: "do I look like a slut?" But according to the page, she also likes literature and wishes she could have met Mother Teresa. It's a hodgepodge of random thoughts and photos—some of them a bit graphic—like many of the personal Web pages on MySpace, which has become the place to swap and post both mundane and racy tidbits that were once reserved for a diary hidden in a bottom drawer.[48]

Framing the story in a way that connects the teen girl's use of MySpace with sexual assault, suggesting "she asked for it"—a blame-the-victim mentality that has stigmatized rape survivors throughout history and further reproduces hegemonic discourses linking feminine sexuality to promiscuity. This story's intention is quite different from the 1957 *America* magazine editorial suggesting that the teen girls attending Elvis Presley's concert exercised too much sexual agency at their own peril, but the end product is similar. Both make the point that girls who articulate sexuality in public either are sluts or have the potential to become sluts.

Although the language in this *Cleveland Plain Dealer* editorial refers in a gender-neutral way to "students" using MySpace, it is later disclosed that these students are from an all-girls high school:

"Your sexxy little bear."

"I'll be ur dirty lil secret."

"The string that holds my thong together," posted with a photo of a young woman swigging a bottle of Miller beer.

They read like come-ons from a soft-core porn site. They aren't.

These are the titles of self-created and often detailed profiles of Northeast Ohio high school students, which are posted on the Internet with such characteristics as age, sexual orientation and whether they're interested in friendship, dating or a serious relationship.

Surf MySpace.com and similar trendy sites and you will read the random musings, inside jokes and personal favorites of typical teendom. Much of what's posted is just that: harmless chatter. But, with a little mining, you'll also trip on questions like, "What kinda sex do you like?" or "Do you think I'm hot?" or "Would you have sex with me?" Some admit they smoke or have been drunk. Many of the teens' Web profiles include photos of them drinking or smoking or posed provocatively in revealing clothes. Many also provide their full name, high school, hometown and other identifying information.

As if the world's sickos needed help finding prey.[49]

In other words, these teen girls use MySpace to project sexuality, ultimately leading to sexual predators being better able to track them. This example further reinforces the understanding that posing "provocatively in revealing clothes" will understandably bring "the world's sickos" to girls' front doorsteps with the sole purpose of hurting them. Like the *Boston Globe* article, this newspaper portrayal of MySpace equates sexuality with sexual violence and allows girls to be blamed for their role as victim.

This victimization might also be tied to the lack of agency teen girls have in telling their stories within the mass media. One commonality pervades the coverage of teen girls in public recreational space over the past century in America and that is the way that the stories are told *about* them rather than including them. The stories primarily quote authorities, experts, and official sources rather than the girls themselves. Sometimes, a reporter will include a colorful quote from the teen girl because she has said something silly, sexually suggestive, or unladylike, which may seem to add to the news value of the story in the sense that the reporter finds it to be both novel and entertaining. But it does not usually make for a more complete story, nor does it afford real agency to the teen girl who is being represented by others.

When girls are able to speak for themselves, a more complicated, nuanced understanding of how they use the Internet usually emerges. For example, "Nicole" from New Jersey tells the story about how, as a budding seventeen-year-old artist in 2007, she photographed herself in a self-portrait, where a guitar covered her otherwise nude body. She had published it on the website deviantart.com, an online community where artists may upload their work with the hope of gaining an audience, meeting fellow artists and collaborators, and possibly even making a sale. She also posted it to her MySpace profile, which was where a problem arose:

> It was an artistic self-portrait that revealed my arms and legs behind a guitar but was not necessarily sexy other than the fact that it alluded to me being naked. The only reason I did post it on my profile was because the photograph received a lot of positive feedback from a website geared toward an artist community, deviantart.com, and I found it to be a work of art rather than a cry for attention. It turned out that my peers and classmates didn't see or appreciate my art as something serious. They were very immature about it, and so I removed the picture from my MySpace profile but not on the art site.

She said her parents were unaware of the photo or the negative attention she got from her classmates, and she imagined they would have been shocked and upset because of "the fact that I was young, and online presence and the dangers associated with it were an especially prominent issue at the time." At the time of the interview, she was a twenty-two-year-old college student studying art and said the incident still affected her: "Overall, it was a disheartening experience that turned me off to continuing self-portraiture as a branch of photography I was interested in. To this day I do not take or post any kind of artistic self-portraits because I feel embarrassed and feel it would be not appreciated with my artistic intentions in mind."[50]

Much like Nicole, another New Jersey teen named Jessica, who participated in a PBS *Frontline* documentary, was also castigated by her peers (and punished by her school principal and parents) when at age fourteen she created an online persona called "Autumn Edows," who became a popular goth-style model with a MySpace page that received hundreds of page views a day. Jessica, who said in the documentary that she was unpopular and sometimes bullied at school, found the online world that she created to validate her beauty and originality, as visitors would comment on the photos of herself that she posted. But a fellow student found the website and showed it to her parents, who sent a link to the principal of her school and in turn called Jessica's parents. Although the images were not nude, the principal said they were far too inappropriate for a girl her age to post online, and her parents were shocked. "It supposedly offended people. Everyone was calling me a whore," she said, choking back tears. "The pictures were really—in comparison to the things I've seen on the Internet— they really were not terrible. Compared to girls who are just taking pictures of their butts, you know, just like with a thong, and that's what other girls would do all throughout my school."

Although her parents initially punished her by having her remove the site and delete all the photos, they eventually realized the site was an important creative outlet for their daughter. Under their supervision, she was allowed to rebuild the site and relaunch her persona with slightly less racy photos.[51] Although Jessica's story was told through a documentary in which both she and her parents spoke for themselves, had it been picked up by a mainstream news outlet, the chances are that as a minor she would not have been identified or allowed to speak. Instead, if it followed the storytelling conventions of many of the news stories analyzed for this chapter, it would have been told as a cautionary tale for parents, without nuance and without Jessica's input.

In the news accounts of girls who are "victimized" by their use of digital media, the reporters often convey a paternalist tone that is similar to the alarmist tenor of stories about the dance halls of the early 1900s and the new "modern" girls who wanted to participate in strenuous running sports in the 1930s to the potential detriment of their reproductive health. But, especially in this discussion of paternalism, a distinction must be made in the cultural construction of the teen girl in the twenty-first century. As early chapters point out, "teen" was not a determined social category until decades into the twentieth century, and girls aged thirteen to nineteen, specifically those with a lower socioeconomic status, were considered "women" who were eligible to marry, bear children, or work full-time in an occupation appropriate for a working-class female.

In the early twenty-first century the category of "adolescent" seems to have expanded for girls, as younger and younger girls have been sexualized in media depictions and older girls, even those in their early twenties, have been increasingly infantilized. Today, "college girls"—not women—often are viewed as living an extended version of their teenage years as they gain an education away from home. While some of the language applied them seems reminiscent of the early 1900s' "working girls" and the 1920s' "modern girls," there seems to be a distinction in that this contemporary application of "girls" applies more universally rather than to a particular social class, race, and ethnicity. The television show *Girls*, which debuted on HBO in 2012, pushes this extension even further as it focuses on the lives of four twenty-something female college graduates who grapple with issues of adulthood and sexuality.

Most female teen Elvis fans in the 1950s would have been expected to be engaged or married by their early to mid-twenties. It is fortunate that young American women are no longer required to be wives and mothers by age twenty-five to properly enact femininity. It is also notable (though not necessarily fortunate) that parents of teens and young adults feel comfortable allowing their kids to remain kids for longer periods as they remain in one another's lives—described by many as the helicopter-parent phenomenon, in which parents "hover" like helicopters in their children's lives, even when they are past the point of childhood.[52] Nonetheless, the cultural construction of adolescence and girlhood has changed in the past few decades, and it is apparent in the media coverage of teen girls' recreational practices, especially as they relate to the Internet.

For example, this 2007 *San Antonio Express* story focused on a "party girl": "Jackie Davis knows people talk trash about her. On her MySpace.com page, the self-described party girl, club promoter and 22-year-old student at the University of Texas at San Antonio has photos of herself dressed to the nines out on the town and on the beach clad in an orange bikini. In one photo, Jackie is wearing a skin-tight black leather Catwoman costume, two triangles of vinyl struggling to cover her silicone-enhanced breasts." The reporter continues, "In these kids" (although the main subject is a twenty-two-year-old college student), "a combination of self-confidence and technological savvy has led to the explosion of Web sites such as YouTube, which allows users to upload homemade videos, and social networking sites such as MySpace and Facebook, where anyone can create a personalized Web site to message friends and post pictures, blogs, videos and music." She equates this unabashed public living with a generational shift, but also finishes the article with a cautionary conclusion about how these pictures, blogs, and media will be online for a "long, long time," reminding us that young women like Jackie really might have something to worry about—despite her self-confidence and technological acumen, two attributes most people would connect to success—because other people will judge her for her rather "public" way of living. Like the working-class girls who went to dance halls in the 1900s and the teen punks who went to potentially dangerous clubs, media narratives suggest that by merely having fun in a public space, a girl could be harmed simply by showing up in a space that was traditionally male dominated.[53]

A 2006 *New York Times* article does the same, describing MySpace in the lead as "the Internet hangout for teenagers and young adults, the content of which is shocking parents and, according to the police, attracting sexual predators." The story, about the fears of parents and educators from both upper-crust and blue-collar cities in Connecticut, noted that "educators throughout the state have also sent home warnings in newsletters and through e-mail messages cautioning parents that students who post personal information on the site, including often-provocative photos, could fall prey to predators posing as cyberspace friends." The language, suggesting social networks could be rife with deviance and deception, seemed intent to grab the attention of the *Times*'s national readership, especially worried parents: "Teenagers often provide information about themselves that is news even to their parents, the police said. Some information is innocent, including pictures of friends and posters of favorite bands. Some is intensely personal, including provocative photos. Other pages offer seemingly innocent links to what are actually pornographic Web sites."[54] Much as the *Times* did in the early 1900s with dance hall stories, this article seemed to suggest that absolutely any teen girl, rich or poor, could fall victim to this social-networking site, and it could ruin her. Again, such reporting, even by an elite newspaper like the *New York Times,* grabs readers' attention and sells papers.

In addition to sexual predators online, teen girls were increasingly represented in 2004 to 2010 as victims of cyberbullying. Cyberbullying, the act of bullying another person through any kind of digital channel (from cell phone texts to social media spaces), is a particularly insidious practice that the media has reported on heavily, particularly after a male college student at Rutgers University committed suicide in 2010, after learning his roommate secretly recorded and broadcast him while he made out with his boyfriend. Although the topic of cyberbullying would appear to apply to both girls and boys and both homosexual and heterosexual youth, news reporters told stories about cyberbullies through considerably gendered discourses. Often, the stories about girls acting as cyberbullies used imagery to paint them as "mean girls." The "mean girl" is a popular archetype in the media as shown through characters like Regina in the 2004 film *Mean Girls* or Blair from the *Gossip Girl* book series and television show, and it appears repeatedly as archetype in popular culture and in news stories about girls.[55] In the 2010 Phoebe Prince story—she was cyberbullied to the point that she committed suicide—all the news accounts noted that older girls in her school bullied her because she had accepted a date with an upper classman. The stories pointed out secondarily that it was not only girls who were being charged with criminal harassment for their bullying campaign that tormented her but two boys as well.[56]

In a story published by the *London Daily Mail* about the case, a psychologist's quote explains that girls are the most common victims of cyberbullying; the language also suggests that the bullies themselves are also girls—adhering to the "mean girl" archetype—even though that was not a finding of the study being discussed in the article. "Girls are far more likely to be victims of cyberbullying than boys, Peter Smith, professor of psychology at Goldsmiths, said. 'Ten years ago psychologists thought of aggression in verbal or physical terms, which traditionally was a male domain. But cyberbullying is more akin to relational or indirect bullying, such as spreading rumours, where girls are more likely to get involved.' "[57] By using archetypes and stereotypes to describe girls bullying others, news stories often tend to diminish the seriousness of the issue and the violence involved; however, stories about girls being physically violent with one another are seen as so far out of the ordinary that they often garner international media attention as an exception to the rule. As the media perpetuates these stereotypes that girls are "mean" (not violent) toward other girls, culture buys into them—again recreating stereotypes of girls as utterly harmless in their roles as aggressors.

Although the majority of news narratives about cyberbullies used gender-neutral language (such as "teens," "youth," or "adolescents") to portray both bullies and their victims, the actual accounts of cyberbullying used

in the stories overwhelmingly described girls being harassed by boys. Furthermore, many of these stories actually were about boys *sexually* harassing
girls online, which has quite different meaning from cyberbullying. For
example, in a *New York Times* article with a headline about "teenage bullies," half of the examples in the article related incidents that most people
would understand as sexual harassment. One of these examples was about
a teacher trying to help after an incident with a sixth-grade girl:

> Recently, Ms. Yuratovac intervened when a 12-year-old girl showed
> her an instant message exchange in which a boy in her class wrote,
> "My brother says you have really good boobs." Boys make many more
> explicit sexual comments online than off, counselors say. "I don't
> think the girl is fearful the boy is going to accost her, but I do think
> she is embarrassed," Ms. Yuratovac said. "They know it's mean, it's
> risky, it's nasty. I worry what it does to them inside. It's the kind of
> thing you carry with you for a lot of years."[58]

As Angela McRobbie points out, the underlying reason for moral panic
is often because conservative forces use it as a means of social control.[59] In
the case of this story, it might seem that girls simply should not be allowed
to use instant messaging because it could potentially harm them for "a lot
of years." And much like Nicole noted after her own incident, even more
social punishment is meted out to girls who send nude or half-nude photos
of themselves online. Stories about teenagers using their mobile phones
for sexting abound in 2010 and 2011, including a positively frightening
one in the *New York Times* story, "A Girl's Photo, and Altered Lives," that
talks about how one fourteen-year-old girl sent a nude photo of herself to
her boyfriend, who broke up with her and sent the photo to other peers,
who then circulated it among hundreds of other peers, calling her a "slut"
in their caption. The girl's life was ruined, and some of the students who
sent the photo were charged with dissemination of child pornography and
arrested; the county prosecutor in the story was quoted saying it was a
"mean-girl drama" in some ways. In this case, the *Times* put fear into the
parents of teen victims and victimizers in its coverage. The story mirrored
others of its kind in its appropriation of teen language (the reporter quoted
the text's caption, "Ho Alert!," for example) and its use of official sources,
like school principals, legal experts, and scholarly experts.[60]

But this story was different, too. First, the victim herself was named and the story was described in detail, from the points of view of her, the boyfriend, the parents, and others. The story also noted the double standard of sexting: "While a boy caught sending a picture of himself may be regarded as a fool or even a boastful stud, girls, regardless of their bravado, are castigated as sluts." Additionally, the story was one of the longest in the *Times* the day it ran, beginning on the front page with a photo (although the photo was not of students involved in the case, it did show two classmates who gave a presentation on the risks of sexting). Finally, the story does not gloss over the fact that the school where the incident took place was economically and racially diverse, rather than a generic middle-class, mostly Caucasian school. Clearly, this makes the piece alarming because it was an alarming situation—rather than because of unfair news-gathering and storytelling devices. Unfortunately, this was a very unusual story among the dozens of stories that could be found about the dangers of sexting to girls.

Race, Class, and Social-Networking Sites

Although class is a less visible piece within the coverage of teen girls and social-networking sites, it can be seen in the coverage of youth and digital divide—stories that discuss how the Internet would improve the lives of young people who do not have access to it. These stories generally do not utilize the rhetoric of moral panic, but they do seem to bring back the theme of "betterment" that the Progressive-era reformers and Women's Division captured in the early twentieth century. The middle-class position of the subjects of news stories are certainly clarified in rather subtle ways—for example, that girls are "mean" and not "violent." These stories undoubtedly are different than the stories about girls in inner-city gangs who are never characterized as "mean" but rather as violent; girls in gangs are "others." In stories about girls online, journalists often appeal to the affluent news consumer, suggesting that "mean girls" and girls who are cyberbullied are the daughters of news consumers—not necessarily of working class, the poor, or "others," including immigrants and girls of color.

Even though girls of color comprise an enormous segment of the adolescents who use the Internet, the few stories that mentioned race were stories about lower-income youth and their lack of access to the Internet. Although digital divide has been a real issue for lower-income teenagers, and although these teens are sometimes African American or Latina, race and class has become somewhat conflated in much of this news coverage. Because few of the articles written about teen girls and social-networking sites described or interviewed individual girls, few articles in general noted the race or socioeconomic status of the girls. But the inclusion of this kind of information in stories about digital divide (and lack of it in other types of stories) might suggest the discussion of the Internet as a recreational space is confined to Caucasian audiences of a higher socioeconomic status.

Additionally, social-networking sites inhabited by girls of color are never mentioned in articles about teen girls' use of the Internet. A search for news about websites popular with African American adolescent girls during the same time that MySpace and Facebook caused such panic in the mainstream media—NevaEvaLand and Black Planet's Teen Chat forums, for example—yielded nothing within the dominant mainstream print and broadcast television. They also yielded nothing in the black press, including the *Chicago Defender* and *New York Amsterdam News,* and nothing on popular entertainment programming geared toward African American audiences, such as BET. These sites provide important space for communication and gender performance among black teen girls online, as Carla Stokes illustrates in her research.[61] Their complete absence from news and popular media demonstrates a silencing effect for these teen girls that is incredibly troubling, as it indicates an even greater lack of political and cultural power on their behalf.

Teen Latinas, who—like other girls of color in the United States—are major users of the popular sites and technologies mentioned throughout this chapter, also are not mentioned specifically in any journalistic discussion of teen girls. They also face the issue of being part of a new generation of Latinos who tend to read and watch broadcasts primarily in English, though as of the publication time of this book, there was no major mass media geared toward English-speaking Latinos.[62]

Other demographics among U.S. teen girls, including Asian, South Asian, and immigrants who have moved to the United States from countries around the globe, are also either invisible within this coverage or simply lumped in a more generalized coverage of a mythical, universal teen girl who is still considered part of a crisis. When fifteen-year-old Phoebe Prince committed suicide, she was portrayed primarily as a victim without much attention to her Irish immigrant status in most of the stories the

U.S. media ran.[63] That status is potentially an important part of the story, however, considering Nelly Elias and Dafna Lemish's research showing that teen immigrants who migrate to other countries tend to use the Internet "to reinforce original cultural identity, and so to gain better status in the new social environment."[64] Had news stories discussed the importance of social media and connection among teen immigrants in new countries, fewer people might have asked why the girl continued to log in, even realizing that she might face bullying online. But this aspect of the Prince story was simply not part of the news frame that most journalists were interested in using. Lisa Nakamura has argued that issues of race, gender, and access to technology are often treated with ambivalence in our "post-Internet" culture, and perhaps this analysis of news is the perfect example of how the ambivalence is enacted.[65]

Moral Entrepreneurship in the Digital Age

As in the case of social reformers against dance halls in the early 1900s and the religious conservatives against punk rock in the 1970s and 1980s, moral entrepreneurs still exist in the digital age. Their motives and agendas must continue to be questioned. In a 2008 column, "Hooking Up Is College's Most Popular Major," in the *Allentown Morning Call*, the author delves into the high school and college phenomenon of casual sex or, as he writes, "hooking up." (It brings to mind Belle Israels's description, "as girls dance or, in other words, display their charms, the boys step out, two at a time, separate the girls, and dance off in couples—the popular form of introduction in the popular dance hall"). The author writes that the practice is "what we used to call promiscuity; we've removed the sting by replacing the stigmatizing label with a cutesy phrase." He quotes a Stanford study that says that 76 percent of college students "owned up to" the practice of hooking up, and that his primary fascination about the practice is "the architecture of the hook-up":

> Students will furtively text-message during classes, then race back to their dorms, hoping for a new invitation to become someone's "friend" on Facebook. Meal times buzz with relevant chatter—whom you've hooked up with, whom you'd love to hook up with, whom you're hooking up with this weekend as a placeholder until that ideal liaison

is achieved. It's not just weekends, either. Because hooking up doesn't require the money or planning of dating, the event can take place whenever. One hears of students who get text or instant messages in the wee hours, then promptly leave their beds for someone else's.[66]

In other words, new media technology—specifically Facebook and text messaging—makes the practice of sexual promiscuity much easier to accomplish. Furthermore, he blames the hook-up phenomenon on girls who have learned that technology mastery makes it far easier for them to "troll for sex": "To my mind, this curiously depersonalized way of arranging the ultimate personal act explains why the practice has flourished. It has to do with young women, who, evidence suggests, embrace the technology of hooking up with a particular, er, passion," he writes. "Just as the Internet became the salvation of the maladroit—enabling millions of people without people skills to reach out to the world while hiding behind a computer screen—hooking up gives young women a means of trolling for sex without shame. Nor do they have to face the embarrassment of dealing with rejection personally or on the phone. The text goes unanswered? Next!"

This journalist, like so many others of his time, uses contemporary language to describe how a girl can put herself in a public space and, because of her inherent lack of morality, enact a courtship ritual for which she should feel ashamed. It brings to mind the description of girls in dance halls that also suggests they should be ashamed for their romantic dalliances. He suggests their lack of embarrassment about their sexuality is as offensive as the act of using text messages to find a sex partner. He continues, referring to two nonfiction books about "hooking up," about which he says is "no coincidence that the authors of the two nonfiction books about hooking up (a) are women and (b) write with nary a trace of judgment. Perhaps for the first time, hooking up has given girls true sexuality parity. One might say coeds today pursue a common degree: a master of bachelors."

The author of the column, Steve Salerno, is a freelance writer and author, and a sometimes contributor to the *National Review*, a biweekly right-wing political magazine. This fact is not revealed in a tagline at the end of the column, nor is Salerno's political agenda revealed in any way. Salerno squarely genders the "problem" of hooking up by vilifying young women and publicly castigating them for pursuing sex, but he also suggests that they are further emboldened to pursue sex with men because they are able to do so through new media—Facebook and text messaging. In this way, Salerno is acting as a moral entrepreneur, and the newspaper is enabling his agenda.

Single moral entrepreneurs in the twenty-first century are in some ways far less powerful than their predecessors. Moral entrepreneurship works quite differently in the contemporary cultural context, in fact. Newspaper readership is no longer as high as in previous decades, so having an editorial published in a newspaper or having a newspaper reporter publish extensive quotations from a moral entrepreneur no longer has the significant reach of decades past.

It could be argued that the contemporary media environment, where every person has the ability to publish a blog or become a curator of others' news via Twitter, is so vast and dispersed that it becomes difficult to single out any specific moral entrepreneurs. The global networked media landscape has decentralized the traditional mass media and in some ways weakened the reach of more localized media. While large media conglomerates are still strong and control the messages sent through their media holdings (most notably in the case of NewsCorp, Murdoch's empire that owns the *Wall Street Journal* and the politically conservative network Fox News in the United States, as well as media worldwide), the blogosphere, YouTube, social networks like Facebook and Twitter, and various mobile apps are all at play in terms of spreading or diluting the messages of moral entrepreneurs.

Yet these varied and scattered online media environments can also demonstrate exactly how strong the dominant cultural narratives about teen girls can be. Often, stories about teen girls online are shared on social-networking sites and their reach is even more extensive than it would have been had it run in only one newspaper, magazine, or broadcast channel. And often participants on social-networking sites reproduce exactly the same types of stories that mainstream media report. In their ability to allow users to comment and discuss news, though, they also offer an opportunity to counteract typical news-gathering and storytelling devices and grant more voice to those who are often overlooked within corporate mainstream journalism.

Nonetheless, in stories about teen girls on social-networking sites, journalists still tend to overrely on quotes from law enforcement authorities or "experts" without questioning their agenda. They rarely interview the teen girls who are using the Internet. They often do not even acknowledge racial or socioeconomic differences among teen girls, nor do they include subtle details that might make a story more complicated or less alarmist.

As a result, most of this reportage continues to foster and perpetuate gender-related crises related to teen girls' use of the Internet and to social media in particular. Much like the stories that were told about teen girls using public recreational space over the past century, the media accounts of girls' Internet use create a policing effect that subtly (or not so subtly) suggests the Internet is no place for a girl.

Complicated Narratives

This chapter clearly shows a disconnect between what most girls believe they are doing online and what the media believes they are doing online. Teen girls see digital media as space for making connections, communicating, articulating identity, and creating and distributing their own media—a space for work, relationships, and recreation. But the mass media (even the online media) creates and perpetuates narratives that place teen girls in the role of either victim or vixen—and, problematically, sometimes insinuates that girls' articulation of sexual identity might be the reason that they are targeted or attacked by sexual predators.

The narrative is further complicated by yet another issue regarding girls' use of social-networking sites—that of the girl as a laborer. While I previously have argued for girls to be represented and understood as cultural producers in their use of the Internet, Sarah Banet-Weiser's view of girls as using the digital environment to position themselves before cameras and offer their bodies as a hypersexualized product is compelling.[67] She views this feminized "self-branding" as a source of labor that produces and normalizes sexist imagery for Internet audiences.[68] Teen girls themselves, then, are a part of the hegemonic process of sexualization that ultimately leads to their marginalization. In this sense, the Internet is hardly a danger zone in which girls act as either victims or vixens, but it is also not simply a "free" space where they always enact personal agency.

One thing is clear, though. Media-generated panics and crises related to teen girls using social networks and mobile apps and having fun in the digital realm will undoubtedly continue into the twenty-first century. Every time a new interactive technology is introduced, and every time a story appears about how that technology can be used in a way that is "deviant" (or even just unladylike), we can be certain that a wave of mass media stories about girls will follow.

AFTERWORD

THE NARRATIVE OF CRISIS SURROUNDING GIRLS AND social-networking sites has been reproduced and perpetuated through the media's representations, but so much of the dominant news and popular media narratives surrounding these representations is simply a continuation of the same type of historically cycled patriarchal discourse that privileges a specific kind of femininity and morality. This discourse was seen in the crisis surrounding dance halls and working girls in the early 1900s, competitive runners in the 1920s and 1930s, Elvis Presley fans in the mid-1950s, and punk rock–styled teen girls in the 1970s and 1980s.

In one respect, this is still a story of public versus private space, and the belief that girls and women should be relegated to the private, domestic space. Teen girls and young women today are still punished, to a certain extent, for placing themselves in the public eye and allowing themselves to be gazed on by men, even when they are simply out enjoying themselves. Furthermore, this sexist narrative places them in the position of being the victim and blamed for it. When they assert themselves, or articulate their gender or sexuality (especially in nontraditional ways), they are punished in various ways—for example, called a slut or drug user by peers, newspaper columnists, or talk show hosts; questioned about whether they will ever be serious citizens or proper mothers; or simply not given the opportunity to comment because they are considered probably too silly and stupid to speak for themselves.

They are further punished for not performing femininity in a way that adheres to the dominant cultural norms of their time, and often the lack of proper performance suggests a moment of crisis. Sometimes, the media coverage about these episodes even rises to the level of moral panic, often validated by individual, moral entrepreneurs pushing an agenda or simply reproducing ideology. The remedy for such panic is usually an enactment of social control over the wayward girls—sometimes through law and policy and sometimes through cultural punishment that tends to further limit how girls interact in public space. For example, the dance hall "evil" ended in the passing of Prohibition. Girls' track and field essentially ended after certain events were banned from the Olympics, and the Women's Division successfully ended competitive strenuous sports at the high school and college level. In both of these cases, however, and in the cases of Elvis and punk rock, a certain type of femininity also became socially accepted by the majority of people in U.S. society—an example of cultural hegemony at work in terms of naturalized gender roles. Teen girls could behave within certain parameters as long as they still enacted femininity in a way that was consistent with the cultural norms of the time. It still remains to be seen whether moral panic about social networking and other online spaces will be policed enough to make much legal or social change, but cyberbullying legislation has been passed in many states and young people have been arrested for passing along nude photographs on cell phones and charged with distribution of child pornography. Further policing, especially as it relates to acceptable technology use among teen girls, certainly will continue.

In addition to adding to the growing body of feminist youth scholarship, the research presented in *From the Dancehall to Facebook* lends necessary historical and cultural context to our understanding of gender, youth, and the Internet. A discernable pattern of moral panic emerged over the century of case studies presented here that makes it easy to see how social-networking sites, as a public recreational space, are contested political terrain on so many levels. In some ways the Internet still functions as a free space where young people can negotiate and articulate identity, but increasingly this experience is yet another place where wealthy corporations own the tools that enable that articulation. The corporations own what is shared on those spaces—and in the case of teen girls who have been online their entire lives, this represents a wealth of information that is often personal and just as often reflective of the hegemonic discourses surrounding those girls. Considering how personalized algorithms on social-networking sites are able to reflect advertising back to the users, private data could also be sold to third parties. Through that process, this is also the information that might be eventually reflected back through other mass media, in a never-ending feedback loop.

As concerning as that should be, the media-generated moral panic about young people online—especially teen girls—distracts from that reality. This discourse, usually telling audiences about scandal, deviousness, and risk, masks so many other potentially insidious happenings online. Reporting that fosters gendered crises and moral panics about teen girls in public recreational space is popular among U.S. audiences; otherwise, news organizations would not bother. Moreover, this type of journalism is not simply episodic but almost cyclical in nature, occurring regularly and often appropriating the same kinds of arguments. The panics seem to depend on the same kind of news-gathering and storytelling practices, but also on the fact that audiences will often accept the arguments and feel anxious about what is being presented. Stories about scandal and deviance will likely continue to abound with regard to the Internet because it continues to be a novel technology with new applications being developed every day; young people often will be the first to discover them—a fact that makes most adults all the more nervous. As media consumers, we should question these stories, the sources behind them, and their motives.

Moreover, this book illuminates how socioeconomic status in particular has been an underlying factor in so much of the news coverage about youth and their leisure time. Although class was rarely mentioned explicitly within media stories, it was an underlying force in each of the crises explored here. Race too was rarely acknowledged in media stories, but the differences in the way the black press covered the panics over teen girls from the white-dominated media were stark, showing that there is not one universal understanding of girlhood and adolescence, nor is there one way of representing it. The coverage also demonstrates how news values can be interpreted differently—perhaps the news value of "novelty" within the white-dominated media did not mean the same within the African American media. Or perhaps, being in a socially marginalized position themselves, black reporters and editors simply interpreted and treated the grand narrative about teen girls in a way that was less sexist and stereotypical.

In the introduction of this book, I recalled the first time I was contacted to act as a media expert to discuss the topic of youth online. Since that time in 2006 I have appeared as a source in roughly forty media stories, ranging from national newspapers to magazines geared toward parents to segments and live panel discussions on daytime TV and evening news programs to online stories to radio shows. All these media appearances have concerned digital media and its effect on young people. I often attempt to inject nuance into my comments, noting that we should not make generalizations about young people's Internet use because it varies so much based not just on issues of gender, race, ethnicity, sexuality, and socioeconomic status but from kid to kid and household to household. Sometimes, my attempts to complicate the issues make it into the story, but often they are edited out. I reconcile my willingness to serve as an "expert" for such stories with the fact that I think I might be able to provide a reasoned, critical voice within news media coverage that often preys on audiences' fears and uses sexist narratives to represent teen girls' use of digital media. I hope to subversively provide the truth as I see it and counteract the panic.

Still, reading back through all of the research that I conducted over the past few years that is presented in this book, I wonder whether in so many years someone might look back at my quotes and label me a moral entrepreneur. Certainly, I don't have a true political agenda, but I do have an agenda as a feminist scholar and journalism professor. I certainly would like to see journalists acknowledge that certain storytelling and news-gathering techniques are flawed, and as a result the stories presented to audiences often tell a sexist, racist, and classist narrative that frames adolescence and gender in troubling ways. This is likely not so different from the goals that Progressive women activists in the early twentieth century in their various crusades, including the one against urban public dance halls. After all, Jane Addams herself was a strong supporter of women's suffrage and her dedication to social justice would certainly make her an advocate for media fairness and feminism.

No researcher, however, would do the work that they do were it not for a sense that, perhaps, by uncovering evidence—in the case of this work, a demonstration of a historical pattern that potentially could be changed—we might make a dent on both audiences' and practitioners' abilities to treat grand narratives more critically. We hope that audiences, instilled with a new sense of critical literacy that helps them more easily detect institutionalized sexism and racism, can spot unfair narratives. We hope that media practitioners become more aware of the pitfalls of conducting journalism and producing media that privilege the voices of some but leave out others. Antonio Gramsci would likely question the ability to overcome the hegemonic discourses that enable such grand narratives to be told repeatedly throughout history and that create circumstances that make audiences so receptive. I, however, remain optimistic.

NOTES

INTRODUCTION.
Media, Panic, and Teen Girls in Recreational Space

1. Raymond Williams, "Base and Superstructure in Marxist Cultural Theory," in *Problems in Materialism and Culture,* ed. Raymond Williams (London: Verso, 1980), 31–49.
2. Judith Butler, *Gender Trouble: Feminism and the Subversion of Identity* (New York: Routledge, 1990), 33, 178.
3. Antonio Gramsci, *Selections from the Prison Notebooks* (London: Lawrence and Wishart, 1971), 10–47.
4. Stuart Hall, Chas Critcher, Tony Jefferson, John N. Clarke, and Brian Roberts, *Policing the Crisis: Mugging, the State, and Law and Order* (London: Macmillan, 1978).
5. Dorothy E. Smith, *Texts, Facts, and Femininity: Exploring the Relations of Ruling* (London: Routledge, 1990), 18.
6. Dawn Currie, *Girl Talk: Adolescent Magazines and Their Readers* (Toronto: University of Toronto Press, 1999); Angela McRobbie, "Jackie: An Ideology of Adolescent Femininity," 1978, in *Popular Culture: Past and Present,* ed. Bernard Waites, Tony Bennett, and Graham Martin (London: Open University Press, 1982), 263–83; M. Gigi Durham, "Adolescents, the Internet, and the Politics of Gender: A Feminist Case Analysis," *Race, Gender and Class* 8, no. 3 (2001): 20–41.
7. Debra Merskin, "Making an About-Face: Jammer Girls and the World Wide Web," in *Girl Wide Web: Girls, the Internet, and the Negotiation of Identity,* ed. Sharon R. Mazzarella (New York: Lang, 2005).
8. Michel Foucault, *The History of Sexuality,* vol. 1, trans. Robert Hurley (New York: Vintage Books, 1990), 69.
9. Carol Brooks Gardner, *Passing By: Gender and Public Harassment* (Berkeley: University of California Press, 1995), 3.
10. Smith, *Texts, Facts, and Femininity,* 17–18; Brian S. Turner, *The Body and Society* (New York: Basil Blackwell, 1985), 49; Susan Bordo, *Unbearable Weight: Feminism, Western Culture, and the Body* (Berkeley: University of California Press, 1993).

11. Barbara Ehrenreich and Deirdre English, *For Her Own Good: 150 Years of the Experts' Advice to Women* (New York: Doubleday, 1978), 9.

12. Sarah Burke Odland, "Unassailable Motherhood, Ambivalent Domesticity: The Construction of Maternal Identity in *Ladies Home Journal* in 1946," *Journal of Communication Inquiry* 34, no. 1 (2009): 61–84.

13. Katherine Stubbs, "A Telegraphy's Corporeal Fictions," in *New Media, 1740–1915*, ed. Lisa Gitelman and Geoffrey B. Pingree (Cambridge, Mass.: MIT Press, 2004), 91–108.

14. Lana F. Rakow, *Gender on the Line: Women, the Telephone, and Community Life* (Urbana: University of Illinois Press, 1992); Carolyn Marvin, *When Old Technologies Were New: Thinking about Electric Communication in the Late Nineteenth Century* (New York: Oxford University Press, 1990).

15. Rosalind Gill, "Figuring Female Sexual Agency in Contemporary Advertising," *Feminism and Psychology* 18, no. 35 (2008): 43, 44; M. Gigi Durham, *The Lolita Effect: The Media Sexualization of Young Girls and What We Can Do about It* (New York: Overlook, 2008).

16. McRobbie, "Jackie"; Linda K. Christian-Smith, *Texts of Desire: Essays on Fiction, Femininity, and Schooling* (New York: Routledge Flamer, 1993); Bronwyn Davies, *Shards of Glass: Children Reading and Writing beyond Gendered Identities* (London: Hampton, 1993); Margaret Finders, *Just Girls: Hidden Literacies and Life in Junior High* (New York: Teachers College Press, 1996); Currie, *Girl Talk;* Sharon R. Mazzarella and Norma Odom Pecora, eds., *Growing Up Girls: Popular Culture and the Construction of Identity* (New York: Lang, 1999).

17. Mary Celeste Kearney, *Girls Make Media* (New York: Routledge, 2006).

18. Alison Piepmeier, *Girl Zines: Making Media, Doing Feminism* (New York: New York University Press, 2009).

19. danah boyd, quoted in Pamela Paul, "Cracking Teenagers' Online Codes," *New York Times,* January 20, 2012; danah boyd and Alice Marwick, "Social Privacy in Networked Publics: Teens' Attitudes, Practices, and Strategies" (paper presented at the Oxford Internet Institute, "A Decade in Internet Time: Symposium on the Dynamics of the Internet and Society," Oxford, U.K., September 22, 2011).

20. Sonia Livingstone, "Children's Use of the Internet: Reflections on the Emerging Research Agenda," *New Media and Society* 5, no. 2 (2003): 147–66; Livingstone, "Taking Risky Opportunities in Youthful Content Creation: Teenagers' Use of Social Networking Sites for Intimacy, Privacy, and Self-Expression," *New Media and Society* 10, no. 3 (2008): 393–411; Cynthia Lewis and Bettina Fabos, "But Will It Work in the Heartland? A Response and Illustration," *Journal of Adolescent and Adult Literacy* 43, no. 5 (2000): 462–69; Rivka Ribak, "Like Immigrants: Negotiating Power in the Face of the Home Computer," *New Media and Society* 3, no. 2 (2001): 220–38; Susannah Stern, "Girls as Internet Producers and Consumers: The Need to Place Girls' Studies in the Public Eye," *Journal of Children and Media* 2, no. 1 (2008): 85–86.

21. Mary Gray, *Out in the Country: Youth, Media, and Rural Visibility in Rural America* (New York: New York University Press, 2009); Sharon R. Mazzarella, *Girl Wide Web: Girls, the Internet, and the Negotiation of Identity*, ed. Sharon R. Mazzarella (New York: Lang, 2005); Mazzarella, *Girl Wide Web 2.0: Revisiting Girls, the Internet, and the Negotiation of Identity* (New York: Lang, 2010).

22. Shayla Thiel-Stern, *Instant Identity: Adolescent Girls and the World of Instant Messaging* (New York: Lang, 2007).
23. Leslie Regan Shade, "Surveilling the Girl via the Third and Networked Screen," in *Mediated Girlhoods: New Explorations of Girls' Media Culture,* ed. Mary Celeste Kearney (New York: Lang, 2011), 261–76; Valerie Steeves, "If the Supreme Court Were on Facebook: Evaluating the Reasonable Expectation of Privacy Test from a Social Perspective," *Canadian Journal of Criminology and Criminal Justice* 50, no. 3 (2008): 331–47; Sarah Banet-Weiser, "Branding the Post-Feminist Self: Girls' Video Production and YouTube," in Kearney, *Mediated Girlhoods,* 277–94.
24. Mary Celeste Kearney, "New Directions: Girl-Centered Media Studies for the Twenty-First Century," *Journal of Children and Media* 2, no. 1 (2008): 82–83; Joan Jacobs Brumberg, *The Body Project: An Intimate History of American Girls* (New York: Random House, 1997); Susan J. Douglas, *Where the Girls Are: Growing Up Female with the Mass Media* (New York: Three Rivers, 1995); Ilana Nash, *American Sweethearts: Teenage Girls in Twentieth-Century Popular Culture* (Bloomington: Indiana University Press, 2006); Kelly Schrum, *Some Wore Bobby Sox: The Emergence of Teenage Girls' Culture, 1920–1945* (New York: Palgrave MacMillan, 2004).
25. Rebecca C. Hains, Shayla Thiel-Stern, and Sharon R. Mazzarella, " 'We Didn't Have Any Hannah Montanas': Girlhood, Popular Culture, and Mass Media in the 1940s and 1950s," in Kearney, *Mediated Girlhoods,* 113–32.
26. Mary Douglas Vavrus, *Postfeminist News: Political Women in Media Culture* (Albany: State University of New York Press, 2002), 47.
27. Sean P. Hier, "Conceptualizing Moral Panic through a Moral Economy of Harm," *Critical Sociology* 28, no. 3 (2002): 311–34.
28. Stanley Cohen, *Folk Devils and Moral Panics: The Creation of Mods and Rockers* (London: MacGibbon and Kee, 1972), 9.
29. Hall et al., *Policing the Crisis,* 29.
30. Ibid., 59.
31. Stuart Hall, "The Rediscovery of 'Ideology': Return of the Repressed in Media Studies," in *Culture, Society and the Media,* ed. Michael Gurevitch, Tony Bennett, James Curran, and Janet Wollacott (New York: Routledge, 1982), 87, 500.
32. Erich Goode and Nachman Ben-Yehuda, *Moral Panics: The Social Construction of Deviance* (Oxford: Blackwell, 1994); Kenneth Thompson, *Moral Panics* (New York: Routledge, 1998); Angela McRobbie and Sarah Thornton, "Rethinking 'Moral Panic' for Multi-mediated Social Worlds," *British Journal of Sociology* 46, no. 4 (1995): 559–74.
33. Charles Acland, *Youth, Murder, Spectacle: The Cultural Politics of "Youth in Crisis"* (Boulder, Colo.: Westview, 1995), 40, 36.
34. Howard S. Becker, *Outsiders: Studies in the Sociology of Deviance* (New York: Free Press, 1963), 18, 148.
35. Shayla Thiel-Stern, Rebecca Hains, and Sharon Mazzarella, "Growing Up White and Female in the American Great Depression: Popular Communication, Media, and Memory," *Women's Studies in Communication* 34, no. 2 (2011): 161–82.
36. Allan Metcalf, "Birth of the Teenager," *Chronicle of Higher Education,* February 28, 2012.
37. Sherry Turkle, *Alone Together: Why We Expect More from Technology and Less from Each Other* (New York: Basic Books, 2011).

38. Rebecca C. Hains, *Growing Up with Girl Power: Girlhood on Screen and in Everyday Life* (New York: Lang, 2012); Sarah Banet-Weiser, "Girls Rule! Gender, Feminism, and Nickelodeon," *Critical Studies in Media Communication* 21, no. 2 (2004): 119–39.

39. Catherine Driscoll, *Girls: Feminine Adolescence in Popular Culture and Cultural History* (New York: Columbia University Press, 2002), 12.

40. Angela McRobbie, "The Moral Panic in the Age of Postmodern Mass Media," in *Postmodernism and Popular Culture*, ed. Angela McRobbie (London: Routledge, 1994), 217.

41. Hall, "Rediscovery of 'Ideology,'" 138–39.

42. Angela McRobbie, *Feminism and Youth Culture* (New York: Palgrave MacMillan, 2000); Carol Gilligan, *In a Different Voice: Psychological Theory and Women's Development* (Cambridge, Mass.: Harvard University Press, 1982); Nash, *American Sweethearts*, 2.

43. Paul Thompson, *The Voice of the Past* (Oxford: Oxford University Press, 2000), 7.

44. Susan J. Douglas, "Girls 'n Spice: All Things Nice?," in *Mass Politics: The Politics of Popular Culture*, ed. Daniel M. Shea (New York: St. Martin's Press, 1999), 47–48.

1. The Dance Hall Evil, 1905–1928

1. Emma Young Dickson, diary entry, April 5, 1918, YMCA Archives, University of Minnesota, Minneapolis; Dorothy Smith, interview by the author, Madison, Wisc., September 1, 2010.

2. Edward Berlin, "Ragtime," in *The Grove Music Dictionary* (Oxford: Oxford University Press, 2009).

3. Elizabeth Israels Perry, *Belle Moskowitz: Feminine Politics and the Exercise of Power in the Age of Alfred E. Smith* (Oxford: Oxford University Press, 1987), 721.

4. Kathy Peiss, *Cheap Amusements: Working Women and Leisure in Turn-of-the-Century New York* (Philadelphia: Temple University Press, 1986), 90.

5. Ibid.

6. Katherine Stubbs, "A Telegraphy's Corporeal Fictions," in *New Media, 1740–1915*, ed. Lisa Gitelman and Geoffrey B. Pingree (Cambridge, Mass.: MIT Press, 2004), 91–108.

7. "Revival Meeting Drunkard: Mrs. Asher's Singing in Saloon Is Interrupted by Man Who Objects to Women," *Minneapolis Tribune*, November 8, 1905.

8. "Girls Testify to Dunne: Victims of Dance Hall Brought before the Mayor," *Chicago Daily Tribune*, June 21, 1905.

9. "Women to Fight Dance Hall Evil," *Chicago Daily Tribune*, June 19, 1911.

10. "Ends Her Dance with Death," *Chicago Daily Tribune*, January 9, 1905.

11. "Want Law to Govern City Dance Halls: Committee for Working Girls Says Many of These Places Are Now a Menace," *New York Times*, January 31, 1909.

12. "Vice Dives Open: Police at Doors; Women and Girls Drink after Legal Hour on Thirty-First Street: Dance Halls Are Lure," *Chicago Daily Tribune*, February 11, 1911; Helen M. Bullis, "Voice of the People," *Chicago Daily Tribune*, March 31, 1913.

13. "Dance Halls under Fire," *Chicago Daily Tribune*, January 10, 1905.

14. "To Candidates, a Few Questions: Women's Civic Leagues Draw Up Queries to Ask Would-Be Aldermen," *Chicago Daily Tribune*, March 1, 1914.

15. Stanley Cohen, *Folk Devils and Moral Panics: The Creation of Mods and Rockers* (London: MacGibbon and Kee, 1972), 9.

16. J. Charles Sterin, *Mass Media Revolution* (New York: Pearson, 2011), 97–98.
17. Barbara Friedman and Janice Hume, "The Penny Press: The Origins of the Modern News Media, 1833–1861," *Journalism History* 31, no. 1 (2005): 56–60.
18. Donald K. Brazeal, "Precursor to Modern Media Hype: The 1830s Penny Press," *Journal of American Culture* 28, no. 4 (2005): 405–14.
19. Joseph W. Campbell, *Yellow Journalism: Puncturing the Myths, Defining the Legacies* (Santa Barbara, Calif.: Praeger, 2001).
20. David Nasaw, *The Chief: The Life of William Randolph Hearst* (New York: Mariner Books, 2001).
21. Arthur Weinberg and Lila Weinberg, *The Muckrakers: The Era in Journalism That Moved America to Reform, the Most Significant Magazine Articles of 1902–1912* (New York: Capricorn Books, 1982).
22. "Want Law to Govern."
23. "Will Fight Evil of Fruit Stores, Probation Officials Hold Them Great Menace to Boys and Girls of City," *Chicago Daily Tribune*, January 1, 1905.
24. Todd Gitlin, *The Whole World Is Watching: Mass Media in the Making and Unmaking of the New Left* (Berkeley: University of California Press, 2003); Rosalind Gill, *Gender and the Media* (London: Polity, 2007); Nancy Walker, *Women's Magazines, 1940–1960: Gender Roles and the Popular Press* (New York: Bedford/St. Martin's Press, 1998).
25. "East Side Dance Halls That Play Havoc with Morals," *New York Tribune*, October 21, 1906.
26. Zvi Reich, "Constrained Authors: Bylines and Authorship in News Reporting," *Journalism* 11, no. 6 (2010): 707–25.
27. "East Side Dance Halls."
28. Ruth Smiley True, *The Neglected Girl* (New York: Survey Associates, 1914), and Katharine Anthony, "Thoity-Thoid Street's West Side Girls Dissected," *New York Tribune*, January 3, 1915, quoted in True, *Neglected Girl*, 72.
29. Katharine Anthony, "Thoity-Thoid Street's West Side Girls Dissected," *New York Tribune*, January 3, 1915, quoted in True, *Neglected Girl*, 70.
30. True, *Neglected Girl*, 72.
31. Tribune Girl, "The Dance-Hall Evil as Tribune Girl Sees It through Others Eyes," *Minneapolis Tribune*, March 22, 1908.
32. Ibid.
33. George Kibbe Turner, "The Daughters of the Poor," *McClure's* 39 (November 1909–April 1910): 45–61.
34. Ibid., 56.
35. David T. Courtwright, *Dark Paradise* (Cambridge, Mass.: Harvard University Press, 1982).
36. Brian Donovan, *White Slave Crusades: Race, Gender, and Anti-vice Activism, 1887–1917* (Urbana: University of Illinois Press, 2006).
37. "Women to Fight."
38. "Want Law to Govern City Dance Halls: Committee for Working Girls Says Many of These Places are Now a Menace, *New York Times*, January 31, 1908.
39. Elizabeth Israels Perry, *Belle Moskowitz: Feminine Politics and the Exercise of Power in the Age of Alfred E. Smith* (Oxford: Oxford University Press, 1987), 1–15.
40. Ibid.
41. "War against City's Vice Centers on Dance Hall: Women Members of the Law and

Order League's Special Committee Will Concentrate Attack on Resorts," *Chicago Daily Tribune*, February 26, 1907.

42. Ibid., and Robert Loerzel, "The Smoking Gun," *Chicago Magazine*, January 2008, 92–95, 198–99.

43. Black males were given the right to vote with the passage of the Fifteenth Amendment to the U.S. Constitution in 1870. Many members of the Progressive movement were also active in campaigning for women's suffrage, though this is not mentioned in any of the coverage of dance halls, and they did not achieve the vote until 1920, with the passage of the Nineteenth Amendment.

44. Louise Carrol Wade, "Settlement Houses," *Electronic Encyclopedia of Chicago* (Chicago: Chicago Historical Society, 2004),45. Sarah Macharia, Dermot O'Connor, and Lilian Ndangam, "The Gender Gap: Women Are Still Missing as Sources for Journalists," *World Association for Christian Communication Report*, September 2010.

46. Perry, *Belle Moskowitz*, 721. Although the stories in this chapter refer to Belle Lindner Israels by her name or by Mrs. Charles H. Israels, she changed her last name to Moskowitz after her remarriage. A longtime Progressive activist, she later became a political adviser and campaign manager to New York governor and presidential candidate Al Smith.

47. Perry, *Belle Moskowitz*, 722.

48. Ibid.

49. Committee of Fourteen, "The Social Evil in New York City," 1910, Social Welfare History Archives (SWHA), University of Minnesota, Minneapolis, xxvii, 53–65.

50. Dorothy Richardson, *The Long Day: The Story of a New York Working Girl* (New York: Century, 1905), 33.

51. Jane Addams, "The Dance Hall Evil," *Charities and the Commons*, December 5, 1908, 364–68, SWHA.

52. Belle Lindner Israels and Julia Schoenfeld, "The Way of the Girl," *Survey* 22, no. 3 (July 1909): 486–96, SWHA.

53. "City Dance Halls: Plan to Put Them in Parks, on Piers," *New York Tribune*, February 3, 1909.

54. Ibid.

55. "Want Law to Govern."

56. "Dance Halls under Fire."

57. "Polite Dances are Shown to Society," *New York Times*, March 26, 1912.

58. Belle (Mrs. Charles H.) Lidner Israels, "The Dance Problem," 1912, *National Conference on Social Welfare Proceedings*, Fort Wayne, Ind.: Fort Wayne Printing Company, SWHA, 140–41.

59. "Business Training Aid to Housewife," *New York Times*, June 15, 1915; "Taft on Playgrounds: Says Nothing Is More Important to the Welfare of City Youth," *New York Times*, May 11, 1909.

60. Beulah Kennard, "Emotional Life of Girls," in *National Conference*, 147.

61. Ibid.

62. "Gov. Hughes Argues for Playgrounds: Necessary for Health and Morals of Children," *New York Times*, September 11, 1908.

63. Joseph Lee, "Housing and Recreation: Rhythm and Recreation," *National Conference*, 133.

64. Ibid, 132.

65. Ibid, 133.

66. Ibid 129–30.

67. Ibid., 139.

68. Addams, "Dance Hall Evil."

69. James R. Grossman, "Blowing the Trumpet: The 'Chicago Defender' and Black Migration during World War I," *Illinois Historical Journal* 78, no. 2 (1985): 82–96.

70. Rodger Streitmatter, *Voices of Revolution* (New York: Columbia University Press, 2001), 142, 145.

71. "Dances Planned for City Buildings," *Chicago Defender*, February 10, 1912.

72. Fenton Johnson, "Race Betterment League Makes Report: National League on Urban Conditions among Members of the Race, Cares for Delinquent Girls and Boys," *Chicago Defender*, February 22, 1913.

73. "Mixing Races," *New York Amsterdam News*, July 4, 1923.

74. "Night Clubs and Dance Halls Hit: Hostesses Placed on Par with Geisha Girls in Committee Report," *New York Amsterdam News*, July 11, 1928.

75. Paul Cressey, *The Taxi-Dance Hall: A Sociological Study in Commercialized Recreation and City Life* (Chicago: University of Chicago Press, 1932), 7.

76. Ibid.

77. Randy McBee, *Dance Hall Days: Intimacy and Leisure among Working-Class Immigrants in the United States* (New York: New York University Press, 2000), 10.

78. Cressey, *Taxi-Dance Hall*, 33.

79. Ibid., 75.

80. "Social Dancing," box 30, folder 3, YWCA Papers, Smith College, Northampton, Massachusetts, quoted in McBee, *Dance Hall Days*, 69.

2. The Rise and Fall of Girls' Track and Field, 1920–1940

1. From this point on I refer to this age group as "girls" and sometimes as "young women," even though the terminology is arguable by later historical standards.

2. Jane Addams, "Some Reflections on the City's Failure to Provide Recreation for Young Girls," *Charities and the Commons*, December 8, 1908.

3. According to Anna Rice, *A History of the World's Young Women's Christian Association* (New York: Women's Press, 1947), the Young Women's Christian Association (YWCA) was more concerned with instilling a sense of spirituality and moral insulation from urban life and was far less concerned with athletics and the physical fitness of the young women it served.

4. American Society of News Editors, "Code of Ethics, or Canons of Journalism," www.scribd.com.

5. Michael Schudson, *Discovering the News: A Social History of the American Newspaper* (New York: Basic Books, 1978), 122–23, 141, 140.

6. Ibid., 145, 148, 159.

7. Linda Steiner, "Critiquing Journalism: A Twenty-First-Century Feminist Perspective," in *Women, Men, and News: Divided and Disconnected in the News Media Landscape*, ed. Paula Poindexter, Sharon Meraz, and Amy Schmitz Weiss (New York: Erlbaum, 2007), 309.

8. William H. Young and Nancy K. Young, *The 1930s* (Westport, Conn.: Greenwood, 2002), 157.

9. Hugh G. J. Aitkin, *The Continuous Wave: Technology and the American Radio, 1900–1932* (Princeton, N.J.: Princeton University Press, 1985).

10. Library of Congress, "The Recordings," *Recorded Sound Reference Center,* www.loc.gov.

11. Andrea Silen, "90 Years Ago in News History: The First Election Results on Radio," *Newseum,* November 1, 2010, www.newseum.org.

12. Susan B. Anthony, quoted in Nellie Bly, "Champion of Her Sex," *New York Sunday World,* February 2, 1896.

13. "The Sports Girl of 1920: How a New World-Wide Style in Field and Track Sports Is Being Set by American College Girls Who Are Every Bit as Athletic as Their Brothers," *Minneapolis Morning Tribune,* April 25, 1920.

14. L. De B. Handley, "Girls Recommend Swimming for Health and Beauty," *Minneapolis Morning Tribune,* May 21, 1921.

15. Susan K. Cahn, *Coming On Strong: Gender and Sexuality in Twentieth-Century Women's Sport* (Cambridge, Mass.: Harvard University Press, 1998), 35.

16. "Miss 1923 = Athlete and Worker," *Minneapolis Morning Tribune,* December 31, 1922.

17. "Sub-Debs and Flappers Follow Example Set by Brothers," *New Orleans Times-Picayune,* February 13, 1921; Anna Louise Shaver, "Fencing Is Fine Exercise, Revived at Newcomb College," *Times Picayune,* February 13, 1921.

18. "They're Growing Heavier and Taller, So Get 'Em Now, Girls!" *Trenton (N.J.) Evening Times,* March 13, 1921.

19. "The Young Lionesses of the Tennis Courts," *Youth's Companion,* February 25, 1926.

20. "Team Play in the Classroom," *Youth's Companion,* February 17, 1921.

21. Emma L. Wilder, "Cardinal Points of the Wisconsin Association for Health, Physical Education, and Dance," November 7, 1930 meeting notes, MSS 833, box 1, folders 4, 6, Wisconsin Historical Society Archives, Madison.

22. Anne Enke, "Pioneers, Players, and Politicos: Women's Softball in Minnesota," *Minnesota History* 57, no. 4 (2002–3): 212.

23. Allen Guttman, *Sports: The First Five Millennia* (Amherst: University of Massachusetts Press, 2004), 156–57.

24. "Why Is a Public Playground?" *Minneapolis Morning Tribune,* July 10, 1921.

25. Guttman, *Sports,* 157.

26. "Prompt Action Halts Jim Crow at Chi YMCA," *The Afro American,* March 18, 1941; and "A Brief History of the YMCA and African American Communities," Kautz Family YMCA Archives website, University of Minnesota, Minneapolis, www.lib.umn.edu.

27. Cahn, *Coming On Strong,* 37.

28. *Colored Workers Bulletin* 1, no. 1 (October 15, 1931), box 74, National Recreation Association Records, Social Welfare History Archives, University of Minnesota, Minneapolis.

29. Ruth Arnett, quoted in Cahn, *Coming On Strong,* 70.

30. Ruth Arnett, "Girls Need Physical Education," *Chicago Defender,* December 10, 1921.

31. Elizabeth Fones-Wolf, "Industrial Recreation, the Second World War, and the Revival of Welfare Capitalism, 1934–1960," *Business History Review* 60, no. 2 (1986): 232–57.

32. Caryne Brown, "Taking the Track," *American History* 31, no. 2 (1996): 46; Enke, "Pioneers, Players, and Politicos," 212.

33. Brown, "Taking the Track," 46.

34. "15,000 at Garden See Helffrich Capture Millrose 600 for the Fifth Time," *New York Times*, February 3, 1927.

35. "New World's Mark Is Made by Hoff," *New York Times*, February 5, 1926. See also "Summaries of Millrose A. A. Games," *New York Times*, February 2, 1928; and "Miss Cartwright Wins Three Titles," *New York Times*, July 5, 1928.

36. Brown, "Taking the Track," 46.

37. "World Mark Is Broken in Women's Track and Field Meet Held at Paddock Field," *Los Angeles Times*, March 28, 1926; "Douglas Park Girls Score 80 Points in Meet," *Chicago Daily Tribune*, August 18, 1929.

38. Susan Cahn, "Cinderellas of Sport," in *Sport and the Color Line: Black Athletes and Race Relations in Twentieth-Century America*, ed. Patrick B. Miller and David Kenneth Wiggins (New York: Routledge: 2003), 249.

39. "Race Girls Shatter American Record," *New York Amsterdam News*, September 19, 1923.

40. Cahn, *Coming On Strong*, 37.

41. "Mabel Jones a Surprise in Women's Meet," *Chicago Defender*, June 9, 1928.

42. Don Van Natta, "Babe Didrikson Zaharias's Legacy Fades," *New York Times*, June 25, 2011.

43. James Roach, "Women in Sports," *New York Times*, December 6, 1931.

44. Susan E. Cayleff, *Babe: The Life and Legend of Babe Didrikson Zaharias* (Urbana: University of Illinois Press, 1996).

45. See, for example, "Babe Didrikson Ruled Out of Amateur Sports," *Tuscaloosa News*, December 13, 1932; "Girl Star Suspended, A.A.U. Rules in Case of Babe Didrikson," *Montreal Gazette*, December 14, 1932.

46. "Auto Dealer Clears 'Babe,' Decision Is Due Saturday," *Milwaukee Sentinel*, December 9, 1932; "Babe Didrikson Off on Mysterious Trip," *Reading Eagle*, December 21, 1932.

47. Associated Press, "Miss Didrikson Signs Manager in Chicago, Then Billiards Engages Her Attention," *New York Times*, December 26, 1932.

48. Associated Press, "Greeks Were Right, Brundage Believes," *New York Times*, December 25, 1932.

49. Van Natta, "Babe Didrikson Zaharias's Legacy."

50. Arthur J. Daley, "Babe Didrikson, Visiting Here, Hopes to Box Babe Ruth in Gym," *New York Times*, January 5, 1933.

51. Judith Butler, *Gender Trouble: Feminism and the Subversion of Identity* (New York: Routledge, 1990), 10.

52. "Babe Didrikson Decides to Wed Wrestling Star," *Herald-Journal* (Spartanburg, S.C.), July 22, 1938.

53. Cahn, *Coming On Strong*, 57.

54. *Colored Workers Bulletin*.

55. Brown, "Taking the Track," 9.

56. Ibid., 43.

57. Blanche Trilling to L. M. Fort, December 5, 1926, Mitchell, S.D., University of Wisconsin Library Archives, Madison.

58. Emma L. Wilder, "Cardinal Points," folders 4, 6.

59. Emma L. Wilder, "Cardinal Points," folders 10–14.

60. Agnes Wayman, "Play Problems of Girls," *Playground* 20 (1927): 548. The periodical was renamed *Recreation* in 1931.

61. A public fight began to oversee the sport, primarily between the AAU and the National Women's Track Athletics Association, which was founded in December 1922 and led by Dr. Harry E. Stewart, the coach of the American women's Olympic meet in Paris earlier that year. "National Body Formed to Rule Girls' Athletics," *Minneapolis Morning Tribune*, December 3, 1922.

62. Cahn, "Cinderellas of Sport," 249.

63. Lillian Schoedler, "Recreation Life for Girls" (address, Recreation Congress, Atlantic City, N.J., October 20, 1924), published in *Playground* 18 (1924): 635.

64. "Mrs. Hoover Names Sports Commission," *New York Times*, April 20, 1923.

65. Schoedler, "Recreation Life for Girls," 635, 637.

66. Brown, "Taking the Track."

67. J. Anna Norris, "Physical Education as a Profession," August 8, 1932, brochure, Women's Occupational Bureau of Minneapolis, Minnesota Historical Society Library Archives, Saint Paul.

68. Edward H. Clarke, *Sex in Education; or, A Fair Chance for the Girls* (Boston: Osgood, 1873), 155, 158.

69. Ruth Ashmore, "The Physical Life of a Girl," *Ladies' Home Journal*, August 1894.

70. "A Girl's Athletics in Summer," *Ladies' Home Journal*, July 1904.

71. E. L. Wolven, "College Sports and Motherhood," *New York Times*, July 3, 1921.

72. "British Study Faults Athletics for Motherhood's Decline," *New Orleans Times-Picayune*, July 2, 1921.

73. Wolven, "College Sports and Motherhood," 42.

74. "Athletics Blamed for Nervous Ills," *New York Sun*, October 5, 1927.

75. Allen Guttmann, "Olympics," in *International Encyclopedia of Women and Sports*, vol. 2, ed. Karen Christensen, Allen Guttmann, and Gertrud Pfister (New York: MacMillan Reference USA, 2001), 823.

76. Sir Percival Phillips, "Women Athletes Collapse," *London Daily Mail*, Aug. 3, 1928, found in Stephanie Daniels and Anita Gabrielle Tedder, *A Proper Spectacle: Women Olympians, 1900–1936* (London: ZeNaNa, 2000), 71.

77. Wythe Williams, "Americans Beaten in 4 Olympic Tests," *New York Times*, August 3, 1928.

78. David Dupuis, "Penetanguishene's First Olympic Star," *Penetanguishene Sports Hall of Fame (Canada)*, www.pshof.ca.

79. Stephanie Daniels and Anita Gabrielle Tedder, "Filming Florence," *Journal of Olympic History* 10, no. 3 (2002): 41–43.

80. See, for example, "May Bar Events for Women from Future Olympic Games," *New York Times*, August 7, 1928; and "Sports for Women Kept in Olympics," *New York Times*, August 8, 1928.

81. "Would Bar Women from the Olympics," *New York Times*, January 4, 1929.

82. Jerome Holtzman, *No Cheering from the Press Box* (New York: Holt, 1995), 260–72.

83. "Women Athletic Heads Meet Here This Week," *New York Times*, December 30, 1928.

84. "Women and the Sport Business," *Harper's Monthly Magazine*, July 1929.

85. Cahn, *Coming On Strong*, 56–57.

86. Blanche Trilling to John R. Tunis, January 1930, Madison, University of Wisconsin Library Archives.

87. Brown, "Taking the Track," 9.

88. "High School Girl Breaks Jump Record: Pennsylvania Lass Shatters American Mark," *Chicago Defender*, June 7, 1931; "Chicago Girl Track Stars Have Eyes on Olympic Team Berths," *Chicago Defender*, August 18, 1956.

89. "Girls Track Meet Won by Hot Tuskegee Team: Marks Tumble," *Chicago Defender*, May 19, 1934; "Tuskegee Girls Leave for East and Olympic Trials, *Chicago Defender*, July 4, 1936; "Standouts of 1939: Woodruff, McDaniel, Rens Five," *New York Amsterdam News*, December 30, 1939; "Tuskegee Girls, with Coach Dead, Win Sixth Title," *Chicago Defender*, July 11, 1942; "Tuskegee Women Smash Two Indoor AAU Records at National Tourney," *Los Angeles Sentinel*, May 6, 1948.

90. See, for example, "Wabash Y Girls Score 27 Points to Win in Track: Hyde Park, Wilson Tie for Second Place," *Chicago Daily Tribune*, June 8, 1947; "Girls Race for Y.M.C.A. Titles," *Chicago Daily Tribune*, June 11, 1950; "Wabash Y.M.C.A. Takes Boys', Girls' Track Titles," *Chicago Daily Tribune*, June 6, 1954; "Playgrounds Track Title Won by Shoop," *Chicago Daily Tribune*, June 12, 1955.

91. "Wabash Y Girls Cop City Title," *Chicago Defender*, June 21, 1947.

92. Bunice Fuller Barnard, "The New Freedom of the College Girl," *New York Times*, March 19, 1933.

93. Ibid.

94. Wolcott Gibbs, "Shall We Pan the Ladies?," *North American Review* 231, no. 4 (1931): 333, 338.

95. See, for example, Larry Liebman, "Official Seeks School Sanction for Girls to Compete in Track," *Los Angeles Times*, July 28, 1963; "Girls to Vie in Track, Field Competition," *Los Angeles Times*, November 17, 1963; "Prep Gals May Soon Get Sportin' Chance," *Chicago Tribune*, November 7, 1971.

96. "Title IX," Office for Civil Rights, U.S. Department of Education, www2.ed.gov.

97. Linda Jean Carpenter and R. Vivian Acosta, "Women in Intercollegiate Sport: A Longitudinal National Study Twenty-Nine Year Update, 1977–2008," http://webpages.charter.net.

98. "Prep Gals."

99. Chan Keith, "The Economics of Sports Equality: 'When She Jumps, Won't Some Things Come Out of Place?'" *Minneapolis Star*, June 6, 1978.

100. Andrew Sprugeon (A.S.) "Doc" Young, "Track for Girls Now 'In' (Barry Help Us)," *Chicago Defender*, August 22, 1964.

101. Ibid.

3. The Elvis Problem, 1956–1959

1. Elaine Tyler May, *Homeward Bound: American Families in the Cold War Era* (New York: Basic, 1988), 20, 22, 24; Ilana Nash, *American Sweethearts: Teenage Girls in Twentieth-Century Popular Culture* (Bloomington: Indiana University Press, 2006), 174; Susan J. Douglas, *Where the Girls Are: Growing Up Female with the Mass Media* (New York: Three Rivers, 1995), 26.

2. Jon Savage, *Teenage: The Creation of Youth Culture* (New York: Viking, 2007), 36.

3. Grace Palladino, *Teenagers: An American History* (New York: Basic Books, 1997), 5.

4. Ellen Wartella and Sharon R. Mazzarella, "A Historical Comparison of Children's Use of Leisure Time," in *For Fun and Profit: The Transformation of Leisure into Consumption,* ed. Richard Butsch (Philadelphia: Temple University Press, 1990), 174.

5. Palladino, *Teenagers,* 18; Kelly Schrum, *Some Wore Bobby Sox: The Emergence of Teenage Girls' Culture, 1920–1945* (New York: Palgrave Macmillan, 2004), 2.

6. Savage, *Teenage,* 36.

7. Wartella and Mazzarella, "Historical Comparison," 174.

8. Schrum, *Bobby Sox,* 18.

9. Savage, *Teenage,* 453.

10. Schrum, *Bobby Sox,* 2.

11. Palladino, *Teenagers,* 51.

12. Mary Celeste Kearney, "Recycling Judy and Corliss: Transmedia Exploitation and the First Teen-Girl Production Trend," *Feminist Media Studies* 4, no. 3 (2004): 269.

13. Schrum, *Bobby Sox,* 14.

14. Kearney, "Recycling Judy and Corliss," 269; Palladino, *Teenagers,* 53.

15. Mary Celeste Kearney, "Birds on the Wire: Troping Teenage Girlhood through Telephony in Mid-Twentieth-Century U.S. Media Culture," *Cultural Studies* 19, no. 5 (2005): 572; Palladino, *Teenagers,* 54.

16. Palladino, *Teenagers,* 54–55.

17. Nash, *American Sweethearts,* 2.

18. Angela McRobbie, "Girls and Subcultures," with Jenny Garber, in *Feminism and Youth Culture,* ed. Angela McRobbie (New York: Routledge, 2000), 16.

19. Rachel Devlin, "Female Juvenile Delinquency and the Problem of Sexual Authority in America, 1945–1965," in *Delinquents and Debutantes,* ed. Sherry A. Innis (New York: New York University Press, 1998), 84.

20. Gil Rodman, *Elvis after Elvis: The Posthumous Career of a Living Legend* (New York: Routledge, 1996), 25.

21. Karal Ann Marling, *As Seen on TV: The Visual Culture of Everyday Life in the 1950s* (Cambridge, Mass.: Harvard University Press, 1996), 175.

22. Schrum, *Bobby Sox,* 124.

23. Palladino, *Teenagers,* 155.

24. Devlin, "Female Juvenile Delinquency," 84.

25. Marling, *As Seen on TV,* 186; "What TV Is Doing to America," *U.S. News and World Report,* September 2, 1955.

26. Raymond Williams, *Television: Technology and Cultural Form* (London: Fontana, 1974), 16, 17.

27. Jack Gould, "New Phenomenon: Elvis Presley Rises to Fame as Vocalist Who Is Virtuoso of Hootchy-Kootchy," *New York Times,* June 6, 1956.

28. Charles Mercer, "Elvis Presley Hit in Letter to Steve Allen," *Corpus Christi Times,* June 19, 1956.

29. A video clip of the performance can be viewed online: "Elvis: Hound Dog (*Steve Allen Show*)," YouTube video, 2:00, posted by motorecka, February 21, 2009, www.youtube.com.

30. John Lardner, "Lardner's Week: Devitalizing Elvis," *Newsweek,* July 16, 1956.

31. Glenn C. Altschuler, *All Shook Up: How Rock 'n' Roll Changed America* (New York: Oxford University Press, 2003), 91.

32. Greil Marcus, "Liner Notes," *Elvis Presley: The Ed Sullivan Shows*, special ed. DVD, October 2006.

33. Marling, *As Seen on TV*, 180.

34. Pat Strodt, interview by the author, Roseville, Minn., June 11, 2012.

35. Marling, *As Seen on TV*, 175.

36. Jack Gould, "New Phenomenon: Elvis Presley Rises to Fame as Vocalist Who Is Virtuoso of Hootchy-Kootchy," *New York Times*, June 6, 1956.

37. William H. Young and Nancy K. Young, *The 1950s* (Westport, Conn.: Greenwood, 2004), 26.

38. Palladino, *Teenagers*, 133.

39. Rodman, *Elvis after Elvis*, 53.

40. Louis Cantor, *Wheelin' on Beale: How WDIA-Memphis Became the Nation's First All-Black Radio Station and Created the Sound That Changed America* (New York: Pharos, 1992).

41. Rodman, *Elvis after Elvis*, 189.

42. Marling, *As Seen on TV*, 170; Judith Butler, *Gender Trouble: Feminism and the Sub-version of Identity* (New York: Routledge, 1990), 11.

43. Walt Christie, "Concert Review: Elvis Presley," *Honolulu Star Bulletin*, November 11, 1956.

44. "Ain't Nothin' but a Hairdo," *Life*, March 25, 1957.

45. Schrum, *Bobby Sox*, 127.

46. Young and Young, *1950s*, 25.

47. Schrum, *Bobby Sox*, 2.

48. Young and Young, *1950s*, 25.

49. Schrum, *Bobby Sox*, 2–3.

50. Ibid.

51. Phyllis Battelle, "Cold-Eyed, Hot-Voiced Elvis Is King of Teens," *St. Petersburg Times*, June 24, 1956.

52. Battelle, "Cold-Eyed, Hot-Voiced Elvis"; Jean Yothers, "Elvis Makes 'Em Shriek, Jump and Yell," *Orlando Sentinel Star*, August 9, 1956; Sylvan Fox, "Elvis Sings, Swings, Leaves Thousands of Teens Hoarse," *Buffalo Evening News*, April 2, 1957.

53. Will Jones, "Squeals Drown Presley's Songs," *Minneapolis Tribune*, May 13, 1956.

54. "Elvis, a Different Kind of Idol," *Life*, August 27, 1956.

55. Bob Krauss, "Hipster Hexes Hysterical Hepsters," *Honolulu Advertiser*, November 11, 1957.

56. Gould, "New Phenomenon"; Dotti Einhorn, "Yes Elvis Did It Again," *Daytona Beach Morning Journal*, August 10, 1956.

57. Max Norris, "Waiting, Waiting for Their Elvis," *Daytona Morning News*, August 10, 1956; Battelle, "Cold-Eyed, Hot-Voiced Elvis."

58. Eddie Condon, "What Is an Elvis Presley?," *Cosmopolitan*, December 1956, 60–61.

59. May, *Homeward Bound*.

60. Battelle, "Cold-Eyed, Hot-Voiced Elvis," 12.

61. Dorothy R. Powers, "Like Him? I Love Him!," *Spokesman-Review*, August 1, 1957.

62. Fox, "Elvis Sings."

63. Eugene Gilbert, "Survey Shows Elvis Skidding," *Robesonian* (Lumberton, N.C.), March 22, 1957.

64. Bosley Crowther, "The Chemistry of Screen Illusion," *New York Times,* November 18, 1956.

65. Powers, "Like Him? I Love Him!"

66. Douglas, *Where the Girls Are,* 61.

67. Drew Pearson, "Drew Pearson Tackles the Elvis Controversy," *Drew Pearson's Washington Merry-Go-Round,* aired January 6, 1957, available at www.youtube.com.

68. Ruth Millett, "The Presley Crush: The Teenage Declaration of Independence," *Spencer Sunday Times,* October 21, 1956.

69. Norman Miller and James McGlincy, "Girls Identify Elvis as Lover," *New York Daily Mirror,* September 28, 1956.

70. Associated Press, "Tactics of Elvis Presley," *Daily (Centralia, Wash.) Chronicle,* September 3, 1957.

71. Condon, "What Is an Elvis Presley?," 61.

72. "Lonely and Shook Up," *Time,* May 27, 1957.

73. Connie Cullum, "Piggy Banks and Boy Friends Shelling Out to Take Presley Fans to Sunday's Shows," *San Antonio Express,* October 14, 1956.

74. Associated Press, "High School Principals Wince at Presley, Blue Jeans, Ducktails," February 25, 1957.

75. Associated Press, "Elvis Dog-Tags Cause Trouble," August 4, 1958.

76. Associated Press, "Elvis Type Denies Sprees with Sisters, Police Probe Murder Link," *Meridan (Wash.) Record,* January 25, 1957.

77. "Elvis," 108, 109.

78. Editorial, "Letters of Note: To FBI Director J. Edgar Hoover," *La Crosse (Wisc.) Register,* May 16, 1956.

79. Ibid.

80. "Beware Elvis Presley," *America,* June 23, 1956.

81. Associated Press, "Elvis Presley Likened to Golden Calf," *Reading Eagle,* April 9, 1957.

82. Judy Healey, interview by the author, August 19, 2012, Minneapolis.

83. Palladino, *Teenagers,* 176.

84. Rodman, *Elvis after Elvis,* 35.

85. Hazel Washington, "Things Happen When Our Hazel Meets Elvis," *Chicago Defender,* March 16, 1957.

86. Baker E. Morten, "From 'Blue Suede' to Pink Cadillacs: A Yarn," *Chicago Defender,* June 23, 1956.

87. Bert Okuley, "Arrival of Elvis Presley, No Puzzle to T-Bone Fans," *Chicago Defender,* August 18, 1956, 15.

88. "Dixiecrats Even Like Rock 'n' Roll by Elvis," *Daily Defender,* October 1, 1956.

89. "B. B. King Hears How Presley Copied Style," *Chicago Defender,* February 2, 1957.

90. Phyllis Battelle, "Teenagers Rally to Aid of Presley," *Daily Defender,* July 5, 1956, and "Cold-Eyed, Hot-Voiced Elvis is King of Teens," *St. Petersburg Times,* Sunday, June 24, 1956.

91. "Delinquency and Public Safety," *Daily Defender,* October 10, 1956.

92. "Jazz Musician Takes on Presley," *Atlanta Daily World,* November 30, 1956.

93. Hilda See, "Fanaticism over Blues, Rock 'n' Roll Is 'Old Hat,'" *Daily Defender,* October 30, 1956.

94. "If Music Be the Food of Love, Play On!," Housewives' Corner, *Daily Defender*, August 8, 1956; "Presley Film Did Okay in Chicago," *Chicago Defender*, January 7, 1957; "Ed Sullivan Praises the Presley Guy," *Chicago Defender*, January 9, 1957.

95. Alan Hanson, "Elvis Presley and Civil Rights: The Role of Rock 'n' Role," *Elvis History Blog*, www.elvis-history-blog.com; David Troedson, "Elvis Presley and Racism," *Elvis Australia* (blog), March 21, 2013, www.elvis.com.au.

96. Renee Graham, "Elvis Divides Opinion 25 Years after the Fact," *Boston Globe*, August 11, 2002.

97. Ibid.

98. bell hooks and Amalia Mesa-Bains, *Homegrown: Engaged Cultural Criticism* (Cambridge, Mass.: South End, 2006).

99. May, *Homeward Bound*.

4. Punk Rock and a Crisis of Femininity, 1976–1986

1. "Donahue on Today Looks at Punk Rock Movement," *The Phil Donahue Show*, February 3, 1982, my transcription and description; clip (labeled 1984) available at www.youtube.com.

2. Lynne Y. Edwards, "Victims, Villains, and Vixens: Teen Girls and Internet Crime," in *Girl Wide Web: Girls, the Internet, and the Negotiation of Identity*, ed. Sharon R. Mazzarella (New York: Lang, 2005), 2–30.

3. See, for example, Dick Hebdige, *Subculture: The Meaning of Style* (New York: Routledge, 1979); Stanley Cohen, *Folk Devils and Moral Panic* (St. Albans: Paladin, 1972); Lawrence Grossberg, "Is There Rock after Punk?," *Critical Studies in Mass Communication* 3 (1986): 50–74; Angela McRobbie, "Rock and Sexuality," with Simon Frith, in McRobbie, *Feminism and Youth Culture*, 138.

4. Cohen, *Folk Devils and Moral Panic*, 9.

5. See note 3.

6. Angela McRobbie, "Girls and Subcultures," with Jenny Garber, in *Feminism and Youth Culture*, ed. Angela McRobbie (New York: Routledge, 2000), 12, 15.

7. Helen Reddington, "'Lady' Punks in Bands: A Subculturette?," in *The Post-Subcultures Reader*, ed. David Muggleton and Rupert Weinzierl (New York: Berg, 2003), 244, 250.

8. Angela McRobbie, "Rock and Sexuality," with Simon Frith, in McRobbie, *Feminism and Youth Culture*, 138.

9. Grossberg, "Is There Rock after Punk?," 67, 52.

10. Ibid., 52.

11. Angela McRobbie, "Settling Accounts with Subcultures: A Feminist Critique," in McRobbie, *Feminism and Youth Culture*, 39.

12. Robert Liebman and Robert Wuthnow, *The New Christian Right* (New York: Aldine, 1983), 31–32.

13. Jan Glidewell, "Of Censorship, Literature, and the Moral Majority," *St. Petersburg Times*, July 20, 1981.

14. Churchill L. Roberts, "Attitudes and Media Use of the Moral Majority," *Journal of Broadcasting* 27, no. 4 (1981): 404–5.

15. C. H. Sterling, "Deregulation," Museum of Broadcast Communications, www.museum.tv.

16. Robert McChesney, *Rich Media, Poor Democracy: Communication Politics in Dubious Times* (Urbana: University of Illinois Press, 1999).
17. Robert J. Thompson, "Television Viewing in the United States," *Encyclopedia Britannica,* www.britannica.com.
18. Charles Acland, *Youth, Murder, Spectacle: The Cultural Politics of "Youth in Crisis"* (Boulder, Colo.: Westview, 1995), 13.
19. John N. Ingham and Lynne B. Feldman, "Ted Turner," *Contemporary American Business Leaders: A Biographical Dictionary* (New York: Greenwood, 1990).
20. Jack Banks, *Monopoly Television: MTV's Quest to Control the Music* (Boulder, Colo.: Westview, 1996).
21. Dead Kennedys, *Nazi Punks Fuck Off,* Subterranean Records, November 1981.
22. "The Day My Kid Went Punk," *ABC Afterschool Specials,* season 16, episode 3, October 23, 1987.
23. "Battle of the Bands," *CHiPs,* season 5, episode 16, January 31, 1982.
24. Jay H., "More Killed by Punk Rock," *Detailed Twang* (blog), January 10, 2007, http://detailedtwang.blogspot.com. "Next Stop, Nowhere," *Quincy, M.E.,* season 8, episode 8, December 1, 1982. A videotaped home recording of the *Quincy* episode is included in the Sarah G. Jacobson Papers donated to New York University's Fales Library Special Collections.
25. Acland, *Youth, Murder, Spectacle,* 4.
26. McRobbie, "Settling Accounts with Subcultures," 39.
27. Norma Coates, "(R)evolution Now? Rock and the Political Potential of Gender," in *Sexing the Groove: Popular Music and Gender,* ed. Sheila Whiteley (New York: Routledge, 1997), 53.
28. Associated Press, "Hair Wild, Girl 'Pleasant,'" *Ocala Star-Banner,* August 25, 1984.
29. "Twin Cities Live Punk Show," KSTP-TV, St. Paul, Minn., original broadcast July 1985, www.youtube.com.
30. Robert Hilburn, "'Positive Punk' Rocks Music Scene," *Los Angeles Times,* December 23, 1983.
31. McRobbie, "Girls and Subcultures," 23.
32. Jack Perkins, "NBC News Reports of Sex Pistols Tour," January 6, 1978, www.youtube.com.
33. Wayne Freedman, "Punk" (San Francisco: KRON-TV, CBS-4, 1983).
34. McRobbie, "Girls and Subcultures," 37.
35. Acland, *Youth, Murder, Spectacle,* 4.
36. Ibid., 5.
37. Ibid., 6.
38. Legs McNeil and Gillian McCain, *Please Kill Me: The Uncensored Oral History of Punk* (New York: Penguin Books, 1997).
39. Kathleen Hallinan, interview by the author, St. Paul, Minn., May 1, 2012.
40. "Teen Delinquency Control a Growth Industry," *Omaha World-Herald,* July 20, 1984; Associated Press, "Teen Gangs Terrorize Shoppers," *Modesto Bee,* December 19, 1980; "Senior Year in Great Neck: A Jubilant Rite of Passage," *New York Times,* April 9, 1984.
41. Associated Press, "Girl Indicted in Suicide," *Tri City Herald,* February 4, 1983; "Teen Girl Indicted in Suicide," *Bonham Daily Favorite,* February 3, 1983; "Girl Indicted in Friend's Suicide," *St. Joseph News-Press,* February 4, 1983.

42. Editorial, "The Children of Milpitas," *Modesto Bee*, December 10, 1981.
43. Paul Galloway, "An Innocent Afloat in the Netherworld of Punk," *Chicago Tribune*, March 25, 1984.
44. Christine Acham, *Revolution Televised: Prime Time and the Struggle for Black Power* (Minneapolis: University of Minnesota Press, 2004).
45. "NAACP Hails Canceling of Punk Rock Band Show," *Orlando Sentinel*, February 28, 1987.
46. Major Robinson, "Why Punk Rock and Blacks Don't Mix," *New York Amsterdam News*, March 11, 1978.
47. Catherine Squires, "Rethinking the Black Public Sphere: An Alternative Category for Multiple Public Spheres," *Communication Theory* 12, no. 4 (November 2002): 446–68.
48. McNeil and McCain, *Please Kill Me*.

5. Policing Teen Girls Online, 2004–2010

1. Mark Weinstein, "Be Careful Sexting with Snapchat!," *Huffington Post*, June 3, 2013; Doug Gross, "Snapchat: Sexting Tool or the Next Instagram?," *CNN.com*, January 10, 2013, http://edition.cnn.com; Rosa Golijan, "Will Google Glass Destroy Your Life?," *NBCnews.com*, May 31, 2013, www.today.com; Larry Magid, "Snapchat Photos Can Be Undeleted and Captured: When It Matters," *Huffington Post*, May 12, 2013; Max Read, "Swedish Teen Girls Riot Over Call for 'Sluts' on Instagram," *Gawker*, December 12, 2012.
2. Mary Celeste Kearney, *Girls Make Media* (New York: Routledge, 2006).
3. Cynthia Lewis and Bettina Fabos, "But Will It Work in the Heartland? A Response and Illustration," *Journal of Adolescent and Adult Literacy* 43, no. 5 (2000): 462–69.
4. Shayla Thiel-Stern, *Instant Identity: Adolescent Girls and the World of Instant Messaging* (New York: Lang, 2007).
5. Sonia Livingstone, "Taking Risky Opportunities in Youthful Content Creation: Teenagers' Use of Social Networking Sites for Intimacy, Privacy, and Self-Expression," *New Media and Society* 10, no. 3 (2008): 393–411; Thiel-Stern, *Instant Identity*.
6. Amanda Lenhart, Rich Ling, Scott Campbell, and Kristen Purcell, "Teens and Mobile Phones," *Pew Internet and American Life Project Report*, April 20, 2010, http://pewinternet.org.
7. Pete Cashmore, "MySpace Hits 100 Million Accounts," *Mashable.com*, May 12, 2006.
8. NewsCorp sold MySpace in 2011 for far less than it paid for it, according to Brian Stetler, "NewsCorp Sells MySpace for $35 Million," *New York Times*, June 29, 2011; Michael Arrington, "MySpace: The $27.4 Billion Gorilla," *AdAge*, June 13, 2006.
9. Tom Standage, *The Victorian Internet: The Remarkable Story of the Telegraph and the Nineteenth Century's Online Pioneers* (New York: Walker, 2007).
10. Roy Wells, "41.6 of the U.S. Population Has a Facebook Account," *Social Media Today*, August 8, 2010; Stetler, "NewsCorp Sells MySpace."
11. danah boyd, "Taken Out of Context: American Teen Sociality of Networked Publics" (PhD diss., University of California, Berkeley, 2008), 62, www.danah.org.
12. Thiel-Stern, *Instant Identity*.

13. boyd, "Taken Out of Context," 62.

14. Sherry Turkle, *Life on Screen: Identity in the Age of the Internet* (New York: Touchstone, 2004).

15. Lynn Schofield Clark, "The Constant Contact Generation: Exploring Teen Friendship Networks Online," in *Girl Wide Web: Girls, the Internet, and the Negotiation of Identity,* ed. Sharon R. Mazzarella (New York: Lang, 2005), 203–22.

16. "Teen and Young Adult Internet Use," *Pew Research Center,* February 3, 2010, www.pewresearch.org.

17. Shayla Thiel-Stern, "Collaborative, Productive, Performative, Templated: Youth, Identity, and Breaking the Fourth Wall Online," in *Produsing Theory in a Digital World: The Intersection of Audiences and Production,* ed. Rebecca Ann Lind (New York: Lang, 2012), 87–104.

18. Nancy K. Baym and danah boyd, "Socially Mediated Publicness: An Introduction," *Journal of Broadcasting and Electronic Media* 565, no. 3 (2012): 320–29.

19. M. Gigi Durham, *The Lolita Effect: The Media Sexualization of Young Girls and What We Can Do about It* (New York: Overlook, 2008).

20. Sharon R. Mazzarella, "Claiming a Space: The Cultural Economy of Teen Girl Fandom on the Web," in Mazzarella, *Girl Wide Web,* 141–60; Kearney, *Girls Make Media.*

21. Debra Merskin, "Making an About-Face: Jammer Girls and the World Wide Web," in Mazzarella, *Girl Wide Web,* 51–67; Susannah Stern, "Expressions of Identity Online: Prominent Features and Gender Differences in Adolescents' WWW Home Pages," *Journal of Broadcasting and Electronic Media* 48, no. 2 (2004): 218–43.

22. Amanda Lenhart, Mary Madden, Alexandra Rankin Macgill, and Aaron Smith, "Teens and Social Media," *Pew Internet and American Life Project,* December 19, 2007, www.pewinternet.org.

23. Dawn Currie, *Girl Talk: Adolescent Magazines and Their Readers* (Toronto: University of Toronto Press, 1999); Angela McRobbie, "Jackie: An Ideology of Adolescent Femininity," in *Popular Culture: Past and Present,* ed. Bernard Waites, Tony Bennett, and Graham Martin (London: Open University Press, 1982).

24. Lynn Schofield Clark, "Dating on the Net: Teens and the Rise of 'Pure' Relationships," in *Cybersociety 2.0,* ed. Steve Jones (Thousand Oaks, Calif.: Sage, 1998), 159–83; Thiel-Stern, *Instant Identity.*

25. Rachel Simmons, *Odd Girl Out: The Hidden Culture of Aggression in Girls* (Orlando, Fla.: Harcourt, 2002); Sharon Lamb, *The Secret Lives of Girls: What Good Girls Really Do* (New York: Free Press, 2002).

26. See, for example, Turkle, *Life on Screen.*

27. Joseph Tobin, "An American Otaku," in *Digital Diversions: Youth Culture and the Age of Multimedia,* ed. Julien Sefton-Green (New York: Routledge, 1999), 106–27.

28. Durham, *Lolita Effect.*

29. Gwen Filosa, "Online Profiles Attracting Sexual Predators, Feds Warn: Teen Sites Being Used as Victim Directories," *Times-Picayune,* March 24, 2007.

30. Justine Cassell and Meg Cramer, "High Tech or High Risk: Moral Panics about Girls Online," in *Digital Youth, Innovation, and the Unexpected,* ed. Tara McPherson (Cambridge, Mass.: MIT Press, 2008), 53–76.

31. Janis Wolak, David Finkelhor, Kimberley J. Mitchell, and Michele L. Ybarra, "Online 'Predators' and Their Victims: Myths, Realities and Implications for Prevention and Treatment," *American Psychologist* 63, no. 2 (2008): 111–28.

32. Amanda Lenhart, "Protecting Teens Online," *Pew Internet and American Life Project*, March 17, 2005, http://pewinternet.org.

33. Sarah Wright, Henry Jenkins, and danah boyd, "Discussion: MySpace and Deleting Online Predators Act, Digital Divide Network," *MIT Tech Talk*, May 24, 2006.

34. Stuart Hall, Chas Critcher, Tony Jefferson, John Clarke, and Brian Roberts, *Policing the Crisis: Mugging, the State, and Law and Order* (London: Macmillan, 1978), 33–34.

35. Lynne Y. Edwards, "Victims, Villains, and Vixens: Teen Girls and Internet Crime," in Mazzarella, *Girl Wide Web*, 2–30.

36. Cicero Estrella, "Soccer Coach Accused of Raping 14-Year-Old: Girl Says She Met Man, 22, on MySpace.com," *San Francisco Chronicle*, August 5, 2006.

37. Conrad deFelbre, "MySpace Helped Girl Meet Sex Offender, Man Charged," *Minneapolis Star-Tribune*, February 15, 2006.

38. Nicole Marshall, "Facebook 'Friend' Charged in Assault: Man Charged with Sexually Assaulting Two Young Sisters after Befriending Them on Facebook," *McClatchy-Tribune Wire Services*, June 2, 2010.

39. Associated Press, "'MySpace' Teen Returns from Middle East," *Fox News*, June 10, 2006, www.foxnews.com.

40. Associated Press, "Michigan Teen, Home Safe and Sound," *CBSNews.com*, June 20, 2006, www.cbsnews.com.

41. "Kara," interview by the author, Minneapolis, September 15, 2012.

42. Kelly Wallace, "The Secret Lives of Teens Online," *CBS Evening News*, August 10, 2009, www.cbsnews.com.

43. Rondrell Moore, "Facebook Dangers," *News 10* newscast (Terra Haute, Ind.: WTHI-TV10), May 25, 2009.

44. Thiel-Stern, *Instant Identity*, 45; Mary L. Gray, *Out in the Country: Youth, Media, and Queer Visibility in Rural America* (New York: New York University Press, 2009).

45. Ashley Grisso and David Weiss," What Are gURLs Talking About?" in Mazzarella, *Girl Wide Web*, 31–55.

46. Wire Reports, "House of Representatives Set to Battle Sexual Predators on MySpace.com," *Columbus Dispatch*, August 10, 2005.

47. Julie Shaw, "Cyberspace Is a Dangerous World for Children," *Philadelphia Inquirer*, October 12, 2005.

48. Keith O'Brien, "Not Guilty," *Boston Globe*, July 9, 2006.

49. "Parents Warned of Teens' Use of MySpace," *Cleveland Plain Dealer*, December 18, 2005.

50. "Nicole," e-mail interview by the author, September 2, 2012.

51. "Growing Up Online," *Frontline*, PBS, January 22, 2008, www.pbs.org.

52. Foster Cline and Jim Fay, *Parenting with Love and Logic: Teaching Children Responsibility* (Colorado Springs: Piñon, 1990), 23–25; Katie Roiphe, "The Seven Myths of Helicopter Parenting," *Slate*, July 31, 2012.

53. Melissa Ludwig, "Look@Me Generation Next Is Living Out Loud and Online," *San Antonio Express*, April 15, 2007.

54. Jane Gordon, "MySpace Draws a Questionable Crowd," *New York Times*, February 26, 2006.

55. Katherine Sweeney, *Maiden U.S.A.: Girl Icons Come of Age* (New York: Lang, 2008).

56. Kayla Webley, "Teens Who Admitted to Bullying Phoebe Prince Sentenced," *Time*, May 5, 2011.

57. Laura Clark, "Parents Could Be Fined 1,000 Pounds over Cyberbullies," *London Daily Mail*, July 26, 2006. This article is the only piece of global media analyzed for the chapter, but the story itself took place in the United States.

58. Amy Harmon, "Internet Gives Teenage Bullies Weapons to Wound from Afar," *New York Times*, August 26, 2004.

59. Angela McRobbie, "Folk Devils Fight Back," *New Left Review* 203, no. 1 (1994): 107–16.

60. Jan Hoffman, "A Girl's Photo, and Altered Lives," *New York Times*, March 26, 2011.

61. Carla Stokes, " 'Get On My Level: How Adolescent Girls Construct Identity and Negotiate Sexuality on the Internet," in *Girl Wide Web 2.0: Revisiting Girls, the Internet, and the Negotiation of Identity*, ed. by Sharon R. Mazzarella (New York: Lang, 2010), 55.

62. David Folkenflik, "The Next Frontier in TV: English News for Latinos," *National Public Radio's Morning Edition*, August 15, 2012, www.npr.org.

63. Russell Goldman, "Teens Indicted after Allegedly Taunting Girl Who Hanged Herself," *ABC News*, March 29, 2010, http://abcnews.go.com.

64. Nelly Elias and Dafna Lemish, "Spinning the Web of Identity: The Roles of the Internet in the Lives of Immigrant Adolescents," *New Media Society* 11, no. 4 (2009): 533.

65. Lisa Nakamura, *Digitizing Race: Visual Cultures of the Internet* (Minneapolis: University of Minnesota Press, 2008), 2.

66. Steve Salerno, "Hooking Up Is College's Most Popular Major," *Allentown (Pa.) Morning Call*, March 27, 2008.

67. Sarah Banet-Weiser, "Branding the Post-Feminist Self: Girls' Video Production and YouTube," in *Mediated Girlhoods: New Explorations of Girls' Media Culture*, ed. Mary Celeste Kearney (New York: Lang, 2011), 277–94.

68. Sarah Banet-Weiser, *Authentic™: The Politics of Ambivalence in a Brand Culture* (New York: New York University Press, 2012).

INDEX

Addams, Jane, 42, 47–48, 57
African American press, 21, 59, 69, 84, 88–89, 168
  on dance halls, 48–50
  on Elvis Presley, 100, 114–18
  on punk rock, 142–43
  See also newspapers
agenda-setting. *See under* mass media
Amateur Athletic Union (AAU)
  and black athletes, 66
  and Babe Didrikson, 70–71 (*see also* Didrikson, Babe)
  sponsoring events for teen girls, 68–69, 76–77
Associated Press, 71, 98, 111, 113, 134

Becker, Howard S., 18, 39
Butler, Judith, 3, 71, 101

Chicago Daily Tribune, 44
  on "bad girls" in dance halls, 27–28, 31, 37–39
  coverage of girls' sports, 69
Chicago Defender (newspaper), 21, 48–49, 67, 69, 85, 114–15. *See also* newspapers
CHiPs (TV show), 132–34
civil rights movement, 87, 118–19

class (socioeconomic), 167–69
  and girls online, 162, 168, 171
  in girls' sports (*see under* girls' sports)
  in moral panic over dance halls: Paul Cressey's work, 50–53; marking girls as vulnerable, 29; as a working-class leisure activity, 24–26, 32–44, 47, 54–55
  in policing of femininity, 18, 37, 53, 119
  used to marginalize teen girls, 2–3, 6
Cohen, Stanley, 13–16, 124–25
Committee of Fourteen, 42–43, 50
Cosmopolitan magazine, 106–7, 110–11, 116
cultural studies, 15–17, 21, 94, 124
cyberbullying, 13, 164–67

Daily Defender (newspaper), 114, 116–17
dance halls, 24–55
  in the black press, 48–50 (*see also* newspapers)
  boys' corrupting influence in, 28, 44–45
  and liquor, 36, 38, 43–44
  in mass media, 12, 25–53
  in public policy, 28, 37, 42
  and race, 36–37, 49–51

dance hall (*continued*)
  and socioeconomic status, 25–26,
    33–38, 44
Didrikson, Babe, 22, 70–72, 74
Donahue, Phil, 121–23, 135, 138, 144
Douglas, Susan J., 11, 23, 92

Facebook, 13, 19, 146–50, 153–54, 157,
  163. *See also* social media
Falwell, Jerry, 128, 130–31
femininity
  as cultural construct: by media, 3–6,
    18–19, 72–73, 100–101, 151, 156; in
    moral panics, 17, 21 (*see also* teen
    girls)
  and domesticity, 5, 7, 39, 89, 91–92,
    127
  and the feminine body: in coverage
    of the punk rock movement,
    134–35, 138–39; in public/private
    spaces, 5; in sports, 61, 71–73, 84
  performance, 8, 10, 54–55, 71, 94,
    119, 123, 163
  in private, 5–6, 46, 89
  in public, 4–6, 16, 26–27, 37, 89, 109,
    127, 170
  in sports (*see* girls' sports)
  See also gender
feminism, 8, 11, 21, 143

gender
  performance, 8, 10, 54–55, 71, 94,
    101, 134
  representations in media, 3–4, 16,
    31, 44, 103–7
  See also femininity
girls' sports, 12, 46, 56–85, 85–89
  and class: programs for immigrant
    girls, 65; for the working class,
    56–57, 68, 72–72, 75, 84–85,
    89–90
  concerns about reproduction, 57,
    78–79
  and girls of color, 65–67, 69, 73–74,
    84–85, 88–89
  in mass media, 12, 56–65, 68–89
girls' studies, 7–11, 21–23, 95, 125
Gould, Jack, 98–99, 106
Gramsci, Antonio, 3, 14
Great Depression, 12, 59, 72

Hall, Stuart, 14, 20–21, 44, 154
hegemony
  and corporate media conglomeration,
    129–31
  in cultural norms of beauty/
    appearance, 7, 151–52
  in media representations of girls and
    youth, 3–4, 126, 151–52, 172
  social agendas disseminated by news
    media, 14–15

identity. *See* femininity; gender
ideology, 15, 20–21
immigration
  in coverage of dance halls, 36–37,
    39–40
  in coverage of girls' sports, 65
  and marginalization of teen girls, 18,
    39, 54, 167–68
Internet, 4, 8–10, 20
  as a dangerous place, 145, 148, 157
  the digital divide, 167–68
  early history of, 146–48
  as public space, 149–51, 164
  and race, 167–69
  See also social media
Israels, Mrs. Charles H. (Belle) 24,
    37–42, 45, 169

journalism
  muckraking, 30–31, 58–60, 148
  professionalization of, 32, 50, 58–61
  See also mass media; news media;
    newspapers

Kearney, Mary Celeste, 8, 11, 93

Ladies' Home Journal magazine, 56, 60,
  79
Life magazine, 94, 104, 112

MacDonald, Florence, 22, 56, 81–82
mass media
  agenda-setting, 44, 80
  coverage of dance halls, 12, 25–53
  coverage of punk rock (*see* punk rock)
  coverage of rock and roll, 95–119
  coverage of Title IX, 87–88
  decentralization of, 129–30, 171
  film, 97–99, 117, 156, 165

Internet media (*see* Internet)
popular media, 6, 20, 95
radio, 58, 60–61, 97–98, 100
reliance on official sources: in
    coverage of dance halls, 27, 33,
    44; in coverage of girls' track and
    field, 59–60; in coverage of Elvis
    Presley, 107; in coverage of social
    media, 153, 160, 166, 171–72;
    upholding patriarchal social
    agenda, 2, 14, 21–22
television: in coverage of punk
    rock, 129–30, 132, 135, 140–41;
    debut of commercial television,
    97–100; in moral panic over Elvis
    Presley, 109, 111; relationship to
    audiences, 20
and youth, 4, 11–12, 17, 94–94, 130,
    137
See also journalism; news media
Mazzarella, Sharon, 8, 10–11, 18, 93
McRobbie, Angela, 7, 15–16, 20–21, 94,
    125–27, 133, 136–37, 166
Minneapolis (Morning) Tribune, 24, 26,
    34–36, 50, 62–63, 65, 104
Moskowitz, Belle. *See* Israels, Mrs.
    Charles H. (Belle)
moral entrepreneurship, 12–13 and
    dance halls, 38–40; definition, 18;
    in the digital age, 169–72; and girls'
    sports, 73–80, 89; and Elvis Presley,
    111–14, 119; and punk rock, 123,
    128–30, 156
Moral Majority, 128–31
and Jerry Falwell, 128, 130–31
moral panics, 1–2, 12–18, 29, 124–25,
    172
    in the black press, 48–50, 117 (*see
        also* African American press)
    and dance halls (*see* dance halls)
    definition, 13–15
    gendered (*see* gender)
    and girls' track and field (*see* girls'
        sports)
    and punk rock (*see* punk rock)
    and rock and roll, 95–114, 117 (*see
        also* Presley, Elvis)
    and social media, 146–49, 167, 172
        (*see also* social media)
    and television, 97–98

and "white slavery," 36–37, 49
MySpace, 13, 168
    and audience, 150
    fear of sexual predation, 153–55,
        158–61 (*see also* social media: fear
        of sexual predators)
    history of, 146–49
    as public space, 163–64
    See also social media

National Amateur Athletic Federation
    (NAAF), 68, 76
    Women's Division, 76–85, 88–90
National Recreation Association (NRA),
    57, 67, 74
new media. *See* social media
news media
    dissemination of ideology, 3, 14–15
        (*see also* ideology)
    exclusion of female voices from
        coverage of girls' issues, 2, 18,
        21–22, 50–53, 60, 82, 107–8, 125,
        143–44
    news frames, 32, 48, 90, 126, 151
    and newsworthiness, 2, 14, 32
    professionalization of, 58–61
newspapers, 29–32, 58–61, 102–3, 129
    African American, 21, 48–49, 59
        (*see also* African American
        press)
    penny press, 29–30, 48
    *See also names of individual
        newspapers*
New York Amsterdam News
    (newspaper), 49–50, 69, 142
New York Times
    coverage of dance halls, 29, 37–38,
        41, 43–46, 48
    coverage of girls' sports, 68, 70–71,
        77, 80–83, 85, 90
    coverage of Elvis Presley, 98–99,
        106, 108
    coverage of social media, 164, 166
New York Tribune, 32–34, 42, 50

Olympic Games
    of 1928, 64–65, 69, 80
    of 1932, 70, 82–83
    International Olympic Committee
        (IOC), 81, 83, 90

patriarchy
  in construction of feminine identity,
    4–5, 16, 89, 94, 152, 158, 162
  in news media, 13–14, 16, 89, 108, 126
  subversion of, 7–8
  The Playground (periodical), 74–75,
    77
Playground Association of America
  (PAA), 46, 57, 64–66
Presley, Elvis, 12, 95–120
  appropriation of black culture, 100–
    101, 107, 115–16, 118
  cultural backlash, 96–100, 102–14
  in media, 95–119
  as sex symbol, 99–10, 107–10, 112
print media. *See* mass media;
  newspapers
Progressive movement, 18, 33, 38–40,
  42, 47–49, 54, 56–58, 68, 92
Prohibition, 42, 53, 56, 58
punk rock, 12
  in the black press, 141–43 (*see also*
    African American press)
  cultural backlash, 121–44
  and drug use, 122–23, 138–40, 143
  gender in, 121–28, 134–37
  history of, 123–24
  and people of color, 141–43
  and Ronald Reagan, 128, 130–31
  style/aesthetic, 121–23, 127–28,
    134–39

Quincy, M.E. (TV show), 121, 131–34,
  140–41

race, 2
  in coverage of dance halls, 36–37,
    49–51
  in coverage of girls' sports, 65–66,
    69, 84, 87–89
  in coverage of punks, 141–43
  in coverage of Elvis Presley, 110,
    114–19
  in coverage of social networking,
    167–70
racism. *See* race
radio. *See under* mass media
Reagan, Ronald, 126, 128–31
rock and roll. *See* Presley, Elvis; punk
  rock

Schoenfeld, Julia, 40, 42–44
settlement house movement, 34, 38–42,
  47
sexism. *See* patriarchy
sexuality, 97, 99–100, 109, 151–52
  negotiation by teen girls: in dance
    halls, 27, 33, 46, 53; as fans of
    Elvis Presley, 101, 103–9; online,
    152, 158–64, 166
Sinatra, Frank, 94, 96, 101, 103
social media, 9, 12, 145–72
  cyberbullying, 13, 164–67
  Facebook, 13, 19, 146–50, 153–54,
    157, 163
  fear of sexual predators, 12, 147–48,
    153–60, 164, 172
  and identity, 147–50, 158, 169
  MySpace (*see* MySpace)
  and promiscuity, 1, 12, 158–64, 169–71
  and sexting, 145, 147, 166–67
  and teen girls of color, 10, 167–69
  See also Internet; mass media; news
    media
social networks. *See* social media
Suffrage Movement, 26, 47, 57, 54–55, 57
and athletics, 61–65

teenagers
  emergence of the term, 19, 57, 61,
    92–94, 102, 162
  See also teen girls
teen girls
  "bobby soxers," 93–94, 96
  cultural construction of, 6, 11,
    94–95, 151 (*see also* femininity: as
    cultural construct)
  definition of, 16, 19, 56
  and leisure/recreation, 3, 16, 38, 46,
    55–56, 150
  as naive, 29, 34, 36, 38, 51, 96, 106–8
  as producers of media, 8–11, 143, 152
  sexualization of, 7, 97, 101, 103, 112,
    125, 151–52, 163, 172 (*see also*
    sexuality)
  and sports (*see* girls' sports)
  as victims, 6–8, 17, 27, 54, 109–10,
    113, 123, 152–53, 155–57, 160, 172
  as whores, 6, 17, 54, 127, 172
  working-class, 12, 18, 24, 29, 32,
    37–38, 41, 47–48, 50–53, 68, 127

television. *See under* mass media
Title IX, 73, 87–88
track and field. *See* girls' sports
Trilling, Blanche, 77, 80, 83, 85, 89–90

Wilder, Emma, 64, 73–74

World War I, 26, 58–59, 62
World War II, 12, 83, 89, 91–92, 102, 139

YMCA and YWCA, 66–67, 84

SHAYLA THIEL-STERN holds a PhD from the University of Iowa and is on the faculty of the University of Minnesota School of Journalism and Mass Communication. She began working in digital media in 1995 and has published articles, book chapters, and one previous book, *Instant Identity: Adolescent Girls and the World of Instant Messaging,* on media, gender, and adolescence. She resides in Minneapolis.